day trips® from
chicago

help us keep this guide up to date

We would love to hear from you concerning your experiences with this guide and how you feel it could be improved and kept up to date. Please send your comments and suggestions to:

editorial@GlobePequot.com

Thanks for your input, and happy travels!

day trips® series

day trips® from chicago

first edition

getaway ideas for the local traveler

elisa drake

travel

Guilford, Connecticut

All the information in this guidebook is subject to change. We recommend that you call ahead to obtain current information before traveling.

To buy books in quantity for corporate use or incentives, call **(800) 962-0973** or e-mail **premiums@GlobePequot.com**.

Day Trips is a registered trademark of Morris Book Publishing, LLC.

Editor: Kevin Sirois
Project Editor: Lynn Zelem
Layout: Joanna Beyer
Text Design: Linda R. Loiewski
Maps: Ryan Mitchell © Morris Book Publishing, LLC.
Spot photography throughout © Maria Dryfhout/Shutterstock

ISBN 978-0-7627-6459-4

Printed in the United States of America
10 9 8 7 6 5 4 3

contents

about the author

Elisa Drake has covered Chicago area travel for more than a decade, including five years as an editor at *Where* magazine in Chicago. Working on this book gave her the opportunity to venture way beyond the city limits, rediscovering some favorite destinations and finding several new ones. Her work has also appeared in a variety of online and print publications including *TimeOut Chicago Kids, Self,* the official *Illinois Travel Guide, ModernMom.com,* and *Recreation Management.* She's a member of the American Society of Journalists and Authors and lives in Chicago with her husband, dog, and two precocious and precious daughters.

acknowledgments

As I sit here at the Starbucks in Lincoln Square contemplating all the people who helped me with this book in so many ways, I think it's fitting to start first with the employees right here who kept me motoring on with cup after cup of coffee and who allowed me to use their window-front counter as my office away from home. I'm immeasurably indebted to a long list of tourism bureau, chamber of commerce, and public relations representatives who assisted in my travels and research. Big thanks to the Globe Pequot team, especially my editor Kevin Sirois, a supportive, sympathetic, and always gracious leader and guide. Thank you to my friends who didn't see me for a while and to several (Beth, Orly, my sister Lauren and her friend Jen) who suggested interesting destinations. My persistent fact-checker Lisette Medina was essential to the final version of this manuscript. And most of all, I could not have completed this book without my family: my husband, Kevin, who cheered me on, talked me up, and did lots of "daddy days" with our two daughters; and my parents, particularly my mom, who spent many of her days of retirement with the girls while I dashed off to my spot at the coffee shop.

 **introduction**

Putting together a list of 25 trips from Chicago wasn't easy. The first dozen or so came to me quickly, as I've been on many of them. But beyond that took a little digging—and I discovered so many potential places that it was ultimately hard to narrow them down. I hope that the trips I chose satisfy the adventurous spirit in you, whether you're traveling alone, with a group, with your family or your best pals. The excursions take you to five states—Illinois, Wisconsin, Indiana, Michigan, and Iowa—and more than 45 cities, towns, and villages. They range from quiet and quaint to big and boisterous, and the attractions run the gamut from educational and historic to just plain fun.

The landscape is equally varied. While much of the Midwest might have been flattened during the ice age, it also bears scenic glacial lakes and canyons and several spared mountainous regions that deserve attention for their downhill skiing. Mother Nature presents stunning displays of pure beauty at numerous state parks, forests, and prairies. Hike the Glacial Drumlin State Trail, Ice Age National Scenic Trail, and the many trails of Starved Rock; explore Rock Cut State Park, Kettle Moraine Forest, Warren Dunes State Park, the Indiana Dunes, and the Midewin National Tallgrass Prairie.

I'm loyal to Lake Michigan and the Chicago River, but these trips also introduce you to activity and scenery along the Mississippi, Milwaukee, Kalamazoo, Fox, and St. Joseph Rivers; as well as Lake Winnebago and Geneva Lake (where the mail boat cruise is a must). Anglers will be hooked by the bountiful fishing in Pewaukee Lake, Lake Winnebago, and Devil's Lake State Park. Looking for simple suntanning days? The beach towns of South Haven, Saugatuck-Douglas, Grand Haven, and even Madison's five area lakes happily oblige. Historic lighthouses in Kenosha, South Haven, Holland, and Michigan City give their waterfronts an iconic photo-op, while the water lends itself to wet and wild times in the Wisconsin Dells. A handful of waterfront casinos win a spot here too, in Joliet, Milwaukee, Michigan City, and Dubuque.

Two trips take you to state capitals: Madison, where the elegant capitol building anchors the city; and Springfield, where Abraham Lincoln's legend comes to life. In the Land of Lincoln, you'll also travel through towns where Route 66 still bustles with nostalgic stops and historic diners and drive-ins. From those great old greasy spoons to outstanding upscale restaurants, the incredible dining options throughout these drives may surprise you. If you visit Racine, the must-try is its signature kringle; in Wisconsin, cheese curds, frozen custard, and beer produced by both corporate giants and inventive microbrewers; in Springfield, the cozy dog reigns; and in Indiana's Amish Country, make a date for a home-cooked homestead meal.

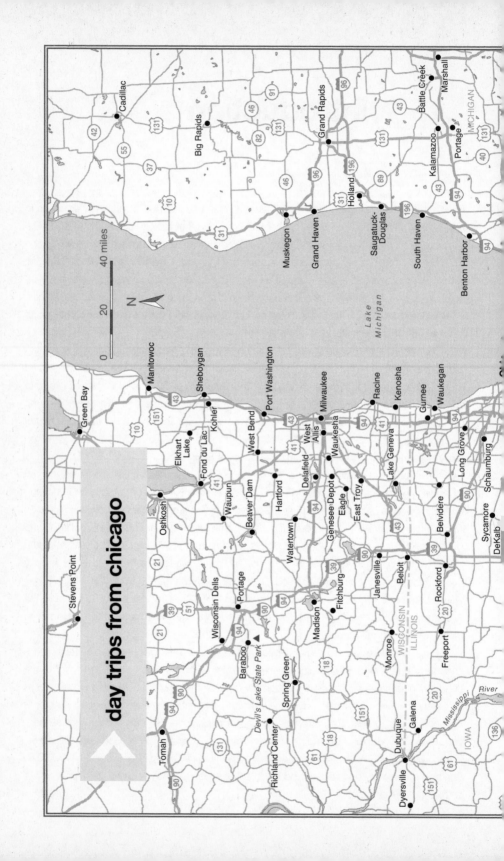

day trips from chicago

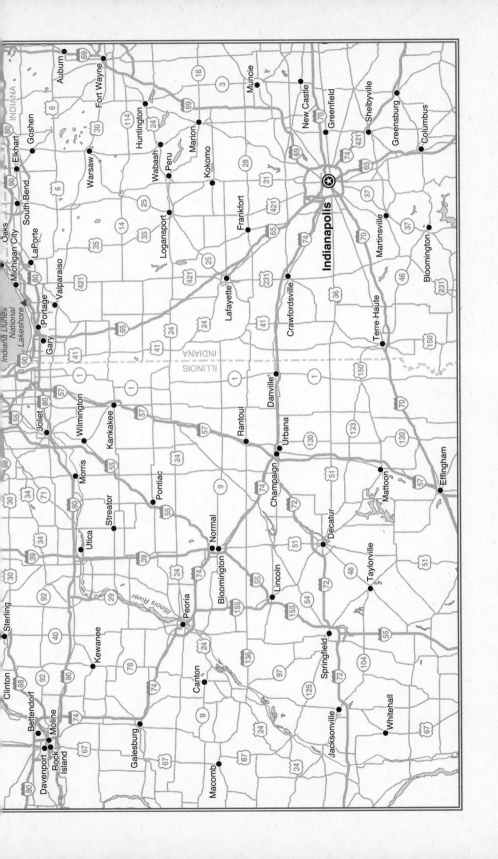

Pick up your own fabulously fresh ingredients at farmers' markets that rival Chicago's—those in Kenosha, Madison, and Milwaukee, in particular. Or get it straight from the source at U-pick apple, blueberry, pumpkin, and peach orchards. The region's wide-open spaces also lend themselves well to gorgeous golf courses and award-winning wineries.

Find out which city is known as the RV Capital of the World and another that claims the world's largest spectator sporting facility. Shop till you drop through grand malls, and turn up treasures at antique centers in Gurnee, Waukesha, Davenport, and several other towns. Tiptoe through the tulips in Holland, Michigan, and tour historic mansions in Galena.

Five college towns make the list: Champaign-Urbana, Bloomington-Normal, Madison, South Bend, and even Peoria. Do some learning of your own at world-class art museums and hidden-away art galleries; two top-notch Native American cultural institutions; and several railway, aviation, and automobile museums. There's more than a day's worth of sightseeing, touring, and activity on each of these 25 trips, so you'd better get going. Fill that tank, hit the road, and have some day-tripping fun.

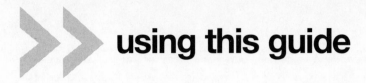 # using this guide

Day Trips from Chicago is organized by general direction from Chicago: north, northeast, east, southeast, south, southwest, west, and northwest. It by no means purports to cover every worthy destination, but rather 25 that I believe make up a varied group that will appeal to couples, families, friends, and fellow travelers, and can be reached by driving from the Loop for 90 minutes up to 3½ hours. I have given most directions from the Loop to the visitor center of each location. One caveat, though: Many of the visitor centers are closed on the weekends, so be sure to check and map your course accordingly.

hours and prices

In the interest of accuracy and because they frequently change, hours of operation and attraction prices are given in general terms. (Note: Most attraction listings mention only that there is an admission fee.) Always remember to call ahead to get the most up-to-date information, as websites are not always reliable. If you have questions, contact the establishments for specifics.

pricing key

The price codes for accommodations and restaurants are represented as a scale of one to three dollar signs ($).

You can assume all establishments listed accept major credit cards unless otherwise noted. For details, contact the locations directly.

accommodations

The price code reflects the average cost of a double-occupancy room during the peak price period (not including tax or extras). Please also note that during peak season in some areas, a two-night stay (or more) is required. Always check online or call to find out if any special discounts are available.

$	less than $100
$$	$100 to $175
$$$	more than $175

restaurants

The price code reflects the average price of dinner entrees for two (excluding cocktails, wine, appetizers, desserts, tax, and tip). You should usually expect to pay less for lunch and/or breakfast, when applicable.

$	$10 to $20
$$	$20 to $40
$$$	more than $40

driving tips

- While we like to rely on GPS these days, it's unfortunately not always accurate, so I recommend that you plan your route before you head out.

- Remember that some highway speed limits are 65 mph, but then crank back down to 55 mph as they reach city limits.

- Like Chicago, other Midwest cities rely on summer weather to embark on road construction projects. Check online to be prepared, and slow down in construction zones.

- Many of these day trips take you along a tollway, so make sure you have cash on hand if you don't have an I-Pass device (or other such toll-paying device).

highway designations

Major highways are typically listed in terms of their numbered designations, such as I-94, but if there's an obvious nickname—part of I-90, for example, is called the Skyway—that is used instead. While US 41 is often referred to as the Edens, I've mostly just kept it as US 41. Outside of the city, there are a lot of addresses with CR, which stands for County Road.

travel tips

General Hours of Operation: Hours for restaurants, shops, and attractions are given in general terms. Because some may close on particular holidays or change hours seasonally, it's best to call ahead before you go.

Seasonal Issues: Winter can mean a slow season and great lodging discounts in some destinations, except during Christmas and New Year's, when popular spots often run on peak-season prices. Winter can also present difficult driving conditions, so be careful—for instance, snowbanks along highways leave very little shoulder lane clear or reduce roads without a shoulder to fewer lanes.

Memorial Day is typically when peak pricing begins for hotels and inns, so if you want to sneak in a stay before that, you'll often get a cheaper rate. Remember that summer in the Midwest does not always mean hot and sunny; plan a few rainy-day options just in case. For fall foliage trips, October usually offers the best viewing; some destinations even offer fall foliage maps to enhance your trip (check online or call the visitor center to find out).

Sales Tax: While it's doubtful that any location you'll visit has a local sales tax as high as Chicago's, it does vary and can add up. If you're interested, call first to find out the specifics. Some attractions will give you prices over the phone and online including tax, but others may not. Be prepared to pay a state sales tax on top of most published prices as well. Hotels rarely include tax or gratuities in their published rates. Such items will sometimes raise a hotel rate by more than 15 percent.

Selected Lodging & Restaurants: Most destinations have chain hotels and restaurants, which are generally not included in the listings in each chapter, as they operate on standards that are similar across the country. The lodgings and restaurants highlighted are typically local to the area.

where to get more information

Day Trips attempts to cover a variety of bases and interests, but if you're looking for additional material, plenty is out there. Most states and cities, and even some smaller towns, have their own tourism bureaus, so for most trips, they are listed as a first "where to go" location. They are a good place to start, often offering comprehensive websites and welcoming calls, emails, or requests for printed visitor guides, brochures, and maps. In addition to the resources in this book, some additional sources of information include:

DuPage County Convention and Visitors Bureau
915 Harger Rd., Suite 240
Oak Brook, IL 60523
(800) 232-0502
www.dupagecvb.com

Heritage Corridor Convention and Visitors Bureau
339 W. Jefferson St.
Joliet, IL 60432
(800) 926-CANAL (2262), (815) 727-2323
801 E. US Highway 6
Utica, IL 61373

(800) 746-0550, (815) 667-4356
www.heritagecorridorcvb.com

The Historical Society of Michigan
5815 Executive Dr.
Lansing, MI 48911-5352
(517) 324-1828
www.hsmichigan.org

Illinois Department of Natural Resources
www.dnr.illinois.gov

Illinois Office of Tourism
(800) 2-CONNECT
www.enjoyillinois.com

Illinois State Historical Society
(217) 525-2781
www.historyillinois.org

Indiana Office of Tourism Development
One N. Capitol, Suite 600
Indianapolis, IN 46204-2288
(800) 677-9800
www.visitindiana.com

Indiana State Parks and Reservoirs
402 W. Washington, Room W298
Indianapolis, IN 46204
(317) 232-4143
www.in.gov/dnr/parklake

Iowa DNR State Parks
Iowa State Park Reservations
502 E. 9th St.
Des Moines, IA 50319
(877) 427-2757
www.iowadnr.gov/parks/index.html

Michigan Department of Natural Resources and Environment
Constitution Hall
525 W. Allegan St.
Lansing, MI 48909
(517) 373-7917
www.michigan.gov/dnr

Pure Michigan: Official Michigan State Tourism
(888) 784-7328
www.michigan.org

State of Iowa Historical Building
(Des Moines)
600 E. Locust
Des Moines, IA 50319
(515) 281-5111
www.iowahistory.org

Travel Iowa: Official Iowa State Tourism
200 E. Grand Ave.
Des Moines, IA 50309
(800) 345-IOWA
www.traveliowa.com

Western Illinois Tourism Development Office
581 S. Deere Rd.
Macomb, IL 61455
(309) 837-7460
www.visitwesternillinois.info

Wisconsin Department of Natural Resources
101 S. Webster St.
PO Box 7921
Madison, WI 53707-7921
(888) 936-7463, (608) 266-2621
www.dnr.wi.gov

Wisconsin Department of Tourism
201 W. Washington Ave.
PO Box 8690
Madison, WI 53708-8690
(800) 432-8747, (608) 266-2161
www.travelwisconsin.com

Wisconsin Historical Society
816 State St.
Madison, WI 53706
www.wisconsinhistory.org

north

day trip 01

north

>>> **shops, drops & danish rolls:**
gurnee, il; kenosha, wi; racine, wi

Past Chicago's North Shore suburbs on I-94, there's space enough for scenic orchards, mammoth malls, and sprawling gardens. While you might be familiar with a few select spots, this day trip breaks that same old, same old mold. After all, let's remember, cities like Kenosha and Racine didn't burn down in their formative years, so there's actually history that dates pretty far back for Midwest standards. While Chicago argues over which of two 1830s homes is the "oldest" (Clarke vs. Noble-Seymour-Crippen), Kenosha generously offers up a whole neighborhood full of pre-Civil War structures. A bit further inland, Gurnee took a little longer to make its mark, but with major attractions and a huge water park resort, it keeps getting stronger. While each area has its own info center, a handy 24-hour Lake County visitor kiosk is located at the Lake Forest Oasis on the Tri-State Tollway I-294/I-94 between IL 60 and IL 176.

gurnee

A pilgrimage to Great America was an anticipated summer ritual when I was growing up. Early years meant going with the family, sometimes even dragging along my unwitting grandparents from New York, who put a smile on and took turns going on kiddie rides with my older sister and me. In high school the kid with the biggest car would pile as many of us in as humanly possible (hey, the seatbelt law wasn't enacted until 1985), and we'd trek out with spending money in our pockets and two dimes to call our parents to let them know we'd be coming home later than planned. Gurnee Mills was always the staple for

2

north day trip 01

back-to-school shopping, and is even more so now. In fact, Gurnee may have begun small, with a population of just under 4,000 as recently as 1973, but it's about 30,000 now, and it's all about the big. Big roller coasters. Big shopping. Big fun.

getting there

From downtown, take I-90/I-94 west (you're going north, of course) and continue on I-94 when I-90 branches off to O'Hare. Soon after you pass the Lake Avenue exit, I-94 merges with US 41 north, the Edens. Be sure you follow US 41 at this point, not the exit to I-94 (you could, but you'd go out of your way west just to come back east). To get to most attractions in Gurnee, you'll take exit 132 (Grand Avenue) off US 41. It's about an hour's drive, but be prepared for traffic, as there always seems to be some construction somewhere on I-94, and part of US 41 is only two lanes. Visit www.plan94.org for construction updates.

where to go

Lake County, Illinois Convention & Visitors Bureau. 5465 W. Grand Ave. Suite 100, Gurnee; (800) 525-3669, (847) 662-2700; www.lakecounty.org. Pick up free visitors guides and tips on where to go. Open Mon-Fri 8 a.m. to 5 p.m.

Cuneo Mansion & Gardens. 1350 N. Milwaukee Ave., Vernon Hills; (847) 362-3042; www.cuneomansion.org. Before reaching Gurnee, take a detour off I-94 into Vernon Hills to check out this majestic Italianate villa. An impressive vision of grand stone staircases, stained glass, and suits of armor, plus breathtaking Jens Jensen–designed gardens, the 100-acre estate was completed in 1918 for GE founder Samuel Insull and purchased in 1937 by businessman John Cuneo, Sr. It remained under the stewardship of John Cuneo Jr. and his wife, Herta, until 2009, when the family foundation donated it to Loyola University to use for educational programming and fine and performing arts events. Guided tours (the only way in) offer a peek at the Cuneos' rich and refined lifestyle, along with many of the family's exquisite antiques, paintings, sculptures, and tapestries. Tours Fri, Sat, and Sun; gardens open Fri, Sat, and Sun 11 a.m. to 3 p.m. Admission; free for Loyola students, faculty, and staff, as well as clergy and military. Tours also available by appointment.

Lambs Farm. 14245 W. Rockland Rd., Libertyville; (847) 362-4636; www.lambsfarm.org. Another pre-Gurnee stop, just off I-94 at US 176, this 72-acre farm started out in 1961 as a pet shop on State Street and now trumps any carnival petting zoo I've ever seen. Sheep, lambs, goats, kids, chickens, rabbits, and super-adorable pygmy goats sidle up for rubs and kisses (on the hands only, please). Need more action? The farm has an 18-hole mini golf course, a kiddie train ride, a cute old-fashioned carousel, and a cow bounce house. Oh, yes, and a pet shop full of pleading pups, kittens, and more (enter at your own risk, if you know what I mean). The facility's pride and joy, though, is its emphasis on employing, assisting, housing, and teaching adults with developmental disabilities. Open daily in season (generally spring through fall) 10 a.m. to 5 p.m. Admission.

Mother Rudd Home Museum. 4690 Old Grand Ave.; (847) 263-9540; www.motherrudd .org. Built in 1844 and now home to the Warren Township Historical Society, this former tavern, inn, and Underground Railway stopover is also one of the oldest structures in Lake County. Displays include a re-created 1930s kitchen and 1900 bedroom, plus historic artifacts and photographs of the Gurnee area. Call for scheduled open house days.

Six Flags Great America. 1 Great America Pkwy.; (847) 249-4636; www.sixflags.com /greatamerica. You could certainly spend an entire day at this longstanding amusement park, what with 14 roller coasters, the interactive Buccaneer Battle, Wiggles World for the littlest ones, the included-with-admission Hurricane Harbor water park and the brand-new Riptide Bay for more wild wet fun. But if you only have half a day, squeeze in a few top thrills. My picks: the beloved Little Dipper from the old Kiddieland grounds; the creaky oldie but goodie American Eagle (I finally mastered that when I was 20); high-speed looper, the Demon; and classic splasher, the Logger's Run. Not scary enough for ya? OK, then, brave guy, try Batman the Ride, claiming to be the world's first inverted, outside-looping coaster; Raging Bull, the fastest coaster at the park; and the crazy headfirst freak-out Superman. Skip the biggest crowds by visiting on a weekday or during April, May, June, or September. Admission starts at around $40 for kids, and parking is extra, but you can get the most for your money with packages, discounts, and deals through the website. Open seasonally. Call or go online for hours of operation.

Tempel Lipizzans. 17000 Wadsworth Rd., Old Mill Creek; (847) 623-7272; www.tempel farms.com. Trot on over to see performances by the graceful, Prince Charming–worthy white horses that are part of the world's largest privately owned herd of this type of horse. Playful brown and black foals begin the show—they'll turn white as they grow—then give it up to the athletic, agile, awe-inspiring adult horses that leap, pirouette, dance in synch, and show off their medieval battle techniques. After the show, browse the historic stables and antique carriage collection. Performances every Wed and Sun, June through Oct. Call about admission prices and off-season facility tours.

Wildlife Discovery Center. 1401 Middlefork Dr., Lake Forest; (847) 615-4388; www .cityoflakeforest.com. This wildlife conservation center on the historic Elawa Farm now houses the largest reptile exhibit in northern Illinois and the nation's largest public display of rattlesnakes, not to mention 800 acres of hiking and biking trails. Stop and say hello to the 14-foot king cobra, the crocodile monitor lizard, the posse of painted turtles (our state reptile, by the way), and Aussie and Harriet, a pair of Australian kookaburras—they're good for a laugh. Open Fri, Sat, and Sun. Modest admission price.

where to shop

Gurnee Antique Center. 5742 Northridge Dr.; (847) 782-9094; www.gurneeantiquecenter .com. More than 200 dealers share their wares in a 24,000-square-foot space. Find top-

olden opportunity

*Tucked in among McMansions and suburban sprawl lies one of my favorite Chicagoland destinations: **Long Grove Historic Village.** Not particularly grand or influential, Long Grove, Illinois, began as the crossroads of two Native American paths and developed in the early 1800s as a German farming town. Long ago, Long Grove residents decided to preserve their historic buildings, their cobblestone walks, and their old-fashioned sensibilities. Today, dozens of independently owned boutiques and restaurants make their homes in restored structures, plaques mark the many landmarks, and the village practically overflows with charm, especially during annual winter holiday festivities. Here, my top 10 spots to hit on your visit:*

*1. **Country House of Long Grove.** 430 Robert Parker Coffin Rd.; (847) 634-2292; www.countryhouseoflonggrove.com. Kitchen gadgets, weather vanes, vintage-style metal signs.*

*2. **Dakota Expressions.** 317 Old McHenry Rd.; (847) 634-8250; www.dakota expressions.com. Native American and southwestern jewelry, crafts, shoes, and accessories.*

*3. **Dog House of Long Grove.** 405 Robert Parker Coffin Rd.; (847) 634-3060; www.thedoghouseoflg.com. In business since 1952, carrying everything from healthy baked pup treats to Halloween costumes, custom-made wooden beds to personalized bowls, plus a kitty corner too.*

*4. **Long Grove Apple Haus.** 230 Robert Parker Coffin Rd.; (847) 634-0730, www.longgroveonline.com. Famous for its "brown bag" apple pie, apple doughnuts, and caramel apples.*

quality, independently appraised 18th-, 19th-, and early 20th-century furniture, glass, jewelry, art, books, clothing, and more. Open daily.

Gurnee Mills. 6170 W. Grand Ave.; (847) 263-7500; www.gurneemills.com. Faced with more than 200 outlets and "value" retailers ranging from Abercrombie & Fitch to Zales, I dare you not to leave laden with shopping bags. The Neiman Marcus Last Call store is the only one in Illinois; the Disney Store Outlet is a parent's very own fairytale; and the Bass Pro Shops is like an outdoorsy amusement park. Browse Bed Bath & Beyond, Kohl's, T.J. Maxx, Sears Grand, Guess Factory Store, H&M, Saks Fifth Avenue Off Fifth—the list goes

5. Long Grove Confectionery. *220 Robert Parker Coffin Rd.; (847) 634-0080; www.longgrove.com. Chocolate-covered everything and outstanding English toffee. Watch them make their homemade fudge.*

6. Ma & Pa's Candy Store. *424 Robert Parker Coffin Rd; (847) 634-0450; www .maandpascandy.com. Nostalgic sweets like sour balls, Pop Rocks and button candy, Sour Patch Kids, and Swedish Fish.*

7. Nifty 50's. *325 Old McHenry Rd.; (847) 478-1932; www.nifty-50s.com. Collectibles from the bobby socks era, such as old Coca-Cola and Betty Boop merchandise, Beatles posters, and Elvis lunch boxes.*

8. Timmy's Sandwiches & Ice Cream. *132 Old McHenry Rd.; (847) 883-8930; www.timmyssandwichesandicecream.tripod.com. Classic sammies done right in an old-timey setting, from a Kendall College Culinary School grad. Ice cream specials too. (Closed Mon.)*

9. The Village Tavern. *135 Old McHenry Rd; (847) 634-3117; www.villagetavern oflonggrove.com. Operating continuously since 1849, now featuring half-pound Angus beef burgers, Wednesday night all-you-can-eat broasted chicken, and live music most nights.*

10. Within Reach. *302 Old McHenry Rd.; (847) 634-2399. Country-quaint home decor, and Within Kid's Reach with hand-painted furniture.*

If you stop here before heading up to Gurnee, take I-90/I-94, following I-94 north, which merges with US 41. Take the Dundee exit west and turn right at McHenry Road (IL 83); at the fork stop, take a left, then a quick right on Old McHenry Road. There's a visitor center in the main parking lot. For more information: (847) 634-0888; www.longgroveonline.com.

on and on. And if you didn't make it to the Wildlife Discovery Center, the Serpent Safari is a kind of mall-ified version. Let's just say, wear your walking shoes and keep track of that credit card max. Open daily.

where to eat

D.W. Anderson's Eatery & Ice Cream Parlor. KeyLime Cove Water Resort. 1700 Nations Dr.; (262) 656-8033; www.keylimecove.com. When an ice cream creation called the Kitchen Sink arrives at the table literally in a kitchen sink, you know you're in for a treat.

This '50s-style diner at the huge KeyLime Cove Water Resort doesn't disappoint in size and humor. A crowd-pleasing selection of salads, sandwiches, burgers, pizza, and fried food—ever seen fries topped with bacon, ranch dressing, and cheddar cheese?—will have you adjusting your belt to the next notch. Open for breakfast, lunch, and dinner. For more on KeyLime Cove, check out the Where to Stay section below. $.

David's Bistro. 883 Main St., Antioch; (847) 603-1196; www.davidsbistro.com. Any place where the kids menu has more than mac and cheese (though they have that too)—think mini "corny" dogs and jumbo fried shrimp—gets points in my book. But it's the grown-up gastronomy that gets the raves. Chef/owner David Maish's quaint storefront eatery features a seasonally changing menu with highlights like New Zealand lamb chops crusted with pine nuts and pecans; pasta with sautéed spinach, portabellas, and sundried tomatoes; and several creative pizzas and soups. His martinis and desserts alone are worth the trip. Open for lunch and dinner. $$–$$$.

Saluto's Italian Restaurant. 7680 Grand Ave.; (847) 356-6900; www.salutosofgurnee .com. This longtime local family-friendly favorite is known for its house salad dressing that people pack up to go, along with its homemade buttercrust pizzas, fresh baked rolls, and family-size portions of pasta. Open Mon for dinner and Tues through Sun for lunch and dinner. $$–$$$.

Timothy O'Toole's. 5572 Grand Ave.; (847) 249-0800; www.timothyotooles.com. Mimicking its sister sports bar near the Mag Mile, the Gurnee location has much of the same drinking, merriment, and hearty bar menu: award-winning wings; baskets of chicken fingers, fried shrimp, and ribs; fish and chips; two meatloaf options; and burgers, salads, and wraps. Be authentic and pair your meal with one of nine different Guinness beer concoctions. Open for lunch and dinner daily and brunch on the weekends. $$.

where to stay

Camping in Chain O' Lakes State Park. 8916 Wilmot Rd., Spring Grove; (847) 587-5512. Can't beat the prices at this camping and RV site bordered by three lakes and the Fox River. Boating activities abound. Just make sure you post your permit and pack plenty of bug spray. $.

KeyLime Cove Water Park. 1700 Nations Dr.; (877) 360-0403; www.keylimecove.com. A tropical adventure comes with your room at this "official resort" of Great America. Opened in 2008 by Famous Dave's restaurant mogul Dave Anderson, the resort does it up with coconut scents in the air (seriously), pastel colors all around, and Jimmy Buffett–like tunes. You might think it's cheesy, but it's all about the getaway experience, with an indoor water park that's 86 degrees all the time, six restaurants, an arcade, live entertainment, and the Paradise Mist Spa. $$$.

The Roxana Bed & Breakfast Hotel. 94 Lippincott Rd., Fox Lake; (877) 769-2621; www
.theroxana.com. Romance comes easy at this historic 1893 bed and breakfast along the
Mineola Bay of Fox Lake. Pull up a swing on the wraparound porch or settle into one of the
leather parlor chairs in front of the fireplace. The 11 guest rooms are decked out in period
pieces, most with private baths and lake views. $–$$$.

kenosha

When Chicagoans think Kenosha, we usually think outlet stores. But K Town offers explor-
ing beyond the racks. Four distinct historic districts and a lighthouse from 1866 highlight the
architecture. The fourth-largest city along Lake Michigan originally served as an automobile
manufacturing hub from about 1902 to 1988, with names like Hudson, Nash, and American
Motors Corporation. These days, it's somewhat quieter, with lots of downtown Chicago
workers using it as their far north—and far cheaper—suburb, commuting quite easily by
Metra, which has its only Wisconsin depot in Kenosha. OK, now you can hit the mall.

getting there

Kenosha is about 20 miles north and slightly east of Gurnee. Jump back onto US 41 head-
ing north, where you'll stay for about 8 miles. After you pass Rosencrans Road, I-94 scoots
back east to join US 41 again, and you'll merge with it at this point. Take exit 344 for WI 50
toward Kenosha. Turn right onto WI 50/75th Street and follow that into town. Like Chicago,
Kenosha streets form somewhat of a grid, but nomenclature is even easier: Numbered
streets run east-west, numbered *avenues* run north-south, and *roads* cross diagonally.

where to go

Downtown Main Office & Visitor Information Center. 812 56th St.; (262) 654-7307,
(800) 654-7309; 24-hour event line: (262) 658-4FUN ext. 3; www.kenoshacvb.com. This
visitor hub is just off Sheridan Road and down the street from the Dinosaur Discovery
Museum. Open Mon through Fri 8 a.m. to 4:30 p.m.

Dinosaur Discovery Museum. 5608 10th Ave.; (262) 653-4450; www.dinosaurdiscovery
museum.org. Though it's hard to equal the wow factor of The Field Museum's T. rex Sue,
this museum comes close, showcasing one of North America's largest exhibits of thero-
pods, the largest terrestrial carnivorous dinosaurs. Plus, it's free. Focusing on the strong link
between birds and theropods, the museum also lets kids dig into fossil-finding at simulated
excavation sites most Saturdays. Open Tues through Sun. Closed Mon.

Jelly Belly Center. 10100 Jelly Belly Lane, Pleasant Prairie; (866) 868-7522; www.jellybelly
.com. Talk about a sweet deal. Tours of this confection factory are free, with freebie bags
of Jelly Belly beans to boot. The fourth-generation-owned company was founded in 1869

and marketed its first eight official Jelly Belly flavors in 1976. There are now more than 50, from toasted marshmallow to margarita, cotton candy to cappuccino. Sample all you want, including dozens of other candies, at the factory store; then bag some up for the road. Open daily 9 a.m. to 4 p.m.

Kenosha Civil War Museum. 5400 1st Ave.; (262) 653-4140; www.thecivilwarmuseum .org. Opened in 2008, this fascinating museum takes a look back at the influences on and effects of the Civil War. Artifacts from six Midwestern states include artillery jackets, hats, and weapons. Board a replica train car and listen to personal stories from Civil War soldiers, nurses, doctors, clergymen, and more; walk into buildings furnished as in 1860; and find out how the war back then changed lives today. Admission; children 15 and under free when accompanied by an adult. Call for hours.

Kenosha's Electric Streetcars. Kenosha Transit Center, 724 54th St.; (262) 653-4287; www.kenosha.org (link to Transportation), or www.kenoshastreetcarsociety.org. Harking back to Kenosha's electric streetcar days (from 1903 to 1932), this 1951 refurbished fleet of streetcars takes riders on a 2-mile loop with 10 stops along the way, including the Southport Marina at the lakefront. Fare is 50 cents for ages 12 and older, 25 cents for 11 and younger. An all-day pass is $2.

National Register Historic Districts. Contact the visitor center for information; (800) 654-7309; www.kenoshacvb.com. Kenosha's four historic districts are definitely worth a walk-through. Homes built before the Civil War dot the Library Park Historic District, while grand mansions of the late 19th and early 20th centuries mark 3rd Avenue's lakefront district. In the Civic Center Historic District, you'll find neoclassical and early-20th-century architecture in a grouping of public buildings. Renovations are giving new life to the many Greek Revival, Italianate, and Classic Revival structures in the Pearl Street Historic District.

Southport Lighthouse Museum. 5117 4th Ave. (better known as Lighthouse Drive); (262) 654-5770; www.kenoshahistorycenter.org. Test your stamina with a climb up to the top of this 55-foot historic 1866 lighthouse. The restored keeper's residence describes the maritime history of the area and the lives of lighthouse keepers. Admission. (Note: Children under 8 are not allowed up.) Open Sat and Sun, generally May through Oct.

where to shop

Kenosha Harbor Market. Spring and summer market at 56th St. & 2nd Ave., late fall and winter market at Rhode Center for the Arts, 514 56th St.; (262) 914-1252; www.kenosha harbormarket.com. Don't tell anyone, but this might be better than Chicago's Green City Market. It has a European feel, with not only home baked goods, fresh flowers, chef demos, locally grown organic produce, meats, cheeses, and eggs, but also live music, ethnic eats, and handmade arts and crafts. Open Sat at the spring and summer location mid-May to mid-Oct; winter location, mid-Oct to mid-May.

Prime Outlets at Pleasant Prairie. 11211 120th Ave., at I-94 and WI 165, Pleasant Prairie; (877) 466-8853; www.primeoutlets.com. Shopaholics get happy at this outlet heaven, where the 90 brand-name outlet stores include Coach, The North Face, Calvin Klein, and Restoration Hardware. The new state-of-the-art guest services center has several fast food options, along with complimentary stroller and wheelchair use, area visitor info, free Wi-Fi, and a lounge for those moments when you just need to sit.

where to eat

Boat House Pub & Eatery. 4917 7th Ave.; (262) 654-9922; www.foodspot.com/boat house. Made-to-order fish specials include the popular Shore Lunch, a fresh catch served with fries, cole slaw, and a roll for less than 10 bucks. Burgers and sandwiches have nautical names like the Tug Boat—roast beef on a toasted French roll with au jus and pepperoncini. Steak, chicken, and salads round out the menu, plus an all-you-can-eat Sunday breakfast buffet and an outrageous list of nearly 20 32-ounce Long Island iced tea cocktails for—get this, city folks—less than $9 each. Boating in? There are 22 private docks too and live entertainment most every Wed, Fri, and Sat. Open daily for lunch and dinner. $–$$$.

Frank's Diner. 508 58th St.; (262) 657-1017; www.franksdinerkenosha.com. Featured on the Food Network series *Diners, Drive-Ins and Dives,* this kitschy train car diner has been cooking up huge pancakes, juicy burgers, and famous five-egg Garbage Plate meals for more than 80 years. Open daily for breakfast and lunch. Last orders are taken half-hour before close. $.

Mangia Trattoria. 5717 Sheridan Rd.; (262) 652-4285; www.kenoshamangia.com. James Beard Award–winning chef Tony Mantuano might be best known for the Mag Mile's magnificent Spiaggia, but Mangia is his hometown hit. This cozy, casual restaurant specializes in authentic Italian pastas and pizzas, as well as the $44 menu in honor of President Obama, a big Spiaggia fan (it's where he proposed to the First Lady). Open for lunch and dinner Tues through Fri and dinner only Sat and Sun. Closed Mon. $$.

where to stay

Merry Yacht Inn. 4815 7th Ave.; (262) 654-9922. You might say this inn is hot. Or it rings your bell. Or it's on fire . . . OK, I'll stop. It's a refurbished 1896 fire station. Walking distance to the harbor and great lake views at an affordable price make it popular with fishing groups. $.

Southport Bed & Breakfast. 4405 7th Ave.; (262) 652-1951; www.southportbnb.com. Roy and Rita Watring run this two-room B&B, just 3 blocks from Lake Michigan. Each room has a private entrance and Jacuzzi bath. The continental breakfast is served right in your room. $.

racine

Translating to "root" in French, Racine got its name when French explorers arrived at the mouth of the Root River by canoe in 1699. Though the Native Americans had other names for the place, Racine stuck with the new white settlers. One of the largest groups of immigrants was the Danish, who founded the oldest Danish Lutheran Church in North America in 1851. They also left a legacy with the famous kringle pastry, a taste of this lakeshore town that's a must-try.

getting there

A straight shot up Sheridan Road (it changes to Alford Park Drive for about a mile) makes for a scenic 25-minute drive north to Racine from Kenosha. To get to the visitor center, make a left at 14th Street, which becomes Washington Avenue after a curve in the road around Washington Park.

where to go

The Real Racine Visitor Center. 14015 Washington Ave., off I-94 and WI 20; (800) 272-2463; www.realracine.com. This Frank Lloyd Wright–inspired structure has everything visitors need to guide their way, including free Wi-Fi. Open daily 9 a.m. to 5 p.m.

Apple Holler. 5006 S. Sylvania Ave., Sturtevant; (262) 884-7100; www.appleholler.com. Open year-round, this 75-acre orchard features more than just apple trees. It has a dinner theater, hearty homestyle-cooking restaurant, wine and gift shop, petting zoo, wagon and sleigh rides, corn maze, and pedal carts. There's also a pumpkin patch in the fall, and pears too. But the apples really do shine, with more than 30 varieties from Viking to Paula Red to Gala. Happy picking.

Fortaleza Hall. 1525 Howe St.; (262) 260-2154; www.scjohnson.com. Joining the iconic Frank Lloyd Wright–designed Administration Building, Research Tower and Golden Rondelle Theater at SC Johnson headquarters is this 60,000-square-foot curvy glass eye-popper from Foster & Partners. Inside is equally impressive. Its centerpiece is Carnaúba, a replica of the Sikorsky aircraft that H.F. Johnson Jr. flew in 1935 to Fortaleza, Brazil, where he discovered the wax that launched his company. Displays and artifacts detail the history and legacy of the SC Johnson family and business, as well as its Frank Lloyd Wright structures, including Wingspan, the 1939 Wright-designed Johnson family home that's now used as an educational and conference center. Free tours are available most weekends; reservations required. Call for details.

Racine Art Museum. 441 Main St.; (262) 638-8300; www.ramart.org. This bold yet inviting 46,000-square-foot space beckons with its back-lit façade of translucent acrylic panels. But the attention mostly goes to the artwork, one of the largest collections of contemporary craft

danish bakeries

In Racine, flaky goodness comes in the shape of a big oval of pastry filled with nuts or fruit. It's called the **kringle,** *and it's the Danish bakery specialty that has turned this small Midwestern town into the Kringle Capital of America.* **Bendtsen's Bakery** *(3200 Washington Ave., 262-633-0365, www.bendtsensbakery.com) claims to be the longest family-owned bakery in town, while* **O & H Danish Bakery** *(4006 Durand Ave., 262-554-1311, www.ohdanishbakery.com) boasts 6,000 square feet of production, deli, and gift shop. Call for hours.*

in North America. Organized by idea instead of media, works by regional and international artists such as Dale Chihuly, Joel Philip Myers, and Lia Cook include paper, ceramics, fiber, glass, metals, and wood. Nominal admission. Open Tues through Sun. Closed Mon.

Racine Lakefront Trolley. (262) 637-9000. Ride 'round Racine in a vintage streetcar for just a quarter. These wheels only come out during the summer, so call for a schedule.

where to eat

Corner House. 1521 Washington Ave. (aka WI 20); (262) 637-1295; www.cornerhouse racine.com. What Lawry's is to Chicago, Corner House is to Racine. Perfectly prepared prime ribs, that is. They've even earned the restaurant a distinction as the Best Place for Prime Rib by *Milwaukee* magazine. Besides that, the menu offers filets, chops, ribs, veal, fish, chicken, lobster, and a drool-worthy dessert menu (think peanut butter ice cream pie and turtle cake). Open daily for dinner. $$–$$$.

Spinnakers. 2 Christopher Columbus Way; (262) 633-8250. If you're looking for a meal with a view, this is the place. Overlooking the harbor and Lake Michigan, it serves a standard menu of burgers, sandwiches, soups, and salads. Open daily for lunch, dinner, and late-night. $.

Wells Brothers Pizza. 2148 Mead St.; (262) 632-4408; www.wellsbrosracine.com. You could get a chicken breast, grilled cheese, or spaghetti here, but that would be silly. This family-owned business is known for its pizza—the authors of *Everybody Loves Pizza* listed it as a top 10. Incredibly thin and how-do-they-do-it crispy, these pizzas have been attracting loyal fans since way back in 1921 when the original Wells brothers, James and Dominic, opened the joint. There's also an all-you-can-eat fish fry every Friday. Open for lunch and dinner Tues through Sat. $.

day trip 02

north

>>> **way more than beer:**
milwaukee, wi

milwaukee

As a kid in the 1970s, for me Milwaukee meant *Happy Days* and *Laverne & Shirley*. I wore a necklace that said "Sit on It" (a la the Fonz) and a T-shirt with an iron-on decal of Laverne and Shirley, best buds who worked at, of course, a brewery. From the 1850s until the late 1990s, beer was key to Milwaukee's growth, and it still plays an important part in its business and pleasure. But these days, Brew City has much more going for it: a world-class art museum and accompanying dynamic art scene; a scenic Riverwalk; active theater and music venues; and the constructive reuse of historic buildings into shopping, dining, and nightlife destinations, many of which bear the striking yellow brick that gave this town its other nickname—Cream City. For us *Happy Days*–era folks, a visit to the statue of the Fonz is a must.

getting there

Take I-90/I-94 west, following the Edens (US 41) north when it splits. Merge back with I-94 west, which is also called I-43 north as you get close to Milwaukee. To get to the visitor center, take the exit toward N. 10th Street. Turn right on Wisconsin Avenue, and the center is about a half-mile down on the left. In the city, the streets are generally a grid, with north-south streets numbered and east-west streets named. East of 1st Street, the streets have names as well. Without traffic it should take about an hour and a half, but be prepared for slow-going due to highway construction around Milwaukee.

N

0   10   20 miles

Brookfield

190

43

94

Milwaukee

94

Waukesha

West Allis

894

Greenfield

894

164

43

36

100

38

32

94

20

41

Racine

36

20

120

Burlington

11

Sturtevant

32

83

142

50

Kenosha

Pleasant
Prairie

94

LAKE MICHIGAN

WISCONSIN
ILLINOIS

Antioch

32

Spring
Grove

Tempel
Lipizzans

Fox Lake

94

Gurnee

120

Waukegan

41

31

176

12

Lamb's Farm

Cuneo Mansion
and Gardens

Wildlife
Discovery
Center

62

22

Long Grove

94

14

Palatine

Arlington Heights

41

90

Elgin

294

Evanston

Schaumburg

Des Plaines

94

Skokie

290

90

14

355

Oak Park

94

90

Wheaton

290

Cicero

Chicago

Berwyn

88

Aurora

Naperville

294

55

94

where to go

Visit Milwaukee Visitors Center. Frontier Airlines Center, inside main rotunda on first floor, 400 W. Wisconsin Ave.; (800) 554-1448; www.visitmilwaukee.org. An award-winning visitor organization that provides destination guides, general visitor guides, shopping guides, and maps. Hours vary based on season and events.

The Bronze Fonz. Along the west side of the Milwaukee River, just south of Wells Street. Immortalizing Henry Winkler's iconic super-cool *Happy Days* character, this bronze statue has become a picture-op stop for fans from all over the world. Standing just a tad taller than Winkler himself, the likeness, created by Wisconsin artist Gerald Sawyer, is fashioned with the Fonz's signature leather jacket, Wrangler jeans, Skate Buckle boots, and two thumbs up.

Discovery World. 500 N. Harbor Drive; (414) 765-9966; www.discoveryworld.org. Several attractions wrapped into one, this 120,000-square-foot lakefront destination features science and technology exhibits, aquariums, a replica of a 19th-century schooner, theaters, and TV and radio studios. Every area is devoted to interactive experiences: Touch a sea urchin, jam with a virtual version of rock 'n' roll legend Les Paul, lie on a bed of nails. Two notes: Exhibits lean toward kids older than 6, and some are closed at times for repairs. Admission. Open Tues to Sun, closed Mon.

Edelweiss Boats. 205 W. Highland Ave.; (414) 276-7447; www.edelweissboats.com. With cruise themes for everything from Sunday brunch to disco to beer and brats, these year-round boat trips tour past sights along the Milwaukee River and Lake Michigan shoreline. The two-hour, three-course dinner cruises make for popular date nights. Prices vary.

Grohmann Museum "Man at Work" Art Collection. Milwaukee School of Engineering, 1000 N. Broadway; (414) 277-2300; www.msoe.edu/manatwork. Milwaukee's newest museum focuses on art that depicts the evolution of organized work. Donated by and named for Milwaukee businessman Dr. Eckhart Grohmann, the collection includes more than 800 paintings and sculptures and spans more than 400 years from farmers to factory workers. A rooftop sculpture garden and three-story atrium lobby highlight the renovated 1924 former bank. Nominal admission. Open daily.

Harley-Davidson Museum. 400 Canal St.; (877) 436-8738; www.h-dmuseum.com. This 130,000-square-foot holy shrine for hog lovers traces Harley history from its humble beginnings in a wooden shack to present-day domination. From the first-known bike ever built to customized models like the 13-foot-long "King Kong," the displays will leave you humming. And yes, you can even get a feel for the power in the Experience Gallery. Fuel up at Café Racer or Motor Bar and Restaurant. Open daily. Admission (children under 5 free). Guided tours available for a nominal fee.

Lakefront Brewery. 1872 N. Commerce St.; (414) 372-8800; www.lakefrontbrewery.com. Boasting regional, national, and worldwide awards out the wazoo, this local phenom may not be the oldest operating brewery in Brew City (that would be Miller), but it's possibly the friendliest and definitely the most innovative—Lakefront developed the first certified organic beer in the US. Tours start off with a glass of suds and end with a coupon for a free pint at a nearby restaurant. Admission includes a souvenir glass too. Tours at 3 p.m. Mon through Fri and 1, 2, and 3 p.m. Sat. First-come, first-served; 50-person maximum per tour (Note: Saturday 3 p.m. tours generally sell out early). Admission.

Milwaukee Art Museum. 700 N. Art Museum Dr.; (414) 224-3200; www.mam.org. The Milwaukee Art Museum's roots date back to 1888, but it made its global mark in 2001 when Santiago Calatrava's stunning new building debuted. Visitors flock to see the opening of its structural "wings" (officially titled the "Burke Brise Soleil") Tuesday through Sunday at 10 a.m. and then to their closing at 5 p.m. But the interior deserves plenty of attention as well, with four floors of galleries containing art from the antiquities to the present, including one of the largest collections of works by Wisconsin native Georgia O'Keeffe. Open Tues through Sun, closed Mon. Admission; free for children under 12.

Milwaukee County Zoo. 10001 W. Blue Mound Rd.; (414) 771-3040; www.milwaukeezoo .org. It's a tough sell for Chicagoans to visit a zoo that's not free, but this one ranks (plus, it's about four times the size of Lincoln Park Zoo). Its 350 species of mammals, reptiles, fish, birds, and invertebrates run the gamut from leopard sharks to snow leopards, Chinese alligators to North American river otters. Don't miss the Apes of Africa exhibit where 15 endangered bonobos make their home. Admission and open hours vary seasonally.

Milwaukee Public Museum. 800 W. Wells St.; (414) 278-2702; www.mpm.edu. This human and natural history museum includes a live butterfly exhibit, modern planetarium, IMAX theater, re-created Milwaukee streets from the 1880s, and the impressive Hebior Mammoth skeleton, discovered less than 30 miles from the museum. Open daily. Call ahead, because in recent years, the museum has been closed on Tuesday during the summer. Admission.

Mitchell Park Horticultural Conservatory (The Domes). 524 S. Layton Blvd.; (414) 649-9830; www.countyparks.com. Rising out of the flatness, the Mitchell Park Conservatory's three iconic, 85-foot-tall glass domes contain a world of beauty, each with a distinct theme. In the Arid Dome are cacti and succulents of the desert; in the Tropical Dome, bright and jungle-y plants of five continents' rainforests; and in the Show Dome, a changing array of seasonal colors. Open daily, hours vary by season. Admission.

Potawatomi Bingo Casino. 1721 W. Canal St.; (800) PAYSBIG; www.paysbig.com. Milwaukee is no Vegas, baby, but this casino wins big, incorporating everything a serious or casual gambler needs under one roof: 3,100 slot machines, a 20-table poker room, a 500-

seat theater, an off-track betting room with more than 100 TVs, a 1,350-seat bingo hall, a buffet, and an award-winning fine-dining steak house. Open 24 hours.

where to shop

Brady Street. (414) BRADYST; www.bradystreet.org. Buildings from the mid-19th through early 20th centuries create a distinctly vintage feel for these 9 east-west blocks that make up Brady Street and run from Lake Michigan to the Milwaukee River—perfect for the indie boutiques and welcoming cafes and wine bars that line the street. Find retro resale at Dragonfly and Annie's 2nd Hand Chic; clothing for fashionable guys at Aala Reed; and classy and sassy kicks at Angelina's Shoe Boutique.

Historic Third Ward. Historic Third Ward Association, 219 N. Milwaukee St., 3rd Floor; (414) 273-1173; www.historicthirdward.org. Perhaps best known for boasting 70 buildings on the National Register of Historic Places and for its hub of artistic activity, including more than 20 galleries and art studios, this area has added great shopping to its fame. Tucked in between the Milwaukee River and I-794, its northern end pulls visitors with the wildly successful year-round indoor Milwaukee Public Market (www.milwaukeepublicmarket.com) that opened in 2005. The nationally acclaimed Spice House is also housed here, as well as fun locally owned women's clothing shop Lela, and Artasia for Asian art, antiques, and housewares.

where to eat

Alterra at the Lake. 1701 N. Lincoln Memorial Dr.; (414) 223-4551; www.alterracoffee .com. Perk up your day with an espresso drink, a blended coffee drink, fresh brewed tea, or a smoothie from this local joint for "Joe." One of nine locations, not to mention its Mitchell airport kiosks, Alterra is a made-in-Milwaukee brew with a huge loyal following and national recognition from *Forbes Traveler Magazine* (one of the country's 10 hottest coffeehouses) and *GQ* magazine (one of 10 places in the nation to "get the best coffee"). Open daily. $.

Bartolotta's Lake Park Bistro. 3133 E. Newberry Blvd.; (414) 962-6300; www.lakepark bistro.com. Chicago's own Adam Siegel, a Kendall College grad who earned his stripes at Spiaggia, helms the kitchen at this romantic French date spot. The James Beard Award-winning chef (for Best Chef Midwest 2008) adheres to traditional French cooking methods in dishes like grilled lamb chops with French green lentils, steak frites, and grilled Scottish salmon with a nicoise olive tapanade. The bistro's setting on a bluff overlooking Lake Michigan doesn't hurt either. Open Mon through Fri for lunch and dinner, Sat for dinner, and Sun for brunch and dinner. $$$.

Hinterland Erie Street Gastropub. 222 E. Erie St.; (414) 727-9300; www.hinterlandbeer .com. The ever-evolving menu at this chic-woodsy downtown gastropub shines the light on fresh flown-in fish, wild game from local ranchers, heirloom produce, and fresh foraged mushrooms. The handcrafted beer features a seasonal brew, and the wine menu pulls from Wisconsin, Spain, Austria, Italy, Napa, and more. Kick back in the cozy lounge, which runs happy hour specials Mon through Fri. Open Mon through Sat for dinner, closed Sun. $$$.

Karl Ratzsch's. 320 E. Mason St.; (414) 276-2720; www.karlratzsch.com. Wiener schnitzel, sauerkraut, sausages, sauerbraten, and homemade strudel? Check. Old-World photos filling the walls? Yep. Displays of old beer steins? That too. After more than a century in business, this landmark German-American restaurant is a visitor favorite. Catch the early-bird specials before 6 p.m. Open for lunch Wed through Sat; open for dinner Mon through Sat; closed Sun (and closed between lunch and dinner hours). $$–$$$.

Kopp's Frozen Custard. 18880 W. Bluemound Rd., Brookfield; (262) 789-9490; www .kopps.com. It's not ice cream. It's frozen custard, and it's got egg yolks and corn syrup and some other tasty stuff. It's also been a must-try treat in Milwaukee since 1950; today's favorite flavors include Swiss chocolate, mint chip, tiramisu, and butter pecan. Fun fact: Kopp's Glendale shop (5373 N. Port Washington Rd.) replaced the Milky Way Drive-in, reportedly the inspiration for the "Happy Days" diner. Want real food first? They have good burgers too. Open for lunch and dinner daily. $.

Mader's Restaurant. 1041 N. 3rd St.; (414) 271-3377; www.madersrestaurant.com. This German mainstay has a slew of claims to fame: host to more US presidents than any other Wisconsin restaurant; place to serve Milwaukee's first legal beer after Prohibition; home to the world's largest Hummel store (in the second-floor Tower Galleries); and a $3 million collection of medieval Germanic weaponry. Oh yes, it also has a menu of German specialties (try the famous pork shank) that wins raves all around. Open Mon through Sat for lunch and dinner, Sun for brunch and dinner. $$$.

Roots Restaurant & Cellar. 1818 N. Hubbard St.; (414) 374-8480; www.rootsmilwaukee .com. Get stellar views of downtown Milwaukee along with dishes made from superbly fresh foods, most of which come directly from local organic farms right to your plate. Menu items at this farmer-chef-owned restaurant have included chicken tagine from the small Nine Patch family farm near Wausau, and grilled haloumi cheese with greens from Roots' own garden. Open daily for dinner and brunch Sun. $$$.

Sanford Restaurant. 1547 N. Jackson St.; (414) 276-9608; www.sanfordrestaurant.com. Seeing accolades like the AAA Four Diamond Award, the Mobil Four Star Award, and a James Beard Award, you know you're going to get top quality. And that's exactly what chef-owner Sanford D'Amato and his wife, Angela, have excelled at for more than 20 years. Housed in the former D'Amato family grocery store, the historic setting now defines contemporary eclectic flavor, particularly apparent in the seven-course Chef's Surprise, offered weekdays. Open for dinner Mon through Sat. $$$.

Sobelman's Pub & Grill. 1900 W. St. Paul Ave.; (414) 931-1919; www.milwaukeesbest burgers.com. Well, the website says it all, doesn't it? Housed in one of Milwaukee's original Schlitz taverns, the downtown grill uses fresh (i.e., not frozen) Black Angus beef patties and rolls baked just for the restaurant. The result is a burger that has blossomed from the occasional order when they opened about 10 years ago to more than 100 served at lunch each day. Non-burger eats are limited, but include apps, chicken sandwiches, and ham and cheese sandwiches. Open daily for lunch and dinner. $.

where to stay

Aloft Hotel. 1230 Old World 3rd St.; (414) 226-0122; www.aloftmilwaukeedowntown.com. Just steps from the Milwaukee Riverwalk, this hip hotel, part of the W Hotel chain, gets kudos for its guest rooms' high ceilings and comfy beds, as well as services like in-room camping for kids, pet-friendly rooms, and eco-friendly design such as in-shower product dispensers rather than plastic throwaways. $$$.

County Clare, An Irish Inn & Pub. 1234 N. Astor St.; (414) 27-CLARE (272-5273); www .countyclare-inn.com. Irish conviviality reigns at this 29-room guesthouse, which makes visitors feel at home (or maybe better) with pillow-top mattresses, handcrafted comforters, whirlpool baths, Wi-Fi, and complimentary breakfast. You can have a good old-fashioned Irish dinner with a pint downstairs. Packages and discounts are often available online. Bonus for downtown Milwaukee: free parking. $$.

Hotel Metro. 411 E. Mason St.; (877) 638-7620, (414) 272-1937; www.hotelmetro.com. Named by *Travel + Leisure* magazine as one of Milwaukee's top hotels, this renovated 1937 Art Deco office building combines elegance with an environmentally friendly approach, using bamboo, cork, and recycled fibers and glass. Master suites are a spacious 720 square feet, with 6-foot whirlpool baths. A rooftop sundeck features a fireplace and reflecting pool. $$$.

Iron Horse Hotel. 500 W. Florida St.; (888) 543-4766, (414) 374-4766; www.theironhorse hotel.com. A century ago, this building served as a warehouse for a bedding company—fitting for its new incarnation as one of Milwaukee's most stylish places to spend the night. Its name also has symbolism: Native Americans referred to the train that traversed the area as the "iron horse," and these days motorcycles are known as iron horses. Within walking distance of the Harley-Davidson Museum, the energy-efficient boutique hotel caters to bike enthusiasts by offering rentals to those who don't have their own iron horse. $$–$$$.

The Pfister Hotel. 424 E. Wisconsin Ave.; (800) 558-8222, (414) 273-8222; www.the pfisterhotel.com. Milwaukee's historically finest accommodations do not disappoint. Since 1893, the Pfister has been the choice for refined service in a grand setting including an art museum–worthy Victorian art collection. The Pfister WELL Spa provides a full menu of pampering treatments, while the indoor pool shows off the hotel's lake and city views from the 23rd floor. Or just sip a cocktail in the 23rd-floor Blu lounge. $$$.

day trip 03

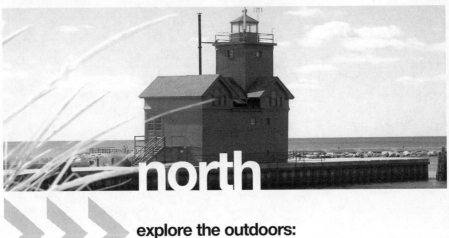

north

During the late 19th century, the fresh springs of this area made many men rich: They touted the springs as "healing waters" and built grand resorts around them. Though the "springs era" is gone here, you'll now find healing of a different kind. My family was not the camping kind, but we had friends who left the 'burbs nearly every year for rustic living at Kettle Moraine. They came back with fish, bug bites, and a healthier state of mind. With its inland lakes and the Fox River, well-maintained parks and long scenic trails, the area's most popular resident is Mother Nature. Glaciers from the last ice age left a varied landscape about 10,000 years ago that Chicagoans envy. It's worth the hassle of toting your bikes and fishing rods—or, in winter, cross-country skis; or just plan to rent equipment there. Waukesha has the largest population of the county, while Delafield is a dot on the map, highlighted because it's a central locale for outdoor adventures.

waukesha

Ranked in 2006 by *Money* magazine as one of the country's "Best Places to Live," Waukesha also boasts some famous hometown celebs including the BoDeans, Les Paul, and Olympic gymnast twin bros Paul and Morgan Hamm. As the biggest city in Waukesha County, and located in the middle of the state's Lake Country, Waukesha offers plenty of outdoor equipment rental agencies for everything from bikes to kayaks.

getting there

Taking about two hours from Chicago, this trip starts as if you're heading toward Milwau-kee: I-90/I-94 west following US 41 (the Edens) north, then merging back in with I-94. Take exit 316 toward I-43 (Airport Freeway) west toward Madison/Fond Du Lac. Continue on I-894 west, then exit at 1B I-94 toward Madison. Take exit 294 (WI 164 north). A left turn leads into Waukesha; a right turn heads toward Pewaukee.

where to go

Waukesha & Pewaukee Convention and Visitors Bureau. N14 W23755 Stone Ridge Dr., Suite 225; (800) 366-8474, (262) 542-0330; www.visitwaukesha.org. Pick up a visitor guide and get more information about the area parks, lakes (there are 77 in the county), and recreation.

Frame Park High Roller Fun Rentals. Frame Park, 1150 Baxter St., behind the Rotary Building; (262) 524-4008, (414) 688-0138; www.highrollerfunrentals.com. Take advantage of Fox River's recreational opportunities with rentals from this company located in Frame Park, a stretch of parkland that features landscaped plantings along the east bank and more of a natural look along the west side. Surrey bikes, pedal go-karts, turbo bikes, paddle boats, and canoes and kayaks all come at reasonable half-hourly rates. Open daily Memo-rial Day through Labor Day, weather permitting; call ahead for spring and fall hours.

Glacial Drumlin State Trail. 810 W. College Ave., Fox River Sanctuary; (262) 646-3025; www.glacialdrumlin.com. This 52-mile east-west biking, hiking, and jogging trail through glacial topography starts at its east end in Waukesha. Mostly a crushed-stone path, its Waukesha leg runs along city streets. Trail users under 16 don't need a trail pass, but those older doing more than hiking should be sure to get a $4 daily pass (or a $20 annual pass).

Pewaukee Lake. Access north of I-94 and south of WI 16, Pewaukee; (262) 691-7275; www.cityofpewaukee.us. The largest lake in Wisconsin's so-called "Lake Country," Pewau-kee Lake measures about 5 miles by 1 mile, a perfect size for inland sailing races, water-skiing, winter ice-boating, and lots of fishing, particularly for muskie (best in spring or fall when the docks are less crowded). White sandy shores make for leisurely summer lolling. From June to September, monthly two-hour historic pontoon tours feature narration by local lake residents. Or hire a guide to teach you a little firsthand fishing knowhow; contact Mike Koepp, (262) 691-8909; or Jim O'Brien, (414) 429-5292.

Retzer Nature Center. S14 W28167 Madison St.; (262) 896-8007; www.waukeshacounty .gov. No wandering aimlessly at this nature center. Each trail comes with color-coded bro-chures, and the manageable 800-foot-long Adventure Trail highlights 30 native Wisconsin animals and plants along the way, perfect for kids. Two observation towers afford panora-mas of the 400-acre surrounding area. Snowshoeing in the winter too. Open daily. Free.

Waukesha County Museum. 101 W. Main St.; (262) 521-2859; www.waukeshacounty museum.org. This museum's home alone is historic, comprising three architecturally interesting and distinct structures—the shell of Waukesha County's second jail built in 1885; a castle-like 1893 Richardson Romanesque former courthouse; and an art moderne/art deco WPA structure from 1938. Permanent exhibits delve into the county's origins; architecture; innovations, inventions, and gadgets; and the Civil War, including the story of a 16-year-old slave who took refuge in the area. Open Tues through Sat. Nominal admission.

where to shop

Allô! Chocolat. 234 W. Main St.; (262) 544-8030; www.allochocolat.com. Treat yourself to a memory trip with candies like Chuckles, Chiclets, candy dots, and Pop Rocks. Or choose from among the shop's famous molded chocolates; Moonstruck truffles in flavors from amaretto to wild huckleberry to Grand Marnier; huge turtles; malted milk balls; green tea-infused hard candies; drinkable truffles (available Friday and Saturday); ice cream; and more. Open Mon to Sat; open Sun during the summer and holiday periods. Hours vary seasonally.

Fox Riverwalk Antique Mall. 250 W. Main St.; (262) 549-4404; www.foxantiques.com. Jam-packed with artwork, jewelry, home decor, tableware, and architectural antiques and artifacts, this 20,000-square-foot space features more than 120 dealers. Grab some complimentary coffee and cookies too. Open daily.

Little Swiss Clock Shop. 270 W. Main St.; (262) 547-2111; www.littleswissclockshop .com. Got the time? You'll have plenty when you stop at this quaint downtown storefront. Since opening as a small watch shop in 1968, it has grown to encompass watches of every kind, plus a wide selection of grandfather, wall, mantel, cuckoo, alarm, and outdoor clocks. Tick-tock . . . time to go. Open daily.

where to eat

Divino Gelato Café. 227 W. Main St.; (262) 446-9490; www.divinogelatocafe.com. Resembling an outdoor Italian piazza, this divine downtown cafe might not be a place to eat, per se, but a place to indulge in creamy delights. Believe it or not, gelato is less fattening than ice cream, so go ahead and order two scoops from a choice of 36 different flavors available daily in summer (24 at other times)—cake batter, caramel and lady kiss, root beer, pumpkin pie, and Snickers, to name a few. Open daily. $.

House of Guinness. 354 W. Main St.; (262) 446-0181; www.houseofguinness.com. Still no substantial eats, but with a name like House of Guinness (H.O.G. by the locals), you know you're in for a bit o' Irish revelry. In a setting of long banquettes, dark wood, and plenty of space at the bar, the beer flows—in addition to the Guinness, there are Bell's, Duvel, Grolsch, Blue Moon, Killian's, and many more—the conversation is easy, and the live bands get Irish eyes smiling every weekend. Open Mon through Sat until the wee hours. $.

La Estacion. 319 Williams St.; (262) 521-1986; www.laestacionrestaurant.com. Make tracks to this Mexican family favorite located in restored railroad train cars. Try the house specialty *parrillada,* a tableside grill of Mexican meats, potatoes, peppers, and onions served with Spanish rice, beans, guac, pico de gallo, and tortillas. The menu also includes whole red snapper, chiles rellenos, grilled steaks, and standard taco, enchilada, and burrito favorites. Open daily for lunch and dinner. $–$$.

Taylor's People Park. 337 W. Main St.; (262) 522-6868; www.peoplesparkwaukesha .com. Located in a historic downtown building, this upscale restaurant and bar has an entirely approachable menu of half-pound burgers, grilled chicken sandwiches, a three-layer grilled cheese (you're in Wisconsin, after all), and a scrumptious weekend brunch of three-egg omelets, crème brulee French toast, and breakfast burritos. Open daily for lunch and dinner, Sat and Sun brunch. $.

where to stay

The Clarke Hotel. 314 W. Main St.; (262) 549-3800; www.theclarkehotel.com. Located in a renovated historic neoclassical building downtown, the Clarke is a chic boutique hotel with 20 rooms appointed with luxurious bedding and Kohler spa showers. A full-service Italian restaurant features nightly specials like the bottomless pasta bowl. $$–$$$.

Country Springs Hotel. 2810 Golf Rd.; Pewaukee; (800) 247-6640, (262) 547-0201; www.countryspringshotel.com. You won't mind the fairly standard rooms when there's a 45,000-square-foot indoor water park on site (for a nominal charge), complete with slides, a lazy river, a zero-depth entry pool, a dump bucket, and an arcade. The independently owned hotel in the Kettle Moraine also offers complimentary continental breakfast daily. $$.

delafield

This petite community about 20 miles northwest of Waukesha is easy to get to. In addition to more outdoor fun, Delafield has a historic downtown that's worth a stroll.

getting there

The scenic route to Delafield, about 25 minutes from Waukesha, follows US 18 west, which is also called Delafield Street and becomes Summit Avenue for awhile. Turn right at County Road C/Kettle Moraine Drive to Main Street to stop at the chamber of commerce first.

where to go

Delafield Chamber of Commerce. 421 Main St.; (262) 646-8100, (888) 294-1082; www .visitdelafield.org. Get the lay of the land and the parks here.

Hawks Inn Historical Museum & Visitors Center Tours. 426 Wells St.; (262) 646-4794; www.hawksinn.org. Built in 1846 for Nelson P. Hawks and his wife, Hannah, this Greek Revival–style inn-turned-museum once saw a revolving door of overnight guests, from farmers to miners. Take a step inside the National Historic Landmark for a look back at its heyday in the mid-1800s when it was both the social and political hub of Delafield. Open for tours Sat, May through Oct, with a Christmas at the Inn event as well. Free.

visit from anywhere

Every town within a 50-mile radius of these three attractions seems to claim them as their own. No matter where you start from, they're worth the trip.

1. East Troy Electric Railroad. 2002 Church St., East Troy; (262) 642-3263; www .easttroyrr.org. When you ride the East Troy Electric Railroad, you ride a slice of history. As Wisconsin's last original electric railroad line, the trains run from East Troy to Mukwonago on tracks that date back to 1907, about 8 miles of which are still used for freight. Joyrides last about 20 minutes, with stops at either end. Cars 24 and 25, Pullman cars built in the 1920s, are used as dining cars now. Admission.

2. Old World Wisconsin. In Eagle, Wisconsin, off WI 67 to Old World Wisconsin, S103 W37890 Hwy 67, follow signs to the site; (262) 594-6301; oldworld wisconsin.wisconsinhistory.org. The Midwest's largest outdoor museum dedicated to the history of rural life, Old World Wisconsin showcases more than 60 authentic historic structures, including a one-room schoolhouse, a blacksmith shop, and a farmstead. Period-dressed actors bring it all to vivid life, while visitors sample the simple life by feeding the livestock, trying hand-crafted toys like stilts, and churning butter. Admission (family admission saves money). Open seasonally (open year-round for prearranged group tours, events, and field trips).

3. Ten Chimneys. Off WI 83 on Depot Road, S43 W31575 Depot Rd., Genesee Depot; (262) 968-4110; www.tenchimneys.org. As much a story as a place, this 60-acre estate was the home of the late legendary acting duo Alfred Lunt and Lynn Fontanne for 50 years. Filled with an array of antique, decorative, and artistic treasures, along with mementos from the couple's lives in the theater—handmade gifts from the likes of Helen Hayes and Noel Coward, letters from protégé Laurence Olivier, photos with Charlie Chaplin—the residence offers guided tours from May through mid-November and serves as an arts education resource. And yes, there really are 10 chimneys. Admission (under 12 not permitted; reservations recommended).

Ice Age National Scenic Trail. Ice Age Trail Alliance; 2110 Main St., Cross Plains; (800) 227-0046; www.iceagetrail.org. This trail isn't technically in Delafield, because it has hundreds of access points, but it does have a fairly new connecting route in Delafield. One of only three national scenic trails in the country contained entirely within one state, it is more than 1,000 miles long. It roughly follows the last outline of the state's most recent glacier, which retreated about 10,000 years ago. If you were to hike the whole thing, you'd be called a "Thousand Miler"; you'd also have very tired feet. But you'd see some extraordinary scenery, including kettles, kames, dells, drumlins, and moraines.

Kettle Moraine State Forest-Southern Unit. Contact Wisconsin Department of Natural Resources for information; (262) 594-6200 direct, (262) 594-6202 for trail conditions hotline; www.dnr.wi.gov. More than 160 miles of connecting trails navigate a diverse and hilly geology of forests and prairies, making for challenging hiking and some of the area's best mountain biking, including a 0.4-mile loop created just for young cyclists. There are also equestrian trails, cross-country and Nordic hiking (a warming house is located on County Highway H south of the Village of Palmyra), snowmobiling, and snowshoeing. Some trails are open only seasonally and closed during wet conditions.

Lake Country Recreation Trail. 600 N. Cushing Park Rd.; www.waukeshacountyparks .com. With a trailhead at Delafield's Cushing Park, this 8-mile paved trail runs along a former train line and suits casual cyclists. It ends at the Landsberg Center trailhead on Golf Road in Pewaukee. Some trail segments are under construction; when complete, the trail will stretch 15 miles, with the west end at Roosevelt Park in Oconomowoc (Jefferson Street). Check the website for updates.

where to stay

The Delafield Hotel. 415 Genesee St.; (800) 594-8772, (262) 646-1600; www.thedelafield hotel.com. Whether you stay in a 500-square-foot king room or the ultimate 1,500-square-foot suite, you are in for a luxury experience. Recognized by *National Geographic Traveler* magazine, *Country Living,* and Chicago's own *CS* for its top-notch treatment, this Preferred Boutique property (there are only 700 across the globe) blankets you with old-world warmth and sophistication, not to mention the very comfy down comforters and in-room massage services available. $$–$$$.

Pedal'rs Inn Bed & Breakfast. 101 James St., Wales; (262) 968-4700; www.pedalrsinn .com. Just a 10-minute drive from Delafield you'll find this amazingly quaint and inviting B&B, offering 4 meticulously decorated rooms, including one with a private stairwell, a fireplace, and a skylight above the whirlpool. Innkeeper Denise (Dee) Nierzwicki brought this 1890s home back to life in 2000, creating a restful sanctuary, perfect for coming back to after an active day of hiking. $–$$.

day trip 04

north

high-end design, low-key vibe:
sheboygan, wi; kohler, wi; elkhart lake, wi

Nine cities comprise Sheboygan County, and while each one has its slice of history, scenery, outdoor recreation, and Native American past, I chose these three for this drive because of their particular distinctions. Sheboygan boasts sought-after Lake Michigan fishing and a prominent arts institution. And you might already know of Kohler, the town built by the bathroom baron himself, but have you *been* to the spa? It's heaven in water. Finally, small but mighty Elkhart Lake explodes from sleepy town to center of attention during Road America races, and balances that out with its own site of serenity at the Aspira Spa.

sheboygan

Some believe Sheboygan got its name from a Chippewa word or phrase for "waterway between the lakes," while others argue it translated to "great noise underground," perhaps referring to the sound of waterfalls upstream from the Sheboygan River. Either way, water definitely was and still is Sheboygan's greatest asset. Like Chicago, Sheboygan makes excellent use of its lakefront status. The swimming, boating, and fishing are phenomenal, so go ahead and bring your swimsuit and take the bait. An acclaimed art center attracts visitors from all over the world, especially for its unique bathrooms.

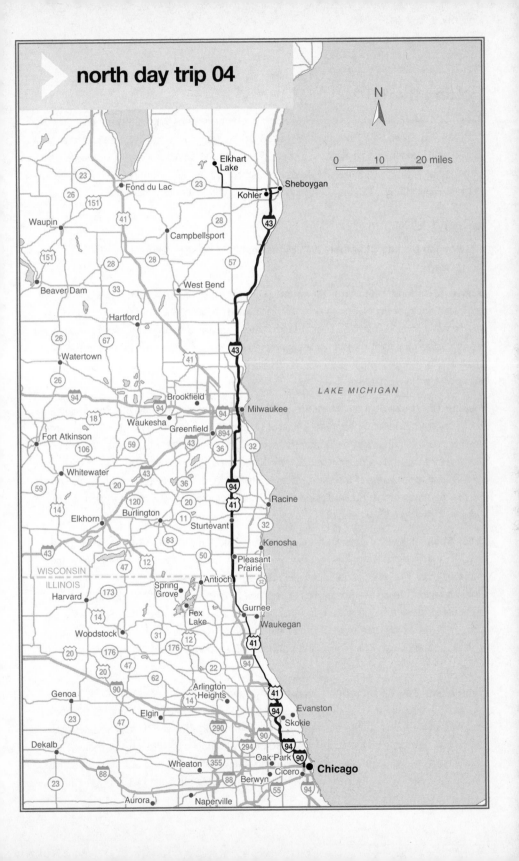

N

0   10   20 miles

Elkhart
Lake

Fond du Lac   23

Kohler   Sheboygan

26

151   28

41   Campbellsport   43

Waupin   57

151   28   28

Beaver Dam   33   West Bend

Hartford

26   67

Watertown   41   43

26

94   Brookfield

18   94

Waukesha   Milwaukee

Fort Atkinson   Greenfield   894

106   59   43   36

Whitewater   43   36   32

59   20   94

14   120   20   41   Racine

Elkhorn   Burlington   11   Sturtevant   32

83   Kenosha

50   Pleasant
Prairie

43   47   12

WISCONSIN   Antioch   32

ILLINOIS

Harvard   173   Spring
Grove

14   Fox   Gurnee

Woodstock   31   Lake   Waukegan

20   176   12   41

20   47   22   94

62   Arlington
Heights

Genoa   90   14   41

23   Elgin   Evanston

47   94   Skokie

Dekalb   290   94

90   Oak Park   90   **Chicago**

Wheaton   355   Cicero

23   88   Berwyn   55

Aurora   Naperville   88   94

LAKE MICHIGAN

getting there

Take I-90/I-94 west; continue on US 41 north, then merge back with I-94 west. Follow I-43 north toward Green Bay. Take exit 126 toward Sheboygan/Kohler to WI 23/Kohler Memorial Drive, which becomes Erie Avenue. If you'd like to stop at the chamber of commerce first, turn right at 14th Street, left on Pennsylvania, right at 9th Street; at a fork in the road, keep left to join 8th Street. Watch out for a couple of new roundabouts in the city.

where to go

Sheboygan County Chamber of Commerce. 621 S. 8th St.; (920) 457-9491; www.she boygan.org.

Above & Beyond Children's Museum. 902 N. 8th St.; (920) 458-4263; www.abkids .org. Not as big or boisterous as the Chicago Children's Museum (not much is), this petite play space ropes kids in with cool stuff like a tree house to climb up, then slide down; a whompamaphone (that's a PVC pipe organ for the uninitiated); a carved and hand-painted, animated miniature circus; and a 200-square-foot blackboard for chalking. Open Tues through Sat. Nominal admission.

Fishing Charters. Boat launch ramps off 8th Street, just north of the 8th Street Bridge; off 14th Street Bridge, in the 1300 block of Niagara Avenue; and in Deland Park, on the lakefront. Call the Sheboygan County Chamber of Commerce, (920) 457-9491. Didn't bring your boat? More than a dozen charter fishing folks are happy to host you aboard theirs to take advantage of some of the state's best sport fishing, particularly salmon and trout. And I love the names of these companies: Sorry Charlie, Contender, Headhunter, and, oh my, Happy Hooker (groan). Seasonal.

John Michael Kohler Arts Center. 608 New York Ave.; (920) 458-6144; www.jmkac .org. This not-for-profit creative hive explores new art forms, focuses on self-taught artists, supports emerging artists, and hopes it all inspires visitors. Opened in 1967 in John Michael Kohler's historic Italian villa home, the center grew by leaps and glassy bounds in 2000 with a state-of-the-art 100,000-square-foot addition that added, among other things, a fab gift shop, cafe, and kids area. And, being Kohler, the restroom fixtures are artwork too, listed in the Discovery Channel's "The World's Ten Best Bathrooms." Donation suggested. Open daily.

Sheboygan County Historical Society & Museum. 3110 Erie Ave.; (920) 458-1103; www.co.sheboygan.wi.us. See four museums in one visit at this cultural complex. Its iconic structure is the former home of prominent Wisconsin judge David Taylor; the stately residence now highlights his long career. An 1864 family homestead, 1867 cheese factory, and 1890s barn, as well as a new space featuring rotating exhibits, round out the experience. Call for tour information. Nominal admission. Open daily Apr through Oct and the Fri after

Thanksgiving through Dec 30 (closed Dec 24 and 25) for the Holiday Memories display. Also open at other times to group tours by arrangement.

where to eat

Duke of Devon. 739 Riverfront Dr.; (920) 458-7900; www.dukeofdevonpub.com. Trinkets and treasures from England fill the walls of this friendly pub. Its scenic riverfront setting makes for a bustling patio come summer. Daily drinks include a sampler of four 6-ounce pours of the restaurant's seasonal draft beers. A list of import bottled beers from Belgium, England, Scotland, and Germany offer up helpful wine-menu-like descriptions. As for food: fish and chips, bangers and mash, Scotch eggs, curries, and mussels in curry sauce or in Stella lager. Open Tues through Sun for lunch and dinner (closes between meals; bar is open all day Fri, Sat, and Sun). $$–$$$.

Field to Fork. 511 S. 8th St.; (920) 694-0322; www.thefieldtofork.com. Veteran self-taught chef and hometown boy Stefano Viglietti—the popular adjacent pizza joint Il Ritrovo is his too—serves up burgers from locally raised grass-fed beef, cheese from homestead cream-eries, and organic bakery goodies. It's all good, actually. And when in Wisconsin . . . try the much-lauded Laack's Dairy Wisconsin white cheddar curds, deep fried and served with honey-Dijon dipping sauce. Open for breakfast and lunch Mon through Sat. $$.

Mucky Duck Shanty. 701 Riverfront Dr.; (920) 457-5577; www.muckyduckshanty.com. Don't let the name or the shack-like look of the building fool you: This family-owned river-front restaurant is serious about its seafood. Choose from nearly a dozen seafood entrees, seven fish sandwiches, three fish pastas, and four seafood salads. Kids' meals are also mostly fish-focused, so let them try breaded shrimp, pan-fried walleye, or broiled scallops. Five different catches on the Friday fish fry menu come with soup and sides. Open daily for lunch and dinner. $$.

Weather Center Café. 809 Riverfront Dr.; (920) 459-9283; www.myspace.com/weather center. With a water and weather theme, this shoreline coffee shop is perfect for a light bite—a healthy, homemade one that includes plenty of vegetarian and vegan sandwiches and pastries. Open daily, breakfast through early dinner. $.

Weissgerber's Seabird Restaurant. 229 S. Pier Dr.; (920) 453-4000; www.weissgerbers .com. This elegant lakefront destination has a business-casual dress code, so swap out the flip-flops and enjoy a fine-dining night of seafood, steak, and chops. The less formal adjoining Blue Point Wine & Tapas Bar makes small plates perfect for sharing, like pork and shrimp potstickers, bruschetta, mushroom ravioli, and truffle risotto. Find something to toast if you can, because the 200-plus wine list has received the *Wine Spectator* Award of Excellence. Dinner only; days and hours change seasonally. $$$.

where to stay

Blue Harbor Resort & Conference Center. 725 Blue Harbor Dr.; (866) 701-BLUE (2583); www.blueharborresort.com. Top-quality and family-friendly, this lakeshore resort greets guests with the world's largest handblown glass fountain in the lobby. Blue Harbor keeps them entertained with an arcade; beautiful lake views; daily crafts, activities, and bedtime storytelling for kids; and Breaker Bay, a huge indoor water park with seven waterslides, an oversize whirlpool, 3 pools, and more. Among the 182 suites, you can choose fireplaces, whirlpools, or an aquarium-themed kid-centric suite with bunk beds. $$$.

kohler

While it was a bit too chilly for golfing when I visited Kohler, a round on the links would have been tough anyway because I would have been too distracted by the milieu: lakefront cliffs, lush greenery, sandy dunes. It's no wonder that John Michael Kohler founded his company here in 1873. Its original products were farm implements, but in 1883, Kohler made his first bathtub as a watering trough for a farmer, and the rest is interior design history. Today the Kohler name is synonymous with quality, and the resort town lives up to it in all categories. Definitely make time for the Kohler factory tour, which includes a look back at some of the first fixtures.

getting there

There are a couple of ways to get to Kohler from Sheboygan, but the most direct route is along County Road PP, also known as Indiana Avenue when it's heading out of Sheboygan. To get to County Road PP, take Pennsylvania Avenue west over the river and make a left onto 14th Street. After about a half-mile, turn right at County Road PP/Indiana Avenue. Take this to Highland Drive in Kohler and turn right. It shouldn't take more than 15 minutes.

where to go

Golf at Kohler. Blackwolf Run: 1111 W. Riverside Dr.; Whistling Straits: N8501 County LS; (800) 344-2838 for advance reservations, (866) 847-4856 for same-day; www.destination kohler.com. Tubs started the town, but tee times are equally important in Kohler these days. Blackwolf Run impresses with its glacial-made terrain. It has received top marks from both *Golf Digest* and *Golf Magazine*, and was host of the 2010 US Women's Open. Whistling Straits features two courses: a breezy lakeshore course and the Irish Course, reproducing the grassy feel of Ireland's best greens. Call for open hours.

Kohler Design Center & Factory Tours. 101 Upper Rd.; (920) 457-3699; www.destination kohler.com. Originally a recreation hall for Village of Kohler residents, the Design Center houses a jaw-dropping display of glimmering bathroom fixtures and a humorously titled

"Great Wall of China" that will have you calling the decorator when you get home. Go deeper into the water wunderkind on a three-hour factory tour hosted by retired employees, which also touches on the company history. Free admission. Center open daily; factory tours Mon through Fri at 8:30 a.m. (tours age 14 and up only; closed-toe shoes required).

Kohler Water Spa. 501 Highland Dr.; (800) 344-2838; www.destinationkohler.com. Soak in the soothing aspects at this award-winning spa, where you're pampered in the latest and greatest Kohler baths and showers. Of course, there's also a full menu of massages, manis and pedis, facials, body treatments, scalp and hair treatments, and get-in-tune-with-your-body energy therapies. A glass-enclosed rooftop deck with whirlpool and fireplace allows for luxurious lounging. Pricing varies per service.

where to shop

The Shops at Woodlake. 725Q Woodlake Rd.; (920) 459-1713; www.destinationkohler .com. Far from your everyday mall offerings, upscale and stylish stores meander away from the Inn at Woodlake past lovely Wood Lake itself. More than 20 specialty boutiques outfit home and body, from Ann Sacks tile to Wisconsin Trader to the Movers & Shakers Kid's Toys shop that will tempt the kid in you too. Open daily.

where to eat

Kohler's dozen restaurants run the gamut from quick cafe sandwiches at the Woodlake Market to comfy pub fare at the Horse and Plow to the romantic, four-diamond pièce de résistance The Immigrant. Call (800) 344-2838 or check out www.destinationkohler.com for information or reservations at any of the restaurants. $–$$$.

where to stay

The American Club. 419 Highland Dr.; (800) 344-2838; www.destinationkohler.com. Built in 1918 to house Kohler immigrant employees who couldn't afford their own homes, the American Club did a 180 in 1981 to become the luxury lodging choice for the most discerning of visitors. One of the poshest resorts in the world, it boasts numerous awards for its accommodations, dining, golf courses, and spa. Elegant Tudor architecture defines its exterior, with American heritage furnishings continuing the traditional feel. But the best part is in each of the 240 rooms: the amazing Kohler whirlpool bath. $$$.

Inn at Woodlake. 705 Woodlake Rd.; (800) 344-2838; www.destinationkohler.com. All dark wood, dark leather, and brilliant white bedding, the rooms at the recently renovated "other" Kohler lodging are decidedly sleek and modern. Kohler luxury extends here with WaterTile bodysprays and WaterTile showerheads—oooh and aaah all you want because they're yours while you're there. Take advantage of the inn's location along scenic Wood Lake by requesting a lakeview room. $$$.

elkhart lake

Named for its supposedly elk heart-shaped lake, this small town vroom-vroomed into history in the 1950s, hosting auto races on some of its public roads. It now boasts an international racetrack that sees hundreds of thousands of visitors at each event. Quieter times are found at Aspira Spa.

getting there

At the northern edge of Kohler, you'll find WI 23/Kohler Memorial Drive. Take it west about 11 miles to the exit for WI 67 north toward Plymouth/Elkhart Lake. Turn left off the ramp and continue for about 5 miles, then turn left at County Road A/E (Rhine Street) to reach the chamber of commerce.

where to go

Elkhart Lake Area Chamber of Commerce. 41 E. Rhine St.; (920) 876-2922, (877) 355-3554; www.elkhartlake.com.

Aspira Spa at the Osthoff Resort. 101 Osthoff Ave.; (877) SPA-2070; www.aspiraspa .com. This one doubles as a "where to stay," because you could definitely bunk down in this beautiful resort on Elkhart Lake, where rooms all offer gas fireplaces and private balconies, and the Pleasures Activity Program keeps kids busy. But back to the spa: With reverence to the lake it sits on—Native Americans believed it to be sacred—and incorporating tenets of feng shui, natural elements, and holistic healing philosophies, the spa was created as "a place to move forward in nature and peace." How exactly? Massages such as kinesiotherapy, lomi lomi, yin yang and crystal chakra balancing; lymphatic treatments; reflexology; Reiki healing; and yoga. Open daily. Pricing varies per service.

Henschel's Indian Museum. N8661 Holstein Rd.; (920) 876-3193; www.henschelsindian museumandtroutfarm.com. Named for the homesteaders who lived side by side with Native Americans from 1849 to 1870, this museum displays relics of the land's past: stone and bone tools, pottery, copper implements, and atlatl, a gadget that Native Americans used to throw their weapons. An excavation revealed the place's sacred history as well, as Wisconsin's oldest burial site of the Red Ocher people, who lived from 1000 to 400 BC. A trout farm here is open for fishing. Keep what you catch, pay per pound, and let the Henschels clean it for you. Open Memorial Day through Labor Day, Tues through Sat in the afternoon (other times by appointment). Nominal admission.

Road America. N7390 WI 67, off County Road J; (800) 365-RACE (7223); www.road america.com. Rev your engines for a radical racing experience at this 640-acre racing park. More than 50 years after the 4.048-mile, 14-turn track was etched into Wisconsin farmland, it is still a driver and fan favorite. Races open to the public take place April through October and feature both vintage and elite sports cars and motorcycles from SCCA Speed World Challenge Series, American Le Mans, AMA, and NASCAR. Try the course on your own four wheels with on-track touring. Ticket prices vary by event (children 12 and under free with paying adult).

where to eat

Lake Street Café. 21 Lake St.; (920) 876-2142; www.lakestreetcafe.com. A popular spot for popping the question, this romantic, white tablecloth restaurant serves an upscale bistro-style menu with traditional starters like escargot and baked Brie en croûte and entrees including Angus beef tenderloin stuffed with garlicky Boursin cheese; orecchiette pasta tossed with Italian sausage and beef ragout; and grilled duck breast. Open for lunch Tues through Sat, and for dinner Mon through Sat. $$.

Paddock Club. 61 S. Lake St.; (920) 876-3288; www.paddockclubelkhartlake.com. In this fine-dining find, executive chef Lynn Chisholm rounds up seasonal ingredients to create fresh pastas like papardelle with porcini mushroom and veal ragout, pan-seared venison chop with a *foie gras* sauce, and grilled lamb loin with goat cheese potato puree. The renovated 100-year-old former tavern has its original tin ceiling and Cream City bricks, and adds large picture windows for people-watching and an open kitchen for food prep-peeking. Open for dinner nightly May 1 through Oct 1, Tues through Sat for the rest of the year. $$$.

Siebkens Resort. 284 S. Lake St.; (920) 876-2600; www.siebkens.com. Even if you're not lodging at this family-owned beachfront resort (which offers Victorian-style rooms or deluxe condo suites), you should check out its Stop-Inn Tavern for burgers and sandwiches or, during Road America race weekends only, its main dining room for more elevated fare in a more formal setting. Friday is pan-fried walleye night; Saturday is prime rib and Cajun prime rib night. Open for dinner nightly Memorial Day through Labor Day, Mon through Sat for lunch, Sunday brunch. Tavern open year-round on Fri and Sat for drinks. $$.

day trip 05

north

>>> **fish & farms:**
fond du lac, wi; oshkosh, wi

Lake Winnebago borders both of these southeastern Wisconsin towns. The largest freshwater lake in the state at 220 square miles, Winnebago hails from the same slice of limestone as does Niagara Falls. It also gives the area a whole lot of fishing lore, culminating in Fond du Lac's well-loved Walleye Weekend in June, along with great seafood restaurants. Non-anglers find recreation in the lush parks and fascinating historic farms.

fond du lac

For an ice cream fiend like myself, Fond du Lac's Kelley Country Creamery beckoned first—and then again. Chicago's urban setting just can't compare to the fresh-churned goodness that comes from milking cows that wander practically at the doorstep. It's this kind of connection with the land, and of course the water, that makes this midsize city so lovely.

getting there

Start on I-90/I-94 west, follow US 41 north, merge back with I-94 for another 33 miles, then stay left to follow signs to I-43 S/I-894 W/Airport Freeway toward Madison/Fond du Lac. Stay on I-894 west. Bear right to continue on US 45 north, aka Zoo Freeway. About 20 miles later, stay in the left lanes to follow US 41 north toward Fond du Lac. Take exit 97 to S. Military Road. Make a right, then turn left at County Road VV/S, Pioneer Road, which will take you to the visitor bureau.

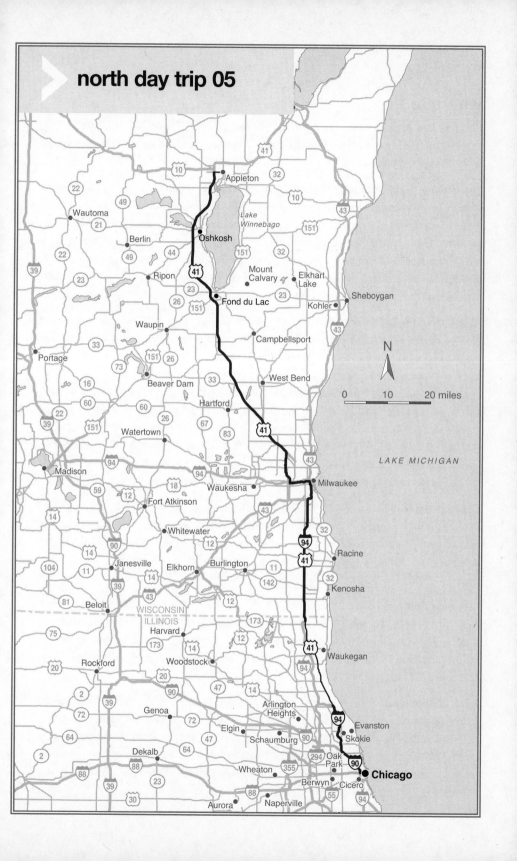

N

0   10   20 miles

LAKE MICHIGAN

where to go

Fond du Lac Area Convention & Visitors Bureau. 171 S. Pioneer Rd.; (920) 923-3010, (800) 937-9123; www.fdl.com. Pick up maps, brochures, event calendars, coupons, and more. Open Mon through Fri.

The Historic 1856 Octagon House & Costume Closet. 276 Linden St.; (920) 923-5656; www.octagonhousefdl.com. Believe in ghosts? The docents at this eight-sided National Historic Landmark do; so did the investigators at the Southern Wisconsin Paranormal Research Group when they studied the house. Not surprising, considering its history as a safe house for the Underground Railroad, its underground tunnel between the house and carriage house, and its nine secret passageways. Chock-full of antique tchotchkes, it also houses the Costume Closet, a fun browse for theater, dress-up, and historic re-enactment.

Kelley Country Creamery. W5215 County Road B; (920) 923-1715; www.kelleycountry creamery.com. When the ice cream is made with milk produced by cows you see grazing the green pastures that surround the shop's 200-acre farm, you better believe this is going to be something special. Karen and Tim Kelley turned their typical dairy farm, in the family since 1861, into an ice cream social in 2010, and it's been a bonanza ever since. It's worth the frequent wait for one of the 16 daily flavors—they've concocted more than 60, including Chew Your Cud (bubble gum–flavored ice cream with bubble gum pieces), Country Bumpkin Pumpkin, Cow Jumped Over the Moon (Blue Moon–flavored with Pop Rocks), and Maple Bacon. Generally open daily during summer and Wed through Sun the rest of the year; call ahead to confirm. Call for creamery and farm tour information.

Lakeside Park. 555 N. Park Ave.; (920) 923-3010. Considered the town's "crown jewel," this 400-acre park at the foot of Lake Winnebago is a triple threat of activity: natural beauty—winding paths, birding, colorful flower displays; a sporty side with ball fields and volleyball; and nostalgia, with its can't-miss antique carousel, kiddie train ride, and bumper boats.

Lakeside Spirit. Board at Lakeside Park marina; for GPS directions, type in 555 N. Park Ave., which is the marina house address; (920) 923-3010 (the visitor center). The only excursion yacht on Lake Winnebago, Lakeside Spirit takes 50 passengers at a time on 90-minute cruises with changing dining themes (Friday means fish fry, of course). Runs seasonally (and for charters). Call for prices.

Lake Winnebago. Winnebago Drive, accessible by County Road K; call the visitor bureau for more information. This is the lake referred to in Fond du Lac's French translation, "base of the lake." It's the second-largest natural freshwater lake in the country, formed by pooling melting glacial ice about 12,000 years ago. Today, anglers know it for its plentiful walleye, as well as bass, bluegill, and muskie. At the lake's Roosevelt Park, you'll find swimming access, though no lifeguards.

Villa Loretto Nursing Home. N8114 County WW, Mt. Calvary; (920) 753-3211; www
.villalorettonh.org. A 15-minute excursion from Fond du Lac, this nursing home is not just
a holy place for senior citizens—it's also home to a menagerie of more than 300 animals,
including standard dogs, cats, and rabbits, as well as llamas, emu, donkeys, miniature
horses, a pot-bellied pig, and a variety of birds. Visit them during guided tours May through
October or feel free to stroll the grounds anytime. Then stop for baked goodies at the Nun
Better Bakery. See? Even nuns have a sense of humor. Open year-round; tours with hay
ride offered May to Oct. Free for strolling. Admission for tours; call to arrange.

where to eat

Cool Beans & Bagels. 131 S. Main St.; (920) 924-9749. This downtown spot is a local
favorite when you're looking for a casual bite to eat or a quick start to your day. Beyond
everyday java, there's Turkish and Lebanese. Open daily. $.

Fond du Lac Seafood Co. LLC. 63 N. Main St.; (920) 517-TUNA; www.fdlseafood.com.
Plan a lakeside picnic with fresh seafood from this friendly downtown fishmonger. They'll
pack up ready-to-devour take-out orders on Friday for dinner. Or choose your own catch to
cook out on your own. Neighboring **Cujak's Wine Market** (47 N. Main St.; 920-922-2499,
www.cujakswinemarket.com) makes a handy stop for your matching vino. Open Tues to Fri
late morning through early evening, Sat late morning until post-lunch. $$.

Schreiner's Restaurant. 168 N. Pioneer Rd; (920) 922-0590; www.fdlchowder.com.
Five moves and more than 70 years later, this legendary establishment is still one of Fond
du Lac's busiest. Now run by Paul Cunningham, who began working here as a busboy in
1969 when he was 15, Schreiner's serves more than 1,500 diners on average each day.
Most of them order Grandma Regina Schreiner's famous New England-style clam chowder
and homemade country-style dessert of the day (think rhubarb pie and mince pie with rum
sauce). Other specials include deep-fried haddock, fried chicken, and broiled ground sirloin
steak, plus burgers, sandwiches, and salads. Open daily for breakfast, lunch, and early
dinner. $.

where to stay

Ramada Plaza. 1 N. Main St. (920) 923-3000; www.ramadafdl.com. Known by locals as
the Retlaw Hotel for its former owner, businessman and hotelier Walter Schroeder (Ret-
law is Walter spelled backward), the historic 1920s red-brick hotel became a psychiatric
facility and nursing home before returning to its original purpose. Though rooms may not
wow, the two-story lobby and generally elegant ambiance do. Watch out for ghosts here
too. $$.

oshkosh

This city of about 64,000 became a household name thanks to the cute kids overalls by OshKosh B'Gosh (the company was established here in 1903). While it's still home to the corporate HQ, it doesn't produce the togs here any longer, so don't be afraid to wear your Levi's when you go exploring this Winnebago County area that boasts one of the nation's best aviation museums as well as the amazingly maintained public gardens of the Paine Art Center.

getting there

Hop back on US 41, heading north for about 30 minutes. Take exit 116 toward WI 44/WI 91/Ripon Road/South Park Avenue. When the road divides, stay left toward WI 44 south. Turn left at the light (44/South Park Avenue). Go about a mile to Waukau Avenue (there's a light) and take a left to head to the visitor center. Forewarning on traffic: Oshkosh's main artery, US 41, is undergoing a major multiyear construction project; check www .us41wisconsin.gov for up-to-date info.

where to go

Oshkosh Convention & Visitors Bureau. 2401 W. Waukau Ave.; (920) 303-9200, (877) 303-9200; www.visitoshkosh.com. Get info on the area 24 hours a day.

EAA AirVenture Museum. 3000 Poberezny Ave.; (920) 426-4800; www.airventuremuseum .org. I've always harbored a secret desire to learn to fly, so the aircraft displays, aviation history, and KidVenture interactive area here got my heart soaring. The museum's collection of sport planes (EAA stands for Experimental Aircraft Association) took off in 1962 with founder Steve Wittman's air racer "Bonzo," and it has grown to include 244 aircraft on display and 30,000 aviation items, of which about 1,000 are showcased. I may never be brave enough to fly, but this was second best. Open daily. Admission.

Oshkosh Public Museum. 1331 Algoma Blvd.; (920) 236-5799; www.oshkoshmuseum .org. Focusing on Oshkosh and the broader Lake Winnebago County, this museum is partially housed in the 1908 Edgar and Mary Jewell Sawyer home, an English Tudor Revival decked out with Tiffany stained glass, stunning hardwood, and an elevator to service the four floors. Besides tours of the house, must-see exhibits include the 1895 Apostles Clock, an 8-foot-tall wonder that comes to life every hour as a top door opens and an angel strikes a gong; and Grandma's Attic, where kids can play old-time dress-up. Open Tues through Sun. Admission.

Paine Art Center & Gardens. 1410 Algoma Blvd.; (920) 235-6903; www.thepaine.org. Big plans for this splendid castle fizzled when the Great Depression hit; built for lumber baron Nathan Paine and his wife, Jessie, the couple never actually lived in it. But in 1946, they established it as a public museum, and it's been open as such ever since. Elaborate stonework, hand-carved woodwork, and architectural features highlight the art-filled interior, while 20 distinct outdoor landscaped spaces vary from English rose garden to woodland plantings with winding paths. Open Tues through Sun. Guided tours available May through Oct (two-week advance reservation required). Admission.

where to eat

Ardy & Ed's Drive-In. 2413 S. Main St.; (920) 231-5455; www.ardyandeds.com. Pulling up to Ardy & Ed's takes you into a time warp of muscle cars, sister singing acts, sock hops, and carhops. Though the menu has expanded since the restaurant's opening in 1948 as an A & W Drive-in serving root beer and hot dogs (there's a host of fried options and burgers these days), the now-famous stop has remained true to its '50s founding, complete with black cows, Coney Island hot dogs, turtle sundaes, and roller-skating carhops. Open Mar through early Oct. $.

Brooklyn Grill. 607 S. Main St.; (920) 230-4477; www.brooklyngrill.com. You're most wanted at this light-hearted eatery with a 1940s Brooklyn gangster theme. Burgers sport names like the Bonnie Or Clyde, the Boot Legger, and the Tommy Gun. A martini list that could beat up any other includes the Oshkosh, a blend of creme de banana, blackberry brandy, Bacardi rum, Myers dark rum, Malibu rum, pineapple juice, sour mix, and a touch of grenadine. Yowza. Open daily from 11 a.m. $.

Caramel Crisp & Café. 200D City Center; (920) 231-4540; www.caramelcrispcafe.com. Watch out, Garrett, this downtown Oshkosh cafe has its own gourmet blend of caramel and cheese popcorn that locals adore. The shop has moved since opening in 1933 next to a movie theater (smart marketing there), but it still makes the same time-honored caramel corn, stirred by hand in small batches that you can practically smell down the street. There are also penny candy jars, homemade fudge, and daily soups, salads, and sandwiches, not to mention modern popcorn flavors like grape, and bacon and cheese. Open daily; closed Sun during winter. $.

Fratellos Waterfront Restaurant & Brewery. 1501 Arboretum Dr.; (920) 232-2337; www .supplerestaurantgroup.com. A Fox River–front location draws huge crowds to this original Fratellos (there are three others in Wisconsin). A menu as long as the Nile keeps them coming back, with everything from filet mignon to baked lasagna to Thai shrimp noodle bowls, plus burgers, sandwiches, meal-size salads, and stone-fired pizzas. Pair anything with one of the house-brewed beers and stick around for live music Saturday nights in the adjacent lounge. Open daily for lunch and dinner. $$.

Lara's Tortilla Flats. 715 N. Main St.; (920) 233-4440; www.larastortillaflats.com. Claiming to be Oshkosh's oldest Mexican restaurant at more than 35 years and counting, Lara's offers a menu of south-of-the-border favorites like quesadillas, empanadas, burritos, tacos,

> ## a magic moment

From Oshkosh, continue following US 41 north to the college town of Appleton, Wisconsin (exit 137 for WI 125/College Ave; turn right onto College Ave). The heart of the 18-community Fox Cities, **Appleton** is known for being the home of **Lawrence University.** Founded in 1847, it was one of the country's first coed colleges and is now an 84-acre campus of about 1,500 students. Although Lawrence provides much of the town's heart and soul, it's a former resident who lends the magic.

Born Erik Ivan Weisz in Budapest, Hungary, **Harry Houdini** lived in Appleton from age 4 till about 13. He loved it so much that long after leaving with his family for New York, he claimed it as his hometown—even going as far as to tell people he was born there. Appleton's **History Museum at the Castle** dedicates its fascinating "A.K.A. Houdini" exhibit to the magic master. Learn about Houdini the person and performer; try funhouse mirrors, a straitjacket, breaking out of a jail cell, unlocking padlocks, and levitating a table. The museum also hands out Houdini walking tour maps that take you to places he was somehow associated with. The museum is open daily during the summer; closed Mon the rest of the year. Admission. 330 E. College Ave., Appleton; (920) 735-9370; www.myhistory museum.org.

and enchiladas, as well as specialty dishes such as tequila lime chicken, cumin ancho-rubbed salmon, and fresh mussels. Open Mon through Sat for lunch and dinner. $.

where to stay

Brayton Bed & Breakfast. 143 Church St.; (920) 267-0300; www.braytonbb.net. Proprietors Nicole and Scott Brayton went above and beyond the basic country-cute when they renovated this historic home near downtown Oshkosh. Originally built in 1867 for a lumberman and his family, the Cream City brick Italianate home was used as a men's boarding house through most of the 20th century. The most romantic of rooms, the Belle, pays honor to the woman who ran that boarding house; it features a two-person bath and a marble and mahogany king bed. Wake up to mouthwatering treats like blueberry bread pudding, chocolate cheesecake muffins, and breakfast calzones. On weekends, mingle over complimentary wine and cheese and late-night goodies. $$.

northeast

day trip 01

northeast

south haven

The first inkling of South Haven as a resort town came in the 1880s when Jewish families from Chicago began landing there for summer stays. It exploded over the next 80 years, at its height boasting more than 200 resorts. But along came the Depression, which sent that number spiraling down to about 45 during the 1960s. Now, a tighter tourist community offers quaint stays at bed-and-breakfasts and lakefront cottages. Its original Native American name, "Ni-Ko-Nong," still fits just fine. It means "beautiful sunsets," and because they take place over Lake Michigan, they truly are. Visitors gather for beach bonfires to watch, and they're never disappointed. Another pastime: blueberry- and peach-picking. South Haven grew out of its heyday in the 1870s, when it shipped lumber to burgeoning Chicago and Milwaukee. As the industry dwindled, the cleared land left it perfect for fruit orchards. Named in 1969 as the World's Blueberry Capital, it still holds the title, celebrating with an annual Blueberry Festival that attracts thousands. From June through October, crops are ripe for the picking; make sure you do.

getting there

Take I-90/I-94 east. Follow signs toward Indiana; continue on I-90/the Skyway. Merge back onto I-94 toward Detroit. Take exit 34 to I-196/US 31 north toward Holland/Grand Rapids. Take exit 20/Phoenix Road. Turn left off the ramp, and the visitor bureau will be down about

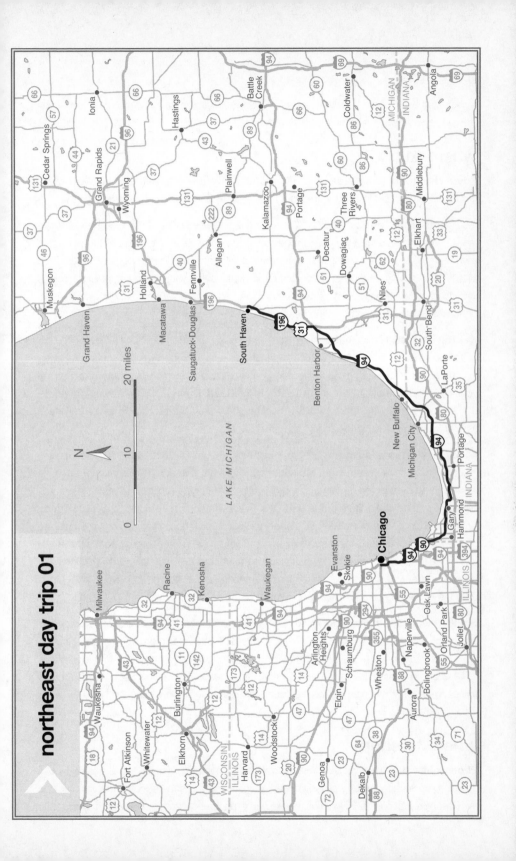

northeast day trip 01

a mile on the left. Be aware that Phoenix Road is the same as Phoenix Street (and even labeled as a highway in some places).

where to go

South Haven Visitors Bureau. 546 Phoenix St.; (269) 637-5252, (800) SO-HAVEN; www .southhaven.org. Get lodging, attraction, U-pick, and dining information here. Open daily.

DeGrandchamp Farms U-Pick. 76241 14th Ave.; (269) 637-3915; www.degrandchamps .com. During busy blueberry season from mid-July to mid- to late August, the picking is easy, and the blueberries are sublime at this neat, 52-year-old U-pick operation off the Blue Star Highway. My family puts this on our must-do list every year, strapping on our buckets (kids too), eating two for every one we collect, and enjoying blueberry pie, cobbler, muffins, pancakes, and just by the bowlful. Seasonal. Pay by the pound.

Kal-Haven Trail. Begins at N. Bailey Ave. and Wells St.; (269) 674-8011; www.vbco.org/ government364491.asp. In its first life this trail was a railroad bed that linked South Haven and Kalamazoo. Now it's a 33.5-mile hiking, biking, and snowmobiling route. Didn't bring your own two-wheeler? Rent them at **Rock 'n' Road Cycle,** 315 Broadway (269-639-0003). Get your trail day pass (or family pass) at the yellow self-pay boxes at the trailheads as well as various Michigan vendors.

Michigan Maritime Museum. 260 Dyckman Ave.; (800) 747-3810, (269) 637-8078; www .michiganmaritimemuseum.org. Learn about the lake we love and its sister Great Lakes at this museum comprising a main building of maritime history, a replica boathouse showcasing rescue crafts and culture of the US Coast Guard in Michigan, an original US Life Saving Service building, the South Pier Lightkeeper's House, and the preserved *Evelyn S.* fish tug that displays workers' clothing and equipment. There's also a new exhibit detailing the history of the Black River. Take a day or sunset cruise aboard the museum's *Friends Good Will* ship—kids enjoy the themed "Pirate Chaser Adventure"—or the new River Launch. Open daily May through early Oct. Nominal admission; cruises extra.

South Haven South Pier Lighthouse. At the end of Water Street and the entrance to the Black River. Call the Maritime Museum (269-637-8078) for more information. Replacing a wood-frame tower built in 1871, this bright red, 35-foot-tall steel structure was built in 1903 and makes a fine photo op no matter the season (stay away when waves make it too dangerous). It has historically been open for visitors for an annual open house. Call for more information.

where to shop

Phoenix Street. Downtown South Haven's strollable main drag is at the top of a hill that looks down to the harbor. Among several dozen shops lining the streets, some favorites include the **Blueberry Store** (525 Phoenix), where sampling is encouraged; **Decadent Dogs** (505

Phoenix) for the pampered pup; **Harbor Toy Company** (409 Phoenix), where kids readily relinquish allowances; and **Bayberry Cottage** (510 Phoenix), an inviting home furnishings and accessories store.

where to eat

Café Julia. 561 Huron St.; (269) 639-7988; www.cafejulia.com. Chicagoans will feel right at home in this cute cafe, sipping none other than Intelligentsia coffee. Pair it with a fluffy omelet, a chocolate-filled croissant, or a seasonal treat like the fall apple butter baby cakes. Lunch features owners Jay and Julia Marcoux's fresh, contemporary menu of panini, salads, and deli sandwiches, including the veggie on seven grain bread with basil pesto mayo. Open daily for breakfast, lunch, and early dinner. $–$$.

Clementine's. 500 Phoenix St.; (269) 637-4755; www.ohmydarling.com. Thankfully there are benches outside this family restaurant, because there's almost always a wait. Orders for the famous pan-fried "mess of lake perch" top the list. Also on the menu: steak, shrimp, pasta, baby back ribs, and the new house specialty, a strawberry-glazed charbroiled chicken breast. Housed in an 1897 former bank building, Clementine's doubles as a sort of ode to South Haven's past, with antiques galore, saloon-type bar, and black and white photos of days gone by. Dig the website name. Open daily for lunch and dinner. $$.

Sherman's Dairy Bar. 1601 Phoenix Rd.; (269) 637-8251; www.shermanicecream.com. This don't-miss dessert stop has been a South Haven staple since the 1950s, when Port Sherman took over a door-to-door milk business from his brothers and churned it into ice cream instead. Still concocting natural rich and creamy goodness, Sherman's offers more than 50 flavors during peak season: from blueberry to a loaded butter pecan, from cappuccino to turtle cheesecake, and, my daughters' pick, Blue Moon (they love that it turns their tongues blue). Open mid-Mar through Oct. Also served year-round at Captain Nemo's, 407 Phoenix St. $.

Tello's Italian Bistro. 524 Phoenix St.; (269) 639-9898; www.tellobistro.com. With flickering candles and jazz music playing, Tello's ranks as one of the more romantic restaurants in South Haven. The menu features made-to-order Italian dishes using local produce and ingredients whenever possible. Pasta orders like Bolognese with roasted pork and beef, and spaghetti with house-made meatballs come in two portion sizes. During summer, open for dinner daily, Fri through Sun for lunch; open during fall daily for dinner and Sat and Sun for lunch; open during winter for dinner only. $$.

where to stay

Carriage House at the Harbor. 118 Woodman St.; (269) 639-2161; www.carriagehouse harbor.com. Choose from 12 gracefully appointed rooms, most with spa tubs, fireplaces, and private porches overlooking the picturesque harbor. Built in 1886, the former residence still offers old-fashioned hospitality, including a gourmet breakfast with items like crème brûlée French toast, lemon scones with Devonshire cream, and spinach bacon strata. Boost the romance factor even higher with an added in-room amenity like a massage, wine and cheese platter, champagne, and chocolate-covered strawberries. $$–$$$.

Lake Bluff Inn & Suites. 76648 11th Ave.; (269) 637-8531; www.lakebluffinnandsuites .com. Located on a bluff with breathtaking views of Lake Michigan, this large inn is great for families, complete with two swimming pools, hot tub and sauna inside, playground, game room, and continental breakfasts. $–$$$.

Last Resort B&B. 86 N. Shore Dr.; (269) 637-8943; www.lastresortinn.com. They say this 1883 structure a half-block from the lake was the first resort in South Haven; thus, the twist on the new name. Innkeepers-slash-artists Mary Hammer and her husband, Alberto Quiroga, revived the place from neglect in 1983 and offer 15 unique rooms, each decorated in an eclectic, comfortable way. A 66-foot wraparound deck seats guests for complimentary breakfast, a grill is available for visitors' use, and a gallery showcases the owners' artwork. Open May through Oct. $$–$$$.

day trip 02

northeast

>>> **calm, cool & art collectors:**
saugatuck-douglas, mi

saugatuck-douglas

It's no secret that Saugatuck-Douglas is one of Chicago's favorite driving destinations . . . and now that *Budget Travel* magazine declared it in 2010 as the "Coolest Small Party Town in America," you really need to go see it for yourself. And yes, it's a party town, but it's also a town for art lovers and artists, lovers and lake loungers, retreat seekers and recreationists. Welcoming girls' weekend girls, road-trippin' families, and same-sex couples alike (it's dubbed "Provincetown of the Midwest" by some), Saugatuck and its adjacent village Douglas have mastered the art of hospitality, not to mention art itself. More than 200 artists of every type live in an area that has a total population of under 2,500. Their presence is complemented by the renowned Ox-Bow art school, affiliated with the Art Institute of Chicago (visitors have included Nick Cave, Ed Paschke, and Claes Oldenburg). Like Chicago, the villages have a river and a Lake Michigan shoreline. Unlike Chicago, they were never reached by railway, so their old-fashioned quaintness, acres of fruit orchards, and resort quality remain. Oval Beach is considered one of the best in the country, so bring your suit. Then bunk down in an array of lodging options, from romantic bed-and-breakfasts to renovated 1950s-era motels to rental homes (call Mill Pond Realty about those, 269-857-1477).

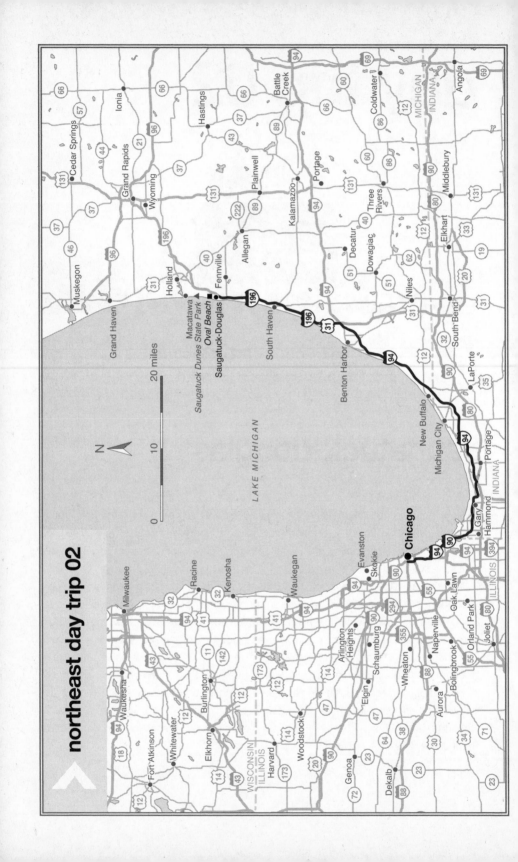

northeast day trip 02

getting there

Take I-90/I-94 east. Follow signs toward Indiana; continue on I-90/the Skyway. Merge back onto I-94 toward Detroit. Take exit 34 to I-196/US 31 north toward Holland/Grand Rapids. Take exit 36 toward Douglas/Saugatuck. Turn right onto old US 31, also known as CR 2 or the Blue Star Highway. The visitor center is just a few minutes down the road.

where to go

Saugatuck/Douglas Convention & Visitors Bureau. 2902 Blue Star Hwy., Saugatuck; (269) 857-1701; www.saugatuck.com. If executive director Felicia Fairchild is around, you'll hit the jackpot on insider info. Either way, pick up a comprehensive visitor guide.

Chain Ferry. 360 Water St., in Wicks Park, Saugatuck; contact the visitor bureau for more information. Resembling something of a lacy hat, this old-fashioned ferry is purport-edly the only one remaining in the country that is pulled by a chain—by hand, no less. Take the quick round-trip across the Kalamazoo River just for fun or pack your suit and towel and hop off at Oval Beach on the other side; it beats the fight for parking and its small fee, though it's about a mile to the shore. Runs Memorial Day through Labor Day. Nominal fee.

S.S. *Keewatin* Maritime Museum. 225 Union St. and Blue Star Highway, Douglas; (269) 857-2464; www.keewatinmaritimemuseum.com. Built in 1907 and retired in 1965, this former Great Lakes passenger ship now offers tours that afford a peek into *Titanic*-era elegance, including first-class staterooms, the Flower Well Lounge with Italian hand-etched and painted skylight windows, the men's lounge with hand-carved wood panels, and the captain's suite. You can also request entry to the engine room and coal-stoked boiler room. Admission varies depending on tour chosen. Generally open Memorial Day to Labor Day (sometimes later in the season).

Oval Beach. Oval Beach Road, near Park Street, Saugatuck; (269) 857-1701; www.sauga tuck.com/beaches.asp. Voted by *Conde Nast Traveler* as one of the best summer shore-lines in the country, considered a top freshwater beach by *National Geographic Traveler,* and named fourth-best inland gay beach by *OutTraveler*, this white sand Lake Michigan beach is a bit like North Avenue Beach, but with big, beautiful dunes. Plus swing sets, concessions, restrooms, and barbecue grills. Parking fee.

The Red Barn Theater. 3657 63rd St. at Blue Star Hwy., Saugatuck; (269) 857-5300; www.redbarnsaugatuck.com. Literally housed in an old red barn, the not-for-profit home of the Lakeshore Arts Alliance showcases local thespians, as well as a film series, musical performances, and cabaret-style shows. Ticket prices vary.

Saugatuck Center for the Arts. 400 Culver St., Saugatuck; (269) 857-2399; www .sc4a.org. A mission to bring arts to the underserved Allegan County, which includes

> ## art galleries galore

I could write a whole separate book on every noteworthy art gallery in Saugatuck and Douglas, but I'm suggesting four to whet your arty appetite.

- ***Button-Petter Gallery.*** *161 Blue Star Hwy., Douglas; (269) 857-2175; www.buttonpettergallery.com. Featuring the works of more than 80 artists in all media, from oils and acrylics to watercolors to glass, drawings, and textiles, as well as a sculpture garden, this 10,000-square-foot gallery is divided into several distinct rooms and practically doubles as an art museum.*

- ***Good Goods.*** *106 Mason St., Saugatuck; (888) 857-6501; www.good goods.com. This Italianate three-story former rooming house showcases ceramics, glass, furniture, and jewelry of more than 200 artists, including folk-arty Sticks works by Sarah Grant.*

- ***Marcia Perry's Ark Gallery & Sculpture Studio.*** *6248 Blue Star Hwy., Saugatuck; (269) 857-4210; www.marciaperry-ark.com. Visit Marcia and her "family" of emotive wooden sculptures that she crafts using sandpaper, chisels, mallets, chainsaw, and power tools. Call ahead to make sure Marcia is in.*

- ***Tuscan Pot.*** *321 Water St., Saugatuck; (269) 857-5550; www.tuscanpot .com. Rachael Hirt hand-paints tiles, sinks, and dishware using the ancient decorative Italian technique of majolica. The results are incredible. You'll be inspired to place an order or book a trip to Italy (or both).*

Saugatuck-Douglas, led to the transformation of a 23,000-square-foot abandoned pie factory in 2003. The center now offers art classes and workshops, rotating exhibits, musical and theatrical performances, a green produce market, and two film festivals—one for kids, and the Waterfront Film Festival (in June), recognized by the Screen Actors Guild as its third-favorite behind Sundance and Cannes. Open Mon through Fri. Free; donations accepted.

Saugatuck-Douglas Historical Museum. Saugatuck Pump House, 735 Park St., Saugatuck; (269) 857-7900; www.sdhistoricalsociety.org. Run by the Saugatuck-Douglas Historical Society, this small museum has a big presence in the area. The structure, built in 1904, served as the town's first pumping station until the 1950s. It was ready for the wrecking ball when a Chicago doctor leased it from the City of Saugatuck and renovated it as his summer cottage. These days, it offers annual exhibits focusing on local history and features a 1,500-square-foot garden with "story stops" that describe the panoramic sights from its elevated location. Open daily Memorial Day through Aug (noon to 4 p.m.); Sat and Sun through Oct. Free admission; donations accepted.

Saugatuck Dune Rides. 6495 Blue Star Hwy., Saugatuck; (269) 857-2253; www.sauga tuckduneride.com. No leisurely jaunt this. It is a roller coaster of ups and downs on the sandy dunes in an open-air jeeplike vehicle they call a "schooner." You'll stop atop a dune for spectacular views where kids can't help but run and roll down (shake out those shoes before getting back into your own car). Launched in 1954 by a local army vet, the company has been operated since 1981 by dune buggy duo Linus and Janice Starring. Open season- ally, generally late Apr through late Oct. Call for prices.

***Star of Saugatuck* Boat Cruise.** 716 Water St., Saugatuck; (269) 857-4261; www .saugatuckboatcruises.com. On this Lake Michigan and Kalamazoo River cruise you'll be pleasantly lulled by the gurgle of the paddlewheels as you travel past quaint cottages, woodlands, and wildlife. The 90-minute narrated trips offer upper and lower deck seating, and snacks and drinks (both alcoholic and non). Runs daily from early May through Sept, then Fri through Mon through mid- to late Oct. Call for ticket prices (cash, debit cards, and checks only).

where to shop

Butler Street. From Culver Street up to about Main, a lively strip of stores is perfect for souvenirs and only-in-Saugatuck finds. At **Saugatuck Spice Merchants** (115 Butler, 269-857-3031, www.spicemerchants.biz), you'll discover a bounty of spice blends, peppers, extracts, powdered chocolate, teas, and coffees. The **Butler Pantry** (119 Butler, 269-857-4875, www.thebutlerpantry.com), housed in a century-old building, carries the greatest kitchen gadgets and gourmet goodies. At **Alle Rue No. 133** (133 Butler, 269-857-5543, www.allerue.com), it's all about French flair, including a fab selection of hats. Pick up any forgotten sportswear at **Saugatuck Traders** (214 Butler, 269-857-4005) or whimsical screen-printed tops at the **T-Shirt Shoppe** (107 Butler, 269-857-4254). **Landsharks** (306 Butler, 269-857-8831, www.saugatucklandsharks.com) has all your chic outdoorsy apparel, plus comfy shoes from Acorn to Uggs. **American Spoon Foods** (308 Butler, 269-857-3084, www.spoon.com) harvests the finest fruits and cooks up some of the best preserves around.

where to eat

Belvedere Restaurant. 3656 63rd St., Saugatuck; (269) 857-5777; www.thebelvedereinn .com. Part of the Belvedere Inn (see "where to stay"), the restaurant is open to the public, and lucky for us. Though elegant with a capital E, there's no dress code, a sign of Ireland native chef Shaun Glynn's welcoming attitude. The prix fixe menu (two, three, or four, plus a kids' selection) includes artfully presented dishes such as grilled asparagus salad, lobster tail, chateaubriand for two, and gratin of veal sweetbreads. Don't miss the traditional English summer pudding with fresh berries. Hours change seasonally and include special event holiday dinners. $$$.

Crane's Pie Pantry Restaurant & Bakery. 6054 124th Ave., Fennville; (269) 561-2297; www.cranespiepantry.com. Head to Fennville, just 15 minutes southwest (Blue Star Highway to 124th Street/Route M-89), for down-home on the farm at its best. Fruit orchards born in the early 20th century (including U-pick cherries, peaches, and apples) surround the restaurant that's cheerfully decorated with a hodgepodge of farm antiques. The menu is mostly of the soups, salads, sandwiches kind, and all lovingly made. Of course, there's the made-from-scratch pie, an award-winning apple, as well as raspberry, peach, rhubarb, blueberry, and more. Or try a "cidersicle," fresh frozen apple cider and honey. Open hours vary seasonally. $.

Everyday People Café. 11 Center St., Douglas; (269) 857-4240; www.everydaypeople cafe.com. Owned by a mom and son team, E.P.C. is unfussy upscale-hip. Flavorful entrees range from an 8-ounce spice-crusted salmon to a gourmet chicken with ricotta dumplings to a pad thai with mushroom soy-peanut sauce. Looking for less? On Saturday and Sunday, the cute Bubbles & Bites menu offers all-you-can-drink champagne with small plates like oysters on the half shell and peel-and-eat shrimp. For weekend dinner, call ahead to put your name on the list to whittle your wait time (which can get lengthy). Open daily for dinner; Sat and Sun for lunch. $$–$$$.

Phil's Bar & Grille. 215 Butler St., Saugatuck; (269) 857-1555. Baked-in-house ciabatta buns for hand-shaped burgers, plus homemade soups, grilled ham and cheese on pretzel bread, specialty fried chicken, and a talked-about gorgonzola dip. It's all good stuff, hidden behind an unassuming storefront bar. Open daily for lunch and dinner. $$.

Restaurant Toulouse. 248 Culver St., Saugatuck; (269) 857-1561; www.restauranttoulouse .com. For more than 20 years, this friendly French spot has been catering to romantic evenings out and casual dinners on the patio. Its seasonally changing menu combines fine-dining elements—like sea scallops in a mushroom and sherry cream sauce, and peppered tenderloin with blue cheese butter and bordelaise sauce—with less fancy fare, including steak frites and a vegetarian Dagwood sandwich. Open for dinner Thurs through Sun. $$$.

Salt of the Earth. 114 E. Main St., Fennville; (269) 561-SALT (7258); www.saltoftheearth fennville.com. This adorable and eco-minded spot has become the new darling of the area. Local entrepreneurs Steve Darpel and Mark Schrock renovated the space, then put in a foundation of top-notch chef, baker, and laid-back vibe. Dishes include wood-fired wild mushroom pizza, pastas, and char-grilled rib eye. Everything from the mayo on the sandwiches to the marshmallows in the wood-fired toasted s'more is made from scratch. Most ingredients come from within 60 miles; there are even 19 Michigan beers. Live music every Friday night and sometimes on Sunday. Open daily for lunch and dinner. $$.

Uncommon Grounds. 127 Hoffman St., Saugatuck; (269) 857-3333; www.uncommon groundscafe.com. For those of us who cherish our morning coffee, this cozy spot under-stands. Steaming selections range from classic lattes, espressos, and cappuccinos to blended mocha, caramel silk, the Milli Vanilli (flavored with vanilla, of course), and the malted mocha (which they claim you can't get anywhere else). A limited but enticing menu offers fresh-baked muffins and scones, house-made granola, egg sandwiches, and mac and cheese. There are also shakes and malts made with gelato, fresh juices, yogurt smoothies, a vegetarian menu, plus free Wi-Fi and patio seating. Open daily for breakfast, lunch, and dinner (closes earlier during the off-season). $.

where to stay

BaySide Inn. 618 Water St., Saugatuck; (269) 857-4321; www.baysideinn.net. Built in 1927 as a boathouse with an upstairs residence, the riverfront structure was partially sub-merged in the water by the time Kathy and Frank Wilson saved it, transforming it into a 10-room bed-and-breakfast. All rooms have private baths and balconies, and the 4 suites have fireplaces. $–$$$.

Boutique Inns of Saugatuck. (269) 857-5777, (877) 858-5777; www.boutiqueinnsof saugatuck.com. You can't go wrong with any one of the three different accommodations comprising Boutique Inns of Saugatuck—**The Belvedere Inn** (a B&B with fine dining), the **Bentley Waterfront Suites,** and the **Bellevue Harbor House**. Run by a former corporate duo from Chicago, each lodging offers something a bit different, but they all share the same genial service. The subtitle of The Belvedere (3656 63rd St.) sort of says it all: a 5-acre "mini Versailles," but built in Frank Lloyd Wright's time and style, with 10 luxurious guest rooms and landscaped gardens. The 4 suites at the downtown Bentley (326 Water St.) all have Kalamazoo River views. Also downtown, the Bellevue (419 Lake St.) is a weekly rental on Lake Kalamazoo that can house eight. $$–$$$.

Lake Shore Resort. 2885 Lake Shore Dr., Saugatuck; (269) 857-7121; www.lakeshore resortsaugatuck.com. The only resort on Lake Michigan with a private beach, the Lake Shore has been getting repeat customers for many years. Take a dip in the large heated pool, stroll along adjacent wooded trails, watch stunning sunsets from the lake-view fire pits, or tool into nearby downtown on free-to-use bikes. Complimentary breakfast is served on decks that afford stunning views of Lake Michigan. The resort is for adults and children at least 13 years old. $$.

The Pines Motorlodge. 56 Blue Star Hwy., Douglas; (269) 857-5211; www.thepines motorlodge.com. You can't help but comment on the cute quality of this place, a renovated

1950s tourist plaza. Though right off the highway, it feels all woodsy with surrounding pine trees, Amish-style wood furnishings, and knotty pine ceilings. Two-night minimum during peak season; closed in winter. $$–$$$.

Ship 'n Shore Motel/Boatel. 528 Water St., Saugatuck; (269) 857-2194; www.shipn shoremotel.com. A favorite among the young and trendy boating crowd, this 40-room motel's greatest asset is its location right on the water. It also boasts one of the largest outdoor heated pools in the area, with landscaping that has the Caribbean in mind, and a new Jacuzzi. Boaters often pull up to the dock for a few nights' stay, bringing with them an upbeat party atmosphere. Continental breakfast is complimentary. $$.

day trip 03

northeast

Together, Holland and Grand Haven snagged a spot as the second "Happiest and Healthiest Place to Live in America," according to a 2010 Gallup index (first is Boulder, Colorado). Both cities have the water at their hearts, with protected sand dunes and soft, sandy beaches lending loads of recreation and natural beauty. Holland is famous for its Dutch flavor in its food, festivals, flowers, fancy footwork of the klompen dancers, and, of course, its grand 12-story-high DeZwaan windmill. In Grand Haven a recently refurbished boardwalk puts a brighter spotlight on Lake Michigan and the Grand River.

holland

While a trip to the Netherlands might cost you a thousand dollars and eight hours, Holland, Michigan, is barely a gas tankful away and a whole lot cheaper. Plus, there's no language barrier. The first white settlers arrived in the area in 1847, immigrants from the Netherlands hoping to trade economic depression and religious oppression for the wealth of the New World. Despite a blow in October 1871 when most of the city burned down (yup, same month and year as the Great Chicago Fire—it was particularly dry that year), like Chicago, Holland fought back and celebrated its 25th anniversary in 1872. By the 1920s, beautiful Lake Macatawa and Ottawa Beach were summer resort destinations, and in 1988, the city became more comfortable in winter too as it completed an impressive 120-mile under-ground snowmelt system (Chicago, are you listening?). But springtime is where it's at in

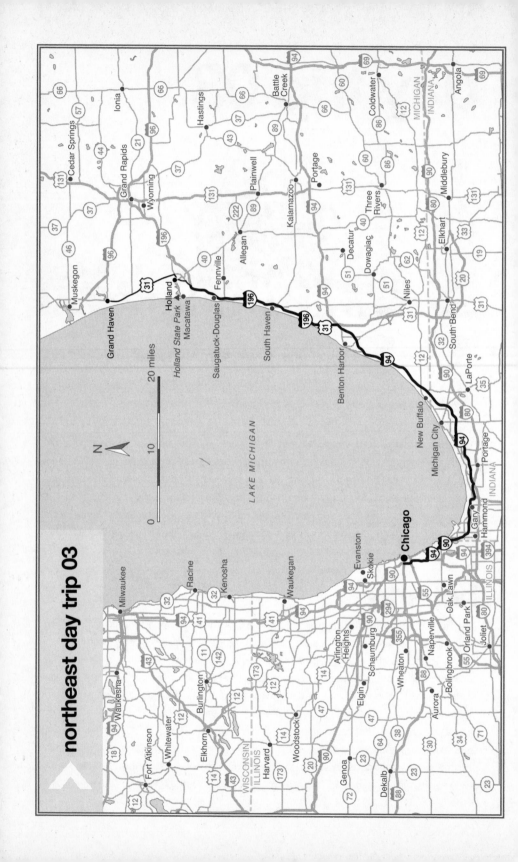

northeast day trip 03

Holland, when the 6 million tulips turn the city into a kaleidoscope of color. As you stroll the streets, look for the collection of bronze statues too. Welkom!

getting there

Take I-94/I-90 east. Stay on I-90 to take the Skyway, then reconnect with I-94. Take exit 34 to enter I-196/US 31 north toward Holland/Grand Rapids. Veer left (exit 44), following I-196 to US 31 north to Holland/Muskegon. Take exit 47B (on the left) toward downtown Holland. Continue for about 2½ miles into downtown.

where to go

Holland Area Convention & Visitors Bureau. 76 E. 8th St.; (800) 506-1299, (616) 394-0000; www.holland.org. Pick up a visitor guide and be sure to say hello to the mascot pug, Lucy. If you're at the bureau when it's closed, there are brochures outside and an events calendar posted on the window. Open Mon through Fri year-round; also open Sat from mid-Apr through mid-Nov, and Sun May through Labor Day. You can tune in to visitor info on the radio at 530 AM once you're in the area.

Holland Museum. 31 W. 10th St.; (616) 796-3329; www.hollandmuseum.org. It's double-Dutch here, showcasing both art and history in a 1914 former post office building. Two 17th-century portraits by Dutch Golden Age artist Michiel van Mierevelt are the pièces de résistance of a collection of more than 50 17th- to 20th-century paintings, along with Dutch artifacts including furniture and costumes. Also operated by the Holland Historical Trust, the Settlers House and Cappon House museums are just a few blocks away. **The Settlers House** (190 W. 9th St.) re-creates the hard-knock life of early Holland settlers, while the Italianate **Cappon House** (228 W. 9th St.) contrasts that with the ornate furnishings of Holland's first mayor and tannery owner Isaac Cappon. Admission for ages 6 and up. Open Mon, and Wed through Sat.

Holland State Park: Ottawa Beach & Big Red Lighthouse. 2215 Ottawa Beach Rd.; (616) 399-9390, camping reservations (800) 447-2757; www.michigandnr.gov. Divided into two sections—one bordering Lake Michigan and one along Lake Macatawa (about a half-mile apart)—Holland State Park comprises the white sandy Ottawa Beach, a 20-mile bike trail that connects to Grand Haven State Park, campgrounds, and cabins. Haul up the 250-plus stairs to Mt. Pisgah Dune and Boardwalk for the best bird's-eye views of the area, as well as the best views of the Big Red Lighthouse, a favorite of photographers with its twin gables and bright crimson color. Park open year-round; camping seasonal.

Nelis' Dutch Village. 12350 James St. (corner of US 31); (616) 396-1475; www.dutch village.com. You'll definitely want to go Dutch at this endearing theme park of sorts. Representing the Netherlands of more than a century ago, it features traditional Dutch orange tile roofs, brick paths, and canals. Not to mention the goats—you can take one for a stroll through town or feed them at the petting zoo. You can also sample cheeses from the Netherlands and take a ride on an antique carousel or the Zweefmolen (swing ride). Don't miss the Dutch dance performances, the 200-year-old windmill, the wooden shoe slide, and a Kiddieland relic, the Petal Pumper Cars, moved here after the Melrose Park amusement park closed in 2009. Bring a dash of Dutch home with you from the shops at Dutch Village—wooden shoes, six-ribboned candles, Sinterklaas items (for Christmas), and more. Shops open year-round; village open Apr through mid-Oct (weekends only Sept and Oct).

Veldheer's Tulip Gardens & DeKlomp Wooden Shoe & Delftware Factory. 12755 Quincy Ave.; (616) 399-1900; www.veldheer.com. I admit, I wasn't there to see spring's spectacular tulip display, its 50,000 daffodils, 10,000 hyacinths, and 20,000 crocuses, but people tell me it's an ocean of blooming beauty. I did see the thousands of Dutch lilies, daylilies, and peonies (they're out from June through mid-October), and it was as pretty as a picture. Besides the flowers and bulbs to buy, Veldheer's boasts the only Delft Dutch pottery production facility in North America—watch the process from liquid clay to mold to 2,000-degree oven to more than 300 different hand-painted items for sale in the shop. Also made on-site are traditional wooden shoes carved on machines imported from the Netherlands. One more attraction here: a farm of nearly 20 bison, including the 14-year-old Tacoma, quite the ladies' man. Open daily. Nominal fee to see bison during tulip season.

Windmill Island. 7th Street and Lincoln Avenue; (616) 355-1030; (888) 535-5792; www.windmillisland.org. This is what you came for, isn't it? To see the only authentic working Dutch windmill in the country, now nearly 250 years old. Shipped here from the Netherlands in 1964, its first visitor in April 1965 was Prince Bernhard of the Netherlands. When it's open, you can climb to the top and look out over 36 acres of landscaped gardens and listen to the history of the old "DeZwaan" (meaning "graceful bird"). Klompen dancers perform on the hour during the summer. Open daily Apr through early Oct. Admission.

where to shop

Holland Clock Company. 210 College Ave.; (616) 796-1277; www.hollandclockcompany.com. You'll go cuckoo for these clocks (sorry, couldn't resist). Opened in 2010 by former electrical engineer Dan Winebrenner, the clock shop has become a must-stop to get German novelty clocks, Dutch-style clocks, German cuckoo clocks with and without the pop-out bird, and other ornamental clocks, both traditional and contemporary. Open daily.

Lizzie Ann's Wool Company. 54 E. 8th St.; (616) 392-2035; www.lizzieannswoolco.com. Stock up on all your knitting needs at this "perl" of a store in downtown Holland. Warm and welcoming owner Lindy Graff named her store in tribute to her mentor in England and carries a rainbow of yarns, plus needles, notions, patterns, buttons, and books. Open Mon through Sat.

Wooden Shoe Antique Mall. 447 US 31 at 16th Street; (616) 396-0353. A defunct wooden shoe factory stepped into new shoes a few years ago as this 11,500-square-foot antique mall, offering dozens of booths with everything from old ad signs to vintage radios to jewelry. The **Wooden Shoe Restaurant** is right next door. Open daily.

where to eat

CityVu Bistro. CityFlats Hotel, 61 E. 7th St.; (616) 796-2114; www.cityflatshotel.com. On the 5th-floor penthouse of the sleekest stay in town (stellar views all around), the CityVu Bistro serves must-try flatbread pizzas featuring crust made from whole wheat flour stone-ground at the DeZwaan windmill. The pizzas are all named for different cities. Of course, you should try the "Chicago," topped with Kalamata olives, artichokes, feta cheese, roasted tomatoes, and mixed greens—I thought it would have steak on it, but for that, there's the "Kansas City" pizza with rosemary seared beef. Weekday lunch features all-you-can-eat soup, salad, and flatbread for less than 10 bucks. A 100-plus wine list, with 24 by the glass too. Open daily for lunch and dinner, Sat also for breakfast, and brunch Sun. $–$$.

New Holland Brewing Company. 66 E. 8th St.; (616) 355-NHBC; www.newhollandbrew .com. This convivial downtown spot pours house-brewed beers that include real pumpkin, hints of chocolate, and other interesting flavors. Menu items go beyond typical pub fare to gourmet pizzas (try the Dixie Luau, breaking barriers with prosciutto, pork belly, grilled pine-apple, red onion, and pickled jalapeno), and sandwiches like grilled portobello and house-made corned beef. New Holland's more recent foray into spirits has resulted in vodka, rum, whiskey, and "hopquila," a distilled barley drink. Open daily for lunch and dinner. $–$$.

Pereddies Restaurant & Deli. 447 Washington Sq.; (616) 394-3061; www.pereddies restaurant.com. This family-owned restaurant has been serving up traditional Italian special-ties (think lasagna, veal Parm, and pasta Bolognese) in a casual white-tablecloth setting for more than two decades. It also has a European-style food market and a comfortable bar (Scusi) that offers the full restaurant menu. $$.

The Piper. 2225 South Shore Dr., Macatawa; (616) 335-5866; www.piperrestaurant.com. People pick the piper for its location, location, location. Situated on Lake Macatawa, the outdoor deck and indoor second-floor dining room and bar all reward you with romantic views of the water and marina. The best part is that the food ranks too: from a seafood combo of salmon and sea scallops on saffron risotto to pan-seared American Kobe beef sirloin and a vegetarian mushroom medley. Plus, build-your-own pizzas offer a whopping 31 toppings. Open daily for dinner from June through Aug; open Tues through Sat the rest of the year. $$.

Windmill Restaurant. 28 W. 8th St.; (616) 392-2726. The locals' go-to breakfast spot, this no-frills family diner has rows of booths and plenty of space at the counter, complete with covered trays of baked goodies. But don't let them tempt you past the biscuits and gravy (you don't see that much around Chicago, right?), omelets, hash browns, and, well, omelet hash browns. Open daily for breakfast and lunch. $.

where to stay

The Beach House at Lake Street. 2047 Lake St.; (616) 886-9243; www.lakemichigan beachhouse.com. Intended for longer stays, this upscale lodging actually offers 8 beach houses to choose from across from Lake Macatawa. Named for other resort towns, each unit includes an equipped kitchen and at least 2 bedrooms and 2 baths, and is immaculately and fittingly decorated to reflect its namesake—like the Southern plantation-style of the Savannah house or the coastal feel of the Charleston. Besides close proximity to beaches, your stay includes access to a heated pool and hot tub, private grill patios, and housekeeping and baby-sitting services. Weekly rentals only from mid-June through late Aug; two- or three-night stays required Sept through June. $$$.

Centennial Inn B&B. 8 E. 12th St.; (616) 355-0998; www.yesmichigan.com/centennial. Originally the home of physician and Holland Mayor Henry Kremers, whose parents were among Holland's original settlers, this renovated 1889 Elizabethan-style home also served as Holland's first hospital, then a fraternity of Hope College, and the first Netherlands Museum. It took on its current use in 1995 when proprietors Rein and Kay Wolfert gave it a loving makeover to offer 6 charming rooms, 3 with working Victorian fireplaces and 1 with a Jacuzzi. Staying here, you're close to downtown and across from scenic Centennial Park. $$.

City Flats Hotel. 61 E. 7th St.; (866) 609-2489, (616) 796-2100; www.cityflatshotel.com. Looking all clean-lined and modern with its ethereal glow at night, this trendy, 56-room hotel opened in 2008 to wide appeal. It was the Midwest's first LEED gold-certified hotel, sporting bamboo linens, dual-flush toilets, and most materials and finishes sourced locally. Soaring 10- to 13-foot ceilings and huge windows give sleek rooms a loft feel. $$–$$$.

Haworth Inn. Hope College Campus, 225 College Ave.; (800) 903-9142, (616) 395-7200; www.haworthinn.com. Located at Hope College in Holland, but open to all guests (Hope parents get a discount), this comfortable hotel is within walking distance of downtown and gets booked fast during tulip time. It offers complimentary continental breakfast too. Tip: Request a room facing away from the downtown street if you want less noise. $$.

grand haven

So what if Grand Haven only launched its Facebook page in summer 2010; it was the country's first municipality to offer city-wide Wi-Fi (though it's not free). Originally a logging and manufacturing town, it has mostly morphed into a mecca for sunbathers and water sport lovers. In fact, the city of less than 12,000 is also said to have one of the top beaches in the country. That makes sense, considering that, of its 7.5 square miles, more than 20 percent is water.

getting there

Grand Haven is about a half-hour north of Holland on US 31. From 8th Street, merge onto US 31 north toward Muskegan. Continue on US 31 about 20 miles. Then turn left at Jackson Avenue, which bends around the river to become Harbor Drive, where you'll find the visitor bureau. To get the heads-up on road construction, check www.michigan.gov/drive.

where to go

Grand Haven Area Convention & Visitors Bureau. 1 S. Harbor Dr.; (800) 303-4096; www.visitgrandhaven.com. Get your grand welcome to the area at this catch-all of information. Open Mon through Fri (and Sat during the summer).

Grand Haven Boardwalk. Call the visitor bureau for more information. A recent face-lift gave this 2.5-mile trail new pavers, new benches, two new sculptures, and a renewed sense of dignity. Perfect for morning jogs and evening strolls, it follows the harbor lined with restaurants and shops and out along the Grand River to Lake Michigan. Bring your camera for photo ops.

Grand Haven State Park: Beach, Lighthouse & Pier. 1001 Harbor Ave.; (800) 447-2757, (616) 847-1309; www.michigandnr.com. This 48-acre park is the site to see the area's historic and iconic pair of red lighthouses, one a typical cylinder shape, the other a cute house-shaped lighthouse. They're connected by a lighted catwalk that presents a brilliant night scene. But back to the beach: Wide expanses of sugary-soft sand offer plenty of space for kite flying, volleyball playing, sandcastle building, and just lounging. Campground reservations can be made at www.michigan.gov/dnr.

Harbor Trolley. Chinook Pier, 301 N. Harbor Dr.; (616) 842-3200. Like the Chicago trolleys that natives rarely ride, this trolley is perfectly suited to visitors. The 30-minute trek takes you around the city with witty narration included. Runs Memorial Day through Labor Day. Nominal fee.

Musical Fountain. On the north shore of the Grand River near Grand Haven State Park; best viewing from Waterfront Stadium, 1 N. Harbor Dr.; (616) 842-2550; www.grandhaven .org/recreation/musical-fountain-schedule. Sure, Chicago's got Buckingham Fountain, but Grand Haven's water wonder incorporates music along with its lights. Local engineer William Morris Booth II designed this 1962 feat of plumbing, which was credited for kick-starting harbor redevelopment. The 20-minute performances show off the fountain's prowess with its 200 colored lights, 8,000 feet of piping, and still-original nozzles and pumps. Sprays of up to 125 feet high, dancing waters, swaying water, fanning water, and curtains of water are part of the choreography. Shows run nightly from Memorial Day through Labor Day.

Rosy Mound Natural Area. 13925 Lakeshore Dr.; (616) 738-4810; www.miottawa.org/ parks. This 164-acre area includes the 200-foot Rosy Mound dune, reached only by the 0.7-mile foot trail, which includes 360 steps. Take a breather at the dune overlooks and take in the peaceful natural setting. You'll eventually reach the beach, but the area is open during non-beach weather too. Open year-round. Nominal parking fees from Memorial Day through Labor Day.

Tri-Cities Historical Museum. 200 Washington Ave. and 1 N. Harbor Dr.; (616) 842-0700; www.tri-citiesmuseum.org. Besides telling the story of Grand Haven, this history museum showcases the communities of nearby Spring Lake and Ferrysburg. Having expanded to fill two buildings since its beginnings in 1952, the museum features exhibits that reflect the people, places, and events that shaped the towns. Open Tues through Sun. Free.

where to shop

Gallery Uptown. 201 Washington Ave.; (616) 846-5460; www.galleryuptown.net. More than 30 award-winning artists showcase their work at this, the oldest co-op gallery in the state. Browse everything from Ann Trowbridge's acrylic paintings of the Michigan landscape to pottery by Steve Zawojski, fired in his hand-built kiln, to woven rugs, towels, and clothing by Marilyn Ryan. Temporary gallery shows feature emerging artists. Open daily.

Mackinaw Kite Company. 106 Washington Ave.; (800) 622-4655; www.mackite.com. Forgot your kite at home? Blow into this colorful shop, one of the world's largest for kites of all kinds: delta, box, foil, birds, classic diamonds, dragons with flowing tails, stunt kites with four lines. If you are suddenly in a kid kind of mood, check out the games, puzzles, yo-yos, and other toys too. Now, get to the beach and go fly a kite. Open daily.

Michigan Rag Company. 121 Washington Ave.; (800) 373-1451, (616) 846-1451; www .michiganrag.com. Not just any ol' T-shirt shop, this place still prints the old-fashioned way: They silkscreen by hand. Plus, the prints are whimsical reminders of your stay in Grand Haven, like the store's bestseller, "Lake Michigan-Unsalted," available in short- or long-sleeve, hooded sweatshirt or crew neck.

where to eat

Bil-mar Restaurant. 1223 S. Harbor Dr.; (616) 842-5920; www.bil-margrandhaven.com. You'll be duly distracted by the Lake Michigan views from this shoreline restaurant. But the food has been bringing people back for nearly 60 years, with signature dishes like a bacon-wrapped turkey tenderloin kebab, grilled lamb chops, and 9-ounce top sirloin with crabmeat topping and hollandaise sauce. $$.

The Grill Room at the Kirby House. 2 Washington Ave.; (616) 846-3299; www.thegilmore collection.com. Since it was built as a hotel in 1873, this downtown structure has seen many a restaurant and inn come and go. It's probably the prime USDA choice beef that has made its latest incarnation one of its most successful. Opened in 1989 by the Gilmore Collection, West Michigan's answer to Chicago's Levy Restaurants, the warmly furnished spot offers a tight menu of steak and seafood. It's one of three eateries in the building—the other two are the family-friendly **Kirby Grill** and wood-fired pizzeria **K2**. Watch out, though: It's rumored to be haunted. Open daily for dinner. $$$.

Odd Side Ales. 41 Washington Ave.; (616) 935-7326; www.oddsideales.com. No fancy decor here, just lots of friendly faces and fun-loving spirit. In fact, this tiny brewery in an old piano factory focuses so much of its attention on its brews that there's nothing to eat, save a few salty nibbles. It's actually a BYOF—bring your own food. Or just sit back and savor sips like a peanut butter cup stout (really!), amber, nut brown ale, pumpkin spice in the fall, or raspberry wheat. $.

Pronto Pup. 313 S. Harbor Dr.; (616) 638-1632; www.grandhavenprontopup.com. Don't blink or you might miss this petite yellow hut along the harbor. For more than 65 years, it's been famous for one thing and one thing only: the made-in-Michigan frankfurter, dipped in a "special batter" and fried up in 100 percent vegetable oil (the eponymous Pronto Pups). Condiments? Just ketchup or mustard. So easy, so simple, so deliciously addictive. Open the first weekend in May through Labor Day, weekends in Sept. $.

where to stay

Harbor House Inn. 114 S. Harbor Dr.; (800) 841-0610; www.harborhousegh.com. Right across from the Grand Haven Boardwalk and within sight of the Grand River and Lake Michigan sand dunes, this Victorian-style bed-and-breakfast comprises 20 rooms and 5 suites in detached cottages. Each room is uniquely decorated, most boasting fireplaces and whirlpool tubs, all privy to the common-area screened-in porch and the sitting area with its own fireplace. Plus, there are buffet breakfasts, tea and coffee, and baked goodies in the evening, and dreamy homemade caramels by your bed every day. $$$.

Lakeshore Bed & Breakfast. 11001 Lakeshore Dr.; (616) 844-2697; www.bbonline.com/mi/lakeshore. If you've ever wanted to live on a lakefront estate, here's your chance. The 4 rooms in this 6,500-square-foot mansion built in 1941 have an American president theme, accessorized with memorabilia and artifacts from George Washington, Abraham Lincoln, John F. Kennedy, Taft, Hoover, Garfield, Reagan, and more. The expansive lawns offer cozy curl-up hammocks, while the 200-foot private beach beckons in warm weather. $$$.

Serendipity Resort Downtown. 200 Franklin Ave.; (616) 842-2761; www.serendipity resorts.com. Six neatly decorated adjoining homes and suites face onto a pool and grilling area and are just blocks from the beach, the Musical Fountain, downtown, and other Grand Haven attractions. Various sizes and options can accommodate more than eight people, so bring the whole gang. $$–$$$.

day trip 04

northeast

take a seat, literally:
grand rapids, mi

grand rapids

Chicago carries substantial clout among furniture and design pros, who work its Merchandise Mart, but Grand Rapids is known as "Furniture City" for its history as a major furniture production market from the late 19th through mid-20th centuries. Even before the city was incorporated in 1850, there were furniture shops popping up around town. The public museum tells the story of the city's furniture glory days, while today, its major contribution is in office furniture, with the headquarters here for $2.3 billion company Steelcase. Grand Rapids has more recently hit architecture-related headlines for LEED leadership in its new art museum. Between taking in the artwork and strolling the stunning Meijer gardens, you really will need to sit down for a spell.

getting there

Just about three hours from Chicago, Grand Rapids is a simple drive. Take I-94/I-90 east. Follow I-90 for the Skyway, then merge back with I-94 east. Take exit 34 to enter I-196/US 31 north toward Holland/Grand Rapids. Take exit 77B toward US 131 south/Kalamazoo. Merge with Mt. Vernon Avenue. Turn left at Pearl Street, then right on Monroe to stop first at the visitor center.

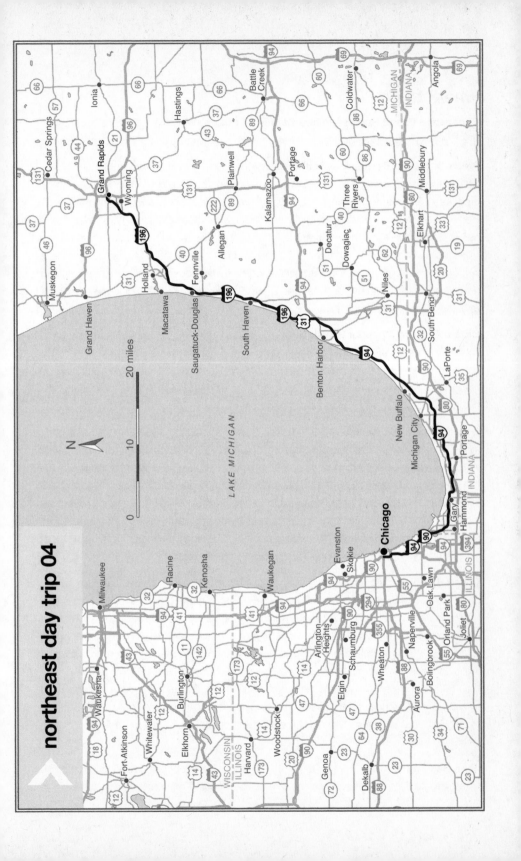

northeast day trip 04

where to go

Experience Grand Rapids Visitors Center. 171 Monroe Ave. NW, Suite 700; (616) 459-8287; www.visitgrandrapids.org. Visit this downtown office to pick up a visitor guide.

Frederik Meijer Gardens & Sculpture Park. 1000 E. Beltline Ave.; (888) 957-1580; www.meijergardens.org. I would venture to say there is nothing like this in the Chicago area. Its 132 acres pack in an amazing sculpture park featuring works by Auguste Rodin, Henry Moore, Mark di Suvero, Magdalena Abakanowicz, Claes Oldenburg, and others; plus nature paths; a 5-acre children's garden that boasts five separate gardens of its own; a tropical conservatory with more than 500 species from all over the world; an arid garden, a woodland shade garden, a Victorian garden, and a carnivorous plant exhibition; an outdoor amphitheater for summer concerts; and a farm garden featuring a 1930s-era farmhouse and barn. Open daily. Admission.

Gerald R. Ford Presidential Museum. 303 Pearl St. NW; (616) 254-0400; www.ford librarymuseum.gov. President Ford grew up in Grand Rapids and is entombed here on the grounds of the museum. Permanent exhibits include a look back at Watergate, featuring the actual break-in tools, a replica Oval Office, and a multimedia exhibit that recalls the 1970s era in which Ford served. Open daily. Admission.

Grand Rapids Art Museum. 101 Monroe Center; (616) 831-1000; www.artmuseumgr .org. Though this art institution celebrated 100 years in 2010, its brand-new home opened in 2007, earning GRAM a thumbs-up from both the art and architecture communities as the first entirely LEED gold-certified art museum in the world. The 125,000-square-foot space includes a three-floor gallery to display exhibits from the museum's renowned collection that includes 19th- and 20th-century American and European paintings and sculpture. It also saves ample room for temporary exhibits such as the recent Princess Diana exhibit that included her wedding dress. Open Tues through Sun. Admission.

Grand Rapids Public Museum. 272 Pearl St. NW; (616) 929-1700; www.grmuseum.org. Learn about Grand Rapids' dynamic heyday as "The Furniture City" in this museum's largest permanent exhibit. Glimpse 120 furniture items and a re-created 1920s furniture market showroom. Other highlights include concerts on the historic Wurlitzer Theater Organ; rides on the 1928 Spillman Carousel, outfitted with 44 hand-carved and jeweled animals; and the most recent addition, "Newcomers: The People of This Place," incorporating more than 600 artifacts and images to tell the story of the various ethnic groups who continue to grow the community. Want more? The museum is also home to the Roger B. Chaffee Planetarium, named after a Grand Rapids–born astronaut who died aboard *Apollo 1*. Open daily. Admission.

John Ball Zoo. 1300 W. Fulton St.; (616) 336-4301; www.johnballzoosociety.org. At 110 acres, this city zoo is almost twice the size as the Lincoln Park Zoo and devotes a whole one-third of an acre to its cherished chimpanzee family. Another zoo pride? The lions of Lake Manyara, in their recently created home, one of the largest lion habitats in the country, offering panoramic and bird's-eye visitor vantage points. Plus, feed budgies, listen to the sounds from 15 different types of frogs, test your courage on a 300-foot zipline and ropes course, ride a camel, and paddle around in a swan boat. Generally open year-round; some exhibits seasonal. Nominal admission (extra fee for some activities).

Robinette's Apple Haus & Gift Barn. 3142 4 Mile Rd. NE; (800) 400-8100; www.robinettes .com. All the frills of a sweet apple farm experience are wrapped up in Robinette's. Pick apples (cherries in July); take a horse-drawn hayride in September and October; watch cider made just about every day during the fall; find your way out of the corn maze; pick up gifts and bakery goods at the shop in the circa-1881 barn. Then taste that fresh cider or try hard cider or apple cherry hard cider, also made here. Open year-round. Nominal fees for some activities.

Urban Institute for Contemporary Art. 41 Sheldon Blvd.; (616) 454-7000; www.uica .org. Placing Grand Rapids squarely in the most thought-provoking of arts scenes, this multidisciplinary arts center incorporates programming in visual arts, dance, film, and music. Look for its brand-new building at 2 W. Fulton in spring 2011. Open year-round. Prices vary depending on the event.

where to eat

The 1913 Room. Amway Grand Plaza Hotel, 187 Monroe Ave. NW; (800) 253-3590, (616) 774-2000; www.the1913room.com. Among the posh Amway Grand's impressive 9 dining options, this one stands on its own gilded pedestal. In 2002, led by self-taught chef de cuisine Christian Madsen, the romantic restaurant received Michigan's first AAA Five Diamond Award and has maintained it since. The rotating menu might include seared Hudson Valley *foie gras*, rosemary roasted kurobuta pork loin and braised belly, and grilled fillet of beef and Maine lobster terrine. Add the velvet booths, Louis XVI–style furnishings, glittering chandeliers, and impeccable service and you've got one memorable meal. Open Mon through Sat for dinner. $$$.

Beltline Bar. 16 28th St. SE; (616) 245-0494; www.4gr8food.com. There might be more authentic Mexican restaurants in town, but this one is by far the most famous (their Facebook page alone has nearly 4,500 fans) and probably the oldest. Opened in 1953, serving not much more than chili dogs, it now has a menu that's as big as the Baja Peninsula—from quesadillas to Cobb salads, chicken enchiladas to shrimp tacos and fajitas. But the house specialty is the "wet burrito," a stuffed flour tortilla topped with secret sauce and Colby cheese. The other don't miss: the margaritas, mixed with any number of the 35 tequilas. Open daily for lunch and dinner. $.

Bistro Bella Vita. 44 Grandville Ave. SW; (616) 222-4600; www.bistrobellavita.com. A pioneer in the farm-to-table movement, Bella Vita even grows its own heirloom produce. The upscale Mediterranean-countryside cuisine might include lamb chops, duck breast, and braised leg over slow-cooked white bean and pork cassoulet, butternut squash ravioli, and outstanding paella. Vegetarian and vegan options too. A global wine list tops more than 100 bottles, the beer list is a connoisseur's dream, and the specialty shaken-tableside martinis are worth the visit alone (try the Pomegranate Punch). Open Mon through Fri for lunch and dinner, Sat and Sun for dinner. $$–$$$.

Electric Cheetah. 1015 Wealthy St. SE; (616) 451-4779; www.electriccheetah.com. From the rosemary grown in reclaimed-wood planters to the homemade crayons for kids to the counter made from concrete and broken glass, this hip spot knows all about sustainability. And it shines in ingredients fresh from the farm (or farmers' market) in dishes like the Michigan farmers pasta, grilled local trout, and orange challah French toast with peach rosemary compote. Most items are jaw-droppingly inexpensive too. Leave 12 minutes to order fresh-baked cookies (seriously, the dough is put on the pan when you order them). Nearby at **Uncle Cheetah's Soup Shop** (1133 Wealthy St. SE), you can savor chef Corey DeMint's delish soups. Open Mon through Sat for lunch and dinner, brunch on Sunday. $$.

Founders Brewing Company. 235 Grandville Ave. SW; (616) 776-1195; www.founders brewing.com. In an airy former trucking terminal, the brewmasters of this mighty microbrewery whip up award-winning magic potions. They do it with skill, enthusiasm, and a sense of humor—evidenced by names like Curmudgeon Old Ale, Double Trouble, and Devil Dancer. The taproom features live music and a view of the brewing facilities. Massive, made-to-order sandwiches on fresh-baked bread include the Tree Hugger with a bevy of good stuff like baby spinach and hummus on six-grain wheat bread; and the Godfather Pepperoni piled with capicola and mozzarella cheese. Expanded production facilities mean more beer coming out of this place, and loyal customers are thrilled. Open Mon through Sat for lunch, dinner, and late-night; Sun opens after lunch. $.

Green Well. 924 Cherry St. SE; (616) 808-3566; www.thegreenwell.com. This gastro-pub had me with its fancy mac and cheese, bubbling with mushrooms, caramelized onions, chicken, bacon, and peas. But its menu covers an eclectic range from jambalaya to Southern clam bake to Michigan maple whiskey chicken. Pair your meal with one of the many wine or beer flights, and you're set. The "green" part comes from its LEED-certified building and locally sourced ingredients, not to mention a down-to-earth atmosphere. Open daily for lunch and dinner. $–$$.

where to stay

Holiday Inn Downtown Grand Rapids. 310 Pearl St. NW; (888) 465-4329; www.holiday inn.com. This Holiday Inn ranks high with visitors for its free parking, downtown location, and indoor pool and whirlpool. Plus, the beds are quite comfy with their pillow-top mattresses and triple sheeting. $$.

Peaches Bed & Breakfast. 29 Gay Ave. SE; (866) PEACHES, (616) 454-8000; www .peaches-inn.com. A tail-wagging hello from resident dalmatian DaChien begins your stay at this beautiful 1916 Georgian manor. Besides the 5 queen guest rooms with private baths, each with original (and tip-top) bathroom fixtures, the house features a cozy living room and library with fireplaces, a cheerful sun room, game room with pool table and original Depression-era murals, patio, gardens, and front porch. It gets its name from a sign in the foyer that harks back to the days when inn owner Jane Lovett's grandfather operated peach orchards in South Haven. $$.

day trip 05

northeast

>>> **brews, zoos & more:**
kalamazoo, mi; battle creek, mi;
marshall, mi

Just off I-94, this trio of Michigan cities takes you from a zoo of airplanes to a zoo with a heart for endangered species, from a microbrewery that's 25 years old to another that boasts a 250-year-old tradition. It features a town that launched the cereal craze and was referred to in a movie as "Wellville." It gives you the key to a castle and the secrets to a museum of magic. You've probably heard of Kalamazoo and Battle Creek, but maybe not little Marshall. It makes up for its petite population (less than 8,000 people) with lovely, small-town living and huge, historic homes. Be sure to make time for a stop at its famous Honolulu House.

kalamazoo

The Glenn Miller Orchestra and Ben Folds Five both sang about Kalamazoo. It's just kind of fun to say, but hard to pinpoint how the name evolved exactly. All stories, however, do suggest the Native American–originated name, bestowed in 1836, has something to do with the sound or look of the Kalamazoo River that intersects and enlivens the city. Hiking trails, classic cars, beer, and airplanes round out the offerings here.

getting there

Take I-94/I-90 east, following I-90, then merging back onto I-94 east. Take exit 74B toward US 131/I-94/Grand Rapids/Three Rivers. Follow the I-94 Business Route at exit 36A toward

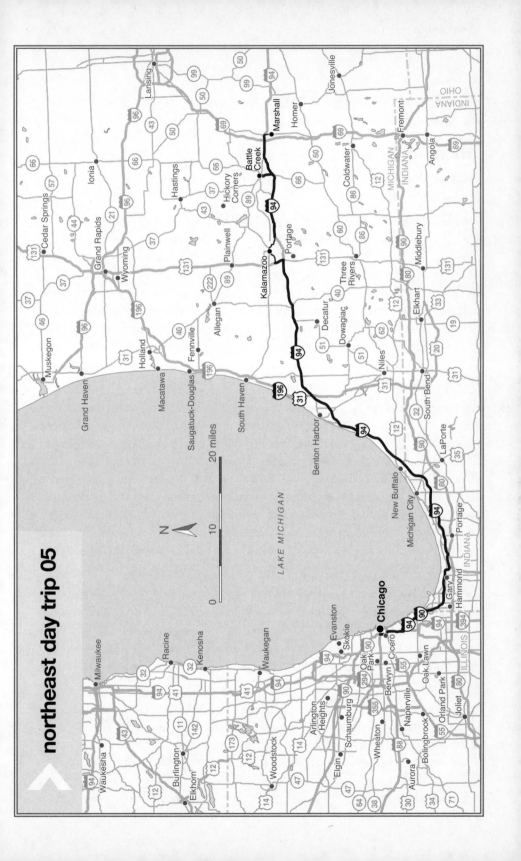

northeast day trip 05

Kalamazoo. Turn right onto Stadium Drive. Take a slight right onto MI 43/Michigan Avenue and follow to the visitor center.

where to go

Discover Kalamazoo Visitors Center. 141 E. Michigan Ave., Suite 100; (800) 888-0509, (269) 488-9000; www.discoverkalamazoo.com.

Air Zoo. 615 Portage Rd.; (269) 382-6555; www.airzoo.org. Founded in 1977 by Suzanne Parish, a former member of the Women Airforce Service Pilots, and her then-husband, Pete, a former Marine Air Corps member, this museum was called the Air Zoo because its first exhibit featured airplanes named the Wildcat, Hellcat, Bearcat, and Flying Tiger. It now features 120,000 square feet of planes, rides, historical artifacts, and real and simulated flight experiences. Take a 3D trip aboard the space shuttle, make like the Wizard of Oz and fly through the air in a Montgolfier hot air balloon, feel the sensation of weightlessness, strap into the Space Ball to experience astronaut training, and peruse the more than 50 historic and modern planes, plus a plane restoration center. Open daily. Free general admission; additional charges for rides.

Gilmore Car Museum. 6865 Hickory Rd., Hickory Corners; (269) 671-5089; www.gilmore carmuseum.org. Did you know that more than 20 different autos were built in and around Kalamazoo? This vintage car museum is a nod to that past. Steer your wheels about 15 miles northeast of the city to see a sampling of Kalamazoo-built cars, plus more than 200 other antique, classic, and collector cars including a Michigan State Police 1937 Ford, a Tucker '48, the Model T, a DeLorean, and the last Checker cab to come off the Kalamazoo-based factory line. The 90-acre setting also includes a vintage Disney movie set, a 1930s gas station, and more. Note: For further area automobile exploration, pick up from the visitor center a Kalamazoo Valley Automobile Heritage Tour brochure (also downloadable at www .discoverkalamazoo.com). Museum open daily May to Oct. Admission (6 and under free).

Kalamazoo Institute of the Arts. 314 S. Park St.; (269) 349-7775; www.kiarts.org. Begun in 1924 with a few volunteers and a simple mission to encourage the appreciation and creation of art, today the 72,000-square-foot KIA, as it's called, brings in a rotating variety of 10 to 15 exhibits each year. It also holds a strong permanent collection of American painting, sculpture, and ceramics. Free tours Sun. Open Tues through Sun. Free general admission.

Kalamazoo Nature Center. 7000 N. Westnedge Ave.; (269) 381-1574; www.naturecenter .org. This 1,100-acre wooded haven recently celebrated its 50th anniversary, making it one of the oldest nature centers in the country. Bring your hiking boots or cross-country skis for a trek through one of the 14 trails covering about 14 miles through everything from prairies to forests. The Interpretive Center features kid-friendly, state-of-the art interactive exhibits, along with a seasonal butterfly and hummingbird garden. Open daily. Nominal fee.

Kalamazoo Valley Museum. 230 N. Rose St.; (269) 373-7990; www.kalamazoomuseum
.org. Science, history, and technology come together in this compact, free museum. Check
out the 2,300-year-old Egyptian mummy—find out if she was a mommy too. Learn about
Kalamazoo's contributions in the automobile, pharmaceutical, musical, and literary fields.
And look back at the history and influences of the area's land, workers, and community.
Open daily. Free general admission.

Parkwyn Village. Parkwyn Drive and Taliesin Drive. A hidden gem for architecture fans, this
community on the west side of Kalamazoo boasts four private homes designed by Frank
Lloyd Wright. You can see them from Asylum Lake Preserve (accessible from Western
Michigan University; parking along Drake Road). Built in 1947, the homes join others in the
neighborhood attributed to Wright's firm Taliesin Associates.

where to eat

Bell's Eccentric Café. 355 E. Kalamazoo Ave.; (269) 382-2332; www.bellsbeer.com.
It might not seem like much to Milwaukee, but around K-Zoo, 25 years is a long time for
a brewery, so they're pretty proud of Bell's. The rustic wood and redbrick cafe is tasting
central for Bell's nationally lauded microbrews. In addition to the 20 or so widely distrib-
uted beers, the cafe offers diners small-batch brews only sold here. A spacious new patio,
outdoor deck, and tranquil green beer garden are popular in warm weather, while a new
indoor music venue gives you one more reason to kick back with a beer here. Oh, yes,
there's food too: sandwiches like barbecue pork, smoked turkey, a classic Reuben, and a
black bean burger. Or just nibble on a soft pretzel with Bell's own mustard. Open daily for
lunch and dinner. $.

Food Dance Café. 401 E. Michigan Ave.; (269) 382-1888; www.fooddance.net. Cheese
from Evergreen Lane Farm & Creamery in nearby Fennville, maple syrup from Jack & Jill
Maple Hill Farm in Paw Paw, chicken and turkey from Otto's in Middleville. Getting the gist?
It's the obsession of owner and chef Julie Stanley to buy local, serve what's in season, and
make great, fresh food. Dishes like baby back ribs in mustard apple sauce, stuffed poblano
pepper, cider-brined pork chop and organic pulled pork sandwich, and the artisan cheese
board will make you grin; the truly service-oriented staff and produce-themed artwork will
keep you smiling. $$.

The Union Cabaret & Grill. 125 S. Kalamazoo Mall; (269) 384-6756; www.millenniumres
taurants.com. In partnership with Western Michigan University, this part-restaurant, part-
music venue caters to a diverse crowd of faculty and students, visitors, and local music
fans of everything from solo pianists to full-blown bands, Afro-Cuban to jazz, and even
the restaurant's own chef Eric Gillish doing his favorite covers. Bustling since it opened in
2002, the Union serves up twists on American standards, like Thai flank steak, lemon and
balsamic-marinated pork chop, and Brazilian-spiced salmon. Be sure to get an order of the
beloved portobello fries too. Open Mon through Sat for lunch and dinner. $$.

where to stay

Henderson Castle. 100 Monroe St.; (269) 344-1827; www.hendersoncastle.com. Situ-
ated high on a hill, this 1895 bed-and-breakfast is listed on the National Register of Historic
Places and exudes a welcoming elegance. You'll be no less than awed by the 5 rooms,
elaborately decorated by proprietors Peter and Laura Livingstone-McNelis to suit their international names, such as Delft tile and original Dutch paintings in the Dutch Room, and green
marble floors and leaded glass windows in the Italian Room. Cool-weather boon: heated
floors and a rooftop hot tub. $$$.

The Kalamazoo House B&B. 447 W. South St.; (269) 382-0880; www.thekalamazoo
house.com. This 1878 Victorian home was beautifully transformed into a 9-room inn,
just steps from downtown restaurants and shops. Gourmet breakfasts enjoyed under
the home's original chandelier include banana nut crunch French toast and cheesy eggs
Benedict. Before heading out for the evening, get to know your fellow guests during social
hour in the parlor, complete with fireplace and leather recliners; then return for late-night
milk and cookies. $$.

battle creek

In the 1870s a man named John Kellogg developed a new breakfast food that would serve
the special diets of patients at the Seventh-day Adventist Church's Battle Creek Sanitarium,
which, by the way, was featured in the 1994 movie *The Road to Wellville.* In the late 1890s,
a former patient named Charles Post pretty much stole one of those recipes and created
Postum cereal, a huge success. Kellogg's brother W.K. bested Post with his debut of Corn
Flakes in 1906, which grew into the cereal giant we know today and which still has world
headquarters in "Cereal City." You might not see Tony the Tiger here, but you will see some
rare red pandas at the zoo.

getting there

From Michigan Avenue in Kalamazoo heading west, turn right onto I-94 BR/MI 96 east
(known here also as King Highway). Keep right to continue toward I-94 east. Stay right to
merge onto I-94. Take exit 98B toward I-194 N/MI 66/Battle Creek. Turn left at Michigan
Avenue and follow to the visitor bureau. The bureau website will give you updates on road
conditions. The drive should take about 40 minutes.

where to go

Battle Creek Convention & Visitors Bureau. 77 E. Michigan Ave., Suite 100; (800)
397-2240, (269) 962-2240; www.battlecreekvisitors.org. This bureau covers all of Calhoun
County and has locations in Marshall and Albion as well. Open Mon through Fri.

Arcadia Brewing Company. 103 W. Michigan Ave.; (269) 963-9690; www.arcadiaales .com. Weekly tours are available in this microbrewery that was established in 1996. Its 250-year-old heritage comes from its imported authentic British equipment and old English methods. At the on-premises TC's Pub, grab wood-fired pizzas and a great barbecue combo for lunch or dinner to go with that ale. Then, back in the Windy City, order up your Arcadia favorites at Delilah's, Guthrie's, or the Map Room. Tours (fee) every Saturday include a logo glass and sample; call for times.

Binder Park Zoo. 7400 Division Dr.; (269) 979-1351; www.binderparkzoo.org. The red panda cubs and giraffe family get lots of attention at this local 433-acre zoo, and understandably so: The pandas are a rare and endangered species, and the giraffes enjoy munching on snacks from visitors' hands. But don't miss the other 140-or-so species including snow leopards, kangaroos, impalas, and zebras. The zoo also has a carousel and a train ride. Open Apr through Oct and for winter holidays. Admission (prices vary seasonally); Lincoln Park Zoo members get half off.

Heritage Mile Walking Tour. Grab a map for this self-guided tour from the visitor center or at Heritage Battle Creek, 165 N. Washington St.; (269) 965-2613; www.heritagebattle creek.org. Battle Creek's downtown area is known as Heritage Mile because of its many historic markers, from the Seventh-day Adventist Church to the art deco Hart Hotel to the Underground Railroad sculpture. The map is divided into two major themes: "The Freedom Saga of Battle Creek," commemorating the town's historic commitment to end slavery, and "Road to Wellness: the Real Story," highlighting Battle Creek's role in promoting healthier lifestyles.

where to eat

Clara's on the River. 44 McCamly St. N.; (269) 963-0966; www.claras.com. Climb aboard for more than just a meal. In this restored 1888 Michigan Central Railroad Depot, multiple rooms feature antiques and photos that highlight a bit of Battle Creek history–original train depot brass lanterns, some of the first cereal boxes ever printed in the city, the station's restored ticket counter. When you're done browsing, settle in with the 17-page menu, from pizza to burgers, sandwiches to seafood, ribs to lasagna. Save room for the signature deep-dish caramel apple pie. But don't worry if you don't finish it—you can come back; this train isn't going anywhere. Open daily for lunch and dinner. $$.

O.T.'s Up-n-Smoke BBQ. 450 NE Capital Ave.; (269) 963-7777; www.otsupnsmokebbq .com. This hole-in-the-wall won the 2010 People's Choice for best ribs in Kalamazoo's annual Ribfest, beating out several big-business types. Try the half-slab, spare ribs, rib tips, or barbecue chicken too, all topped—or served with—the secret sweet-tangy sauce. Accompany with simple sides of coleslaw, fries, baked beans, greens, and corn bread. For dessert? Sweet potato pie. Open daily for lunch and dinner (closes early on Sun). $.

where to stay

Greencrest Manor B&B. 6174 Halbert Rd.; (269) 962-8633; www.greencrestmanor.com. Built in 1935 in the French-Normandy style, this 10,000-square-foot estate sits on more than 14 acres of expansive lawn and gardens and overlook scenic St. Mary's Lake. It combines all the right elements for a dreamy retreat: winding staircases, grand entrance chandelier, marble fireplace, floral wallpapers, and lovingly renovated rooms. Of the 8 rooms, 6 boast private bathrooms, the ultimate VIP Suite with a double whirlpool and fireplace. $$–$$$.

marshall

You know you're in Marshall when you see the Brooks Memorial Fountain at Kalamazoo and Michigan Avenues, a Greek-style landmark built in 1930 and inspired by the "Temple of Love" fountain in Versailles. It's one of the younger landmarks in a city of more than 850 19th-century homes and buildings—so many that Marshall itself has been designated a National Historic Landmark District.

getting there

Another half-hour east is Marshall. Head out of town east on the I-94 business loop, also known as Michigan Avenue, the same Michigan Avenue that you'll wind up on in Marshall. Take a slight right to Junction MI 96. Turn left onto the MI 96/I-94 business loop east. As you enter the traffic circle in Marshall, just continue following the I-94 business loop to the chamber of commerce.

where to go

Marshall Area Chamber of Commerce. 424 E. Michigan Ave.; (800) 877-5163, (269) 781-5163; www.marshallmi.org. Open Mon through Fri year-round and also Sat during the summer.

American Museum of Magic. 107 E. Michigan Ave.; (269) 781-7570; www.american museumofmagic.org. There's a trick around every corner of this one-of-a-kind museum founded in 1978 by the late manic magic fanatic Robert Lund, a writer by profession. Housed in a beautifully restored 1868 Victorian structure (wife Elaine did most of that), the museum bursts at the seams with part of Lund's storehouse of more than 500,000 magic-related items dating from the 16th century to the present—it's one of the largest collections in the world. Look for escape apparatus used by Houdini, Doug Henning's "Zig Zag" machine for sawing his assistant in thirds, Harry Blackstone's levitating skull, and thousands of showbills, programs, books, magazines, photos, letters, performer scrapbooks, and more from illustrious illusionists and many unknowns. Open June through Oct; call for hours. Nominal admission.

Cornwell's Turkeyville USA. 18935 15½ Mile Rd.; (800) 228-4315, (269) 781-4293; www
.turkeyville.com. This 400-acre family-owned farm proves turkey isn't just for Thanksgiving.
Get all turkey all the time at the farm restaurant: sliced, smoked, pulled, roasted, or shredded
Mexican-style. See one of Turkeyville's professional dinner theater shows. Stop by the old-time
ice cream parlor, where the five-scoop Super Tom sundae is less than $5. Get more treats
at the Country Store: old-fashioned candies, 10 flavors of homemade fudge, and fresh-baked
exploding cheese bread, plus gifts and souvenirs. On scheduled weekends, take a ride aboard
the eighth-scale model railroad train. Visit the turkeys frolicking around the farm, along with barn
rabbits, goats, and a donkey. There's also a playground as well as flea markets and art shows.
Oh, and you can pick up a fresh Turkey Day bird here too. Open daily. Free general admission.

Honolulu House Museum. 107 N. Kalamazoo Ave.; (269) 781-8544; www.marshall
historicalsociety.org. This historic landmark house definitely does not keep up with the
Joneses. Built in 1860 for former chief justice of the Michigan Supreme Court Abner Pratt,
it's a replica of homes Pratt admired during his years serving in Hawaii as US counsel to
the Sandwich Islands. Fifteen-foot ceilings and 10-foot doors, walls covered in tropically
themed murals, and an ornate ebony, teak, mahogany, and maple staircase that rises to a
platform on the roof. It's now the home of the Marshall Historical Society, which continually
works to restore and repair. Open May through Oct and by request. Nominal admission.

where to shop

Michigan Avenue. From Marshall Avenue to Sycamore Street; (269) 781-5183; find
shop contact information at www.marshallmainstreet.com. Stroll Marshall's historic turn-
of-the-20th-century downtown for a shopping experience that's the complete opposite of
Chicago's Michigan Avenue. Peaceful and friendly with mom-and-pop shops like **Hodges
Jewelers**, selling handcrafted jewelry (117 W. Michigan); a rainbow of beads at **Just Bead
It** (125 W. Michigan); contemporary artwork at **Blue Hour Gallery** (127 W. Michigan); new,
used, and vintage guitars at **Love Vintage Guitars** (130 W. Michigan); gifts and accessories
at the **Mole Hole** (150 W. Michigan), famous for its 1927 Barton Theater organ that is still
played; and antique glassware at **Marshall Town & Country Antiques** (151 W. Michigan).

where to stay

National House Inn. 102 S. Parkview; (269) 781-7374; www.nationalhouseinn.com. Overlooking Marshall's quaint Fountain Circle, this restored 1835 bed-and-breakfast is listed on
the National Register of Historic Places and is acclaimed as the oldest operating accommodations in Michigan, not to mention one of the oldest brick structures in Calhoun County.
Its 15 inviting rooms are done up in either antique-y country style or Victorian. Some feature
electric fireplaces; others, winning views of the courtyard gardens. Wake up to a home-
cooked breakfast, lounge by the wood-burning fire in the upstairs parlor, take afternoon tea
in the downstairs parlor, and munch on fresh-popped popcorn nightly. $$.

east

day trip 01

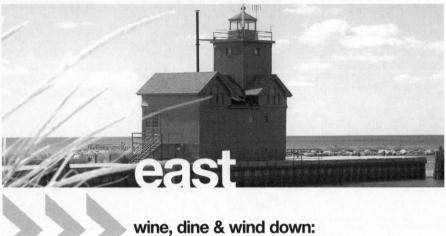

east

wine, dine & wind down:
michigan city, in; new buffalo, three
oaks & sawyer, mi (harbor country)

This trip is a quick one as far as distance (about an hour and a half to the farthest stop, Sawyer, Michigan), but there's so much to see and do, you'll probably want to make it an overnight or two to take it all in. Before you begin, though, be sure you understand the geographic distinctions here. Michigan City is in Indiana and is separate from Michigan's eight-city Harbor Country where New Buffalo, Three Oaks, and Sawyer are located. I learned this from the Harbor Country Chamber of Commerce when I mentioned that the day trip started with a stop in Michigan City; I had to assure them I wouldn't try to squeeze Michigan City into Harbor Country. Perhaps Michigan City is most famous in the Windy City for its excellent outlet shopping—and that, it is. Harbor Country cities brim with quaint bed-and-breakfasts for comfy lodging after a rough day of wine tasting, dune hiking, and even a little card playing at the two casinos in the area.

michigan city

An easy train ride from Chicago on the South Shore Line, Michigan City is a bona fide historic hub. Nearly two dozen historic structures dot its downtown, including the 1866 Vielhack House (402 E. 8th St.), the oldest house in the district, and the Barker Mansion, open for tours; a fascinating military museum; a zoo created almost entirely out of New Deal funds; and, of course, the iconic lighthouse.

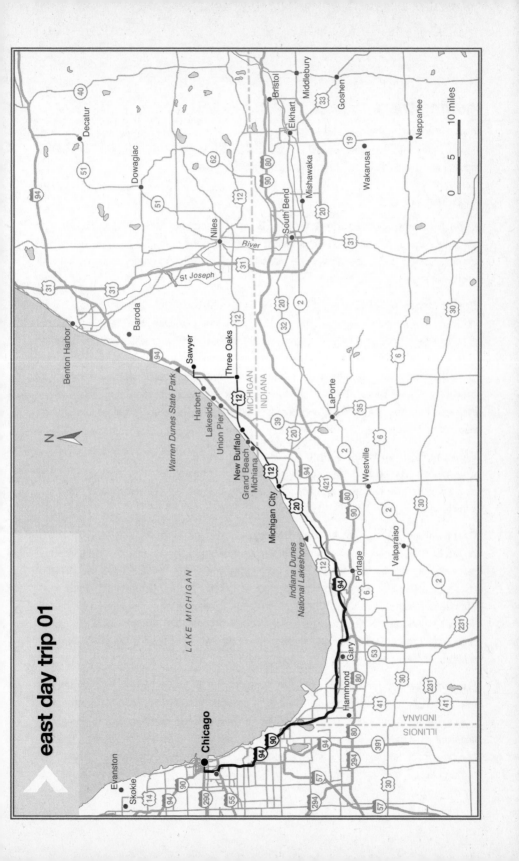

east day trip 01

getting there

If you're not riding the rail, take I-90/I-94 east and follow I-90/the Skyway toward Indiana. Merge back onto I-94 east toward Detroit. Exit at 22B to US 20 east toward Porter. Continue until Franklin Street and turn right to the visitor bureau.

where to go

LaPorte County Convention & Visitors Bureau. Marquette Mall, 4073 S. Franklin St.; (219) 872-5055, (219) 326-8115; www.michigancitylaporte.com. Besides the usual brochures, guides, and maps, this bureau also has its own rotating gallery of locals' artwork and a gift shop. Open daily.

Barker Mansion. 631 Washington St.; (219) 873-1520; www.emichigancity.com. If it were not for a philanthropic teenage girl, this 38-room English manor-style mansion may not have survived. Originally built in 1857, it was expanded in 1905 by wealthy railway magnate John H. Barker, who lived there only five years before he and his wife both died. Their only child, Catherine, was 14 at the time, but kept the home; she later donated it to the city as a historic cultural center. Take a tour to check out the elaborate marble and woodwork, imported European furnishings, and original belongings of the Barker family. Guided tours year-round Mon through Fri three times daily. Nominal admission.

Blue Chip Casino Hotel & Spa. 777 Blue Chip Dr.; (888) 879-7711, (219) 879-7711; www.bluechipcasino.com. Try your luck in the 65,000 square feet of gaming with a little bit of everything: poker, slots, blackjack, mini baccarat, craps. See "where to stay" for more information.

Great Lakes Museum of Military History. 360 Dunes Plaza, W. US 20; (800) 726-5912; (219) 872-2702; www.militaryhistorymuseum.org. Tip your hat to the servicemen and -women of wars from the Revolutionary to the Iraq at this modest, 2,500-square-foot museum. It features everything from Confederate currency to a 12-pound Civil War cannonball to firearms from the US military and a rare WWI Marine uniform. Feel a bit military yourself when you get your own dog tag made. Memorial Day through Labor Day, open daily Tues through Sun; Labor Day through Memorial Day, open Tues through Sat. Nominal admission.

Lubeznik Center for the Arts. 101 W. 2nd St.; (219) 874-4900; www.lubeznikcenter .org. Originally known as the Blank Center for the Arts, this contemporary art center got a new name and a new building in 2002. The larger space, curvy shape, airy galleries, and lakefront location gave it more attention and has allowed the center to present a growing number of rotating exhibits, performances, classes, and after-hours events. Open Tues through Sun. Free admission.

loop the loops

*Working as an editor at a Chicago visitor publication, I always chuckled when the city would conjure up a name for an event that wasn't an event at all, but rather lots of events all gathered into one basket as a way to introduce them in a new and colorful way. That's what northern Indiana's **Art and Earth Trail** is all about—and it's a great concept for us day-trippers. There are seven loops, to be exact, each with anywhere from 15 to 40 stops along the way. They take drivers from LaPorte to LaGrange, from Valparaiso to Wakarusa, and focus exclusively on authentic experiences and only-in-Indiana kinds of places. Places where visitors are warmly welcomed, where a farmer chats you up about his grandfather who started the business, and where you can ride aboard a real steam train. Stops include a miniature horse stable, local artists' studios, and U-pick orchards of apples, blueberries, and peaches. You'll dine at family-owned restaurants, and witness the simple life of the Amish people, taste their foods, and check out their famous furniture shop country stores. The drives are a smart and easy way to see even more of northern Indiana. Get maps of the routes and all the stops included at the Michigan City LaPorte County Convention & Visitors Bureau, 4073 S. Franklin St., (219) 872-5055, at all other member visitor bureaus, at Art and Earth Trail participants, or online at www.artandearthtrail.com.*

Old Lighthouse Museum. Heisman Harbor Road, Washington Park; (219) 872-6133; www.oldlighthousemuseum.org. This beacon on the beach tells a rich history of lighthouse keepers and technology and the changing needs of the ships that passed it. Built in 1858 of Joliet limestone and Milwaukee Cream City brick, its 1973 restoration by the Michigan City Historical Society turned this oldest remaining lighthouse in Indiana into a museum. It now houses exhibits on Lake Michigan shipwrecks, Abraham Lincoln's funeral train stop in Michigan City, local maritime history, and more. But the best part? A climb up the tower into the lantern room. Open Tues through Sun Apr through Oct. Call for hours. Nominal fee.

Washington Park Zoo. 115 Lakeshore Dr.; (219) 873-1510; www.washingtonparkzoo .com. A retired animal trainer and his brown bear partner Jake were the forerunners of this friendly 15-acre zoo in 1925. Completely designed and developed with labor financed through President Roosevelt's New Deal and other post Depression-era policies, the zoo roared into the next decade and continued to grow. The iconic castle that houses the small mammal exhibit is actually a replica of the "corps castle" logo of the US Army Corps of Engineers. Animals now number close to 200, from a Bengal tiger to a ball python, a pot-bellied pig to a Madagascar hissing roach, with an Australian Avian Adventure Exhibit that allows you to hand-feed the free-flying parakeets. Open seasonally. Nominal admission.

where to shop

Lighthouse Place Premium Outlets. 601 Wabash St.; (219) 879-6506; www.premium outlets.com. You've been here already, haven't you? (If you're a woman living in or around Chicago, I'm betting you have.) If not, you'll be surprised that it's not your typical outlet shopping. Upscale offerings among the 120 stores include Coach and Columbia Sportswear, DKNY, and comfy shoe king Ecco. Be sure to check the website to focus your shopping efforts on stores hosting special sales. Open daily.

where to eat

Matey's Restaurant. 110 Franklin St.; (219) 872-9471; www.mateysrestaurant.com. With its lakefront locale and seating for more than 200, this nautically themed, multi-option restaurant attracts a crowd. Its tri-level Caribbean-style Tiki Deck is the hot spot during summer—all colorfully Florida Keys–like with fruity blended drinks and a light bar menu. Inside, the Chart Room offers a full selection of steaks, chops, chicken, and seafood, while the Cocktail Lounge serves the same menu in a more laid-back atmosphere. And yet a fourth area, the Sports Bar, comes with video games, pool table, big TV screens, and rowdiness—plus, baskets of finger-licking fried food, sandwiches, and an all-you-can-eat perch and by-the-pound prime rib special. Open daily for lunch, dinner, and late-night dining. $$.

Shoreline Brewery. 208 Wabash St.; (219) TRY-HOPS (879-4677); www.shorelinebrewery .com. Beer is the star of the show here, but the food isn't too shabby either. Stuffed chicken breast, meal-size salads, seared scallops, barbecue baby backs, oatmeal stout-braised lamb shank—and, with that, back to the beer. Usually about a dozen on tap and more in bottles, the tastes range from Shoreline's popular Stella Blue, a light ale with blueberry hints, to its chocolate-tinged Smokestack Porter and its hearty, World Beer Cup competition-winning Beltaine Scottish Ale. Can't decide? Try a sampler or tap into your server's suds smarts. Open daily for lunch and dinner. $$.

Swingbelly's Restaurant. 100 Washington St.; (219) 874-5718; www.swingbellys.org. In an old train station, with Amtraks still rumbling by, Swingbelly's has casual charm. It also has lake views all around, worthy lake perch, talked-about 8-ounce burgers, and tasty clam chowder. You'll be in good hands, too, with hostess Kelly Siegmund, who recently won a LaPorte County Recognition of Service Excellence Award given to top-notch front-line service employees. Open daily for lunch and dinner. $$.

where to stay

Blue Chip Casino Hotel & Spa. 777 Blue Chip Dr.; (888) 879-7711, (219) 879-7711; www.bluechipcasino.com. When it comes to Michigan City accommodations, Blue Chip is the biggest game in town—486 rooms and suites in two towers. You could book it as just a bed or you could make it that Las Vegas weekend you never had. Besides the gaming,

do the dunes

*Chicago area summer camps often feature field trips around the southern tip of Lake Michigan to the **Indiana Dunes**. But the dunes may never have existed if it weren't for the 1898 research of University of Chicago botanist Henry Cowles, who described their rare ecosystem, a staggering 1,135 native plant species. After decades of persistence and passion, this initial recognition finally led to the official designation in 1966 of the first 8,300 acres of the **Indiana Dunes National Lakeshore**. It has since expanded to include more than 15,000 acres of dunes, beaches, hiking trails, historic homes, campgrounds, and more. Bird-watchers get an eyeful, with more than 350 species of loons, cormorants, hawks, falcons, and other feathered beauties. The tiny town of **Beverly Shores** is known along the dunes route for its five relocated homes from Chicago's 1933-34 Century of Progress. Though there are 15 miles of shoreline here, lifeguards are on duty only at West Beach, where you'll also find a decent bathhouse. More than a dozen trails range from the easy ¾-mile Pinhook Bog Trail to the rugged three-loop, 5-mile Cowles Bog Trail that makes a colorful hike come fall. For cross-country skiing, head to the Ly-co-ki-we Trail, and, of course, be sure to trek the 126-foot-high Mt. Baldy Trail (living sand dune), rerouted recently due to erosion at a rate of 4 inches per year.*

*For more information: **Indiana Dunes National Lakeshore Visitor Center,** 1215 N. SR 49, Porter; (219) 926-7561; www.nps.gov/indu.*

there are five restaurants and bars, including the ubiquitous buffet, an upscale steakhouse, a 24-hour diner, a sports bar, and a lounge with live music. Finally, the spa offers a full range of treatments for head, toes, and everything in between. Room options range from standard to a 1,575-square-foot luxurious loft suite. $$–$$$.

new buffalo, three oaks & sawyer

In Chicago we're accustomed to new neighborhood names being used to boost an area's appeal (think West Loop). Such is the history behind the grouping of eight cities into what's known as Harbor Country, a trademarked name conceived by a passionate group of people in 1981 to describe these quaint southwestern Michigan towns. Part scenic harbor, part quiet country, the area comprises New Buffalo, Three Oaks, and Sawyer, as well as

Michiana, Grand Beach, Union Pier, Lakeside, and Harbert. Since the renaming, Harbor Country has seen quite a rebirth, with fixer-upper homes turned into beautiful summer cottages and family-owned inns, with once-forgotten beaches now active destinations, and with rolling hills now growing acres of grapevines. I think it's fitting that New Buffalo had the country's first highway travel information center in 1935. Who would have thought that more than 75 years later, it is welcoming more visitors than ever.

getting there

Follow US 12 north about 10 miles to New Buffalo. Take a right onto Whittaker to start at the chamber of commerce.

where to go

Harbor Country Chamber of Commerce. 530 S. Whittaker St., Suite F, New Buffalo; (269) 469-5409; www.harborcountry.org; www.newbuffalo.org; www.3oaks.org. Find out about all the towns in Harbor Country at this central site of information. Open Mon through Fri.

Acorn Theater. 107 Generations Dr., Three Oaks; (269) 756-3879; www.acorntheater .com. Owners Kim Clark and David Fink split their time between this eclectic arts center and jobs in Chicago (Clark, a screenwriting teacher at DePaul; Fink, on the boards of both the Poetry Center and the Chicago Improv Festival). In what locals thought was an act of craziness, the two men took 20,000 square feet of a century-old dilapidated former corset stay factory and transformed it into this welcoming 250-seat theater. It features performances most Friday and Saturday nights ranging from solo guitarist Tim Sparks to Chicago's own poetry slam founder Marc Smith to "The Judy Show" to folk-blues singer Maria Muldaur. Every Thursday features music videos from the 1960s through today. Prices vary.

Dinges' Farm. 15219 Mill Rd., Three Oaks; (269) 426-4034; www.harborcountry.com/ guide/dingesfarm. This family-owned farm comes alive in fall with 20 varieties of pumpkins including a Cinderella style, Baby Boo, and the famous Atlantic Giant, as well as 25 different colorful gourds. A day of fun includes tractor- and horse-drawn hayrides, petting zoo, haunted house, corn tunnels and corn mazes, and requisite hot apple cider. Pick up gifts in Ye Old Craft Barn or pick your own Concord grapes. Open daily Sept and Oct. Some fees.

Four Winds Casino. 11111 Wilson Rd., New Buffalo; (866) 4WINDS1 (494-6371); www .fourwindscasino.com. A pretty big deal for a beach town, Four Winds has all the trappings of a traditional casino. Decorated with a woodsy theme, its spacious 130,000-square-foot gaming area includes 3,000 slots from pennies (just my speed) to dollars, blackjack, craps, poker, baccarat, keno, roulette, and more. Consider yourself a VIP? Ask for the High Limits Room. Staying awhile? The posh hotel offers 165 rooms and suites, and dining and nightlife include a steakhouse, buffet and fast-food/deli, martini bar, sports bar, and live music club.

While grownups play, the Kids Quest program (extra fee) gives children 6 to 12 a place to play too. Free admission. Open 24 hours.

Fruitful Vine Tours. (269) 978-8777; www.fruitfulvinetours.com. Tour and taste your way through Michigan's own Napa without having to worry about a designated driver. This luxury wine tour company offers three options: private tours for groups up to 14 people; hop-on tours where you'll join others for stops at three or four wineries (including lunch on the Saturday tours); or the Wine-o-Wagon tour that travels by tractor-pulled wagon to four wineries in off-roading style. Bike tours too (that sounds risky to me). Tours daily. Prices vary.

New Buffalo Railroad Museum. 530 S. Whittaker St., New Buffalo; (269) 469-5409; www .newbuffalo.com/museums.shtml. This small museum housed in a replica depot recalls the railway history that had a big hand in developing Michigan's economy and that of the town itself. Kids will get a kick out of the miniature train display. Open Mon through Thurs.

Round Barn Winery, Distillery & Brewery. Barn location: 10983 Hills Rd., Baroda; (800) 716-9463. Tasting room only: 9185 Union Pier Rd., Union Pier; (269) 469-6885; www.round barnwinery.com. Moved from its original location in rural Indiana and reconstructed in Baroda, the namesake Amish-made round barn is the icon for this wine, spirits, and beer producer. Founder Rick Moersch appreciated its shape as perfect for making "good spirits," because there are no corners for "bad spirits" to hide. Tours are only available Dec through Apr for groups of 20 by reservation. But you can visit the barn to taste those good spirits, as well as the vineyard's winery and microbrewed beer. Open daily for tastings.

Warren Dunes State Park. 12032 Red Arrow Hwy., Sawyer; (269) 426-4013; www.michigan .gov/dnre. Sand dunes that soar 240 feet above Lake Michigan. Dune forests that are home to oaks, maples, deer, and fox. Three miles of beachfront. Six miles of hiking. Wildflowers abounding. It's enough to make you want to say, "ahhhh." Thanks go to Edward K. Warren, local millionaire with a soft spot for the outdoors, who originally purchased this land for preservation in the early 20th century. You can run, sun, hike, windsurf, and cross-country ski in the winter, but please stay away from the creek. There's a trend of visitors covering themselves in the creek's natural clay, which has resulted in a polluted creek that's damaging the ecosystem there (and it just dries out your skin anyway). No on-site equipment rental. Open year-round.

where to eat

Brewster's. 11 W. Merchant St., New Buffalo; (269) 469-3005; www.brewstersitaliancafe .com. Way back in 1992, before the wood-fired pizza craze descended on Chicago, this little (and I mean that literally) cafe by the lake was serving them up to happy diners. Brewster's is still known for thin crust loveliness, but also the quaint setting, outdoor garden patio, welcoming attitude, and tight daily changing menu of fresh pastas, seafood, chicken, and steak. An amazingly reasonably priced dinner for two includes salads, a pizza, entrée, and cookies and coffee. Open for lunch and dinner daily. $$–$$$.

Fitzgerald's Bistro, Pub & Restaurant. 5875 Sawyer Rd., Sawyer; (269) 426-FITZ (3489); www.fitzsawyer.com. Crab cakes with loads of real fresh crab; fish with hand-cut chips; hanger steak grilled to perfection; moist sticky toffee pudding. Sure is a departure from your typical off-the-highway stop. This cheerful local part-Italian, part-French (the croque sandwiches are a winner), and part-American eatery has become a visitor favorite too, especially with free live jazz on Thursday nights and summer weekend barbecues on the patio. Open daily for lunch and dinner. $$$.

Kite's Kitchen & Retro Café. 801 W. Buffalo St.; (269) 469-1800. Chef-owner Judy Kite-Gosh left a corporate job in Chicago in 1993 to pursue her passion for cooking. A champion of sustainable cooking techniques (she even has her own PBS show called *Farm Fresh to You*), Kite-Gosh soon had a loyal following of diners who appreciate her use of locally sourced ingredients in breakfast dishes like free-range-egg omelets and gingersnap pancakes, and lunch items such as organic all-beef meatloaf on multigrain bread with chili sauce and beef stew. Besides the environmental benefits, Kite-Gosh argues that dishes made with fresh, seasonal ingredients just taste better. I'm not arguing with that. Open Wed through Sun for breakfast and lunch. $–$$.

Red Arrow Roadhouse. 15710 Red Arrow Hwy., Union Pier; (616) 469-3939; www .redarrowroadhouse.com. Sporting a big "Eat" sign and a bunch of stuffed game as decoration, this is a roadhouse with white tablecloths and a respectable menu too. Dishes range from its signature "broasted" chicken to pan-roasted catfish jambalaya, panko- and Parmesan-crusted chicken to pulled barbecued pork sandwiches and big, juicy burgers too. Nearly 20 wines come by the bottle or glass, and the fresh fruit pies are served warm with ice cream. $$.

Redamak's. 616 E. Buffalo St.; (269) 469-4522; www.redamaks.com. George and Gladys Redamak ran this Red Arrow Highway stop for about 30 years until George passed away and Gladys sold it to regulars Jim and Angie Maroney in 1975. The Maroney family has owned it since, expanding, improving, and updating everything from the kitchen to the parking lot to the screened-in porch to the menu. But some things have remained the same: namely, the famous cut-and-ground-on-site Redamak burger, the down-home country-style service with a smile, and the reasonable prices (pretty much everything's under 10 bucks, many less than $5). In addition to burgers, try breaded eggplant, corned beef, Italian beef, brats, thinly sliced ham, tuna, and deep-fried perch specials on Friday. Got kids? Save time for the game room and "Red," the fire engine. Cash only. Open daily for lunch and dinner, March 1 to October 24. $.

where to stay

Elephant Walk Cottages. 9679 Greenwood Dr., Union Pier; (630) 205-1270, (269) 469-0977; www.elephantwalkcottages.com. Less than 2 blocks from the beach, this little compound of cottages amid lush greenery works well for extended family get-togethers because the gorgeous main house sleeps 12 and attaches to 2 cottages (there are 5 total). Owner Roger Voegele plays up the elephant theme in decor like tables with faux-tusk legs and elephant heads on cottage entrances, elephant-y trinkets, and posters of the eponymous 1954 Elizabeth Taylor movie. Voegele travels the world and also operates the nearby Harbert Antique Mall, affording a trove of more decorative treasures for his cottages. The main house has a fireplace, 2 balconies, and a screened porch with an outdoor dining table. Open May through Dec. Weekly rentals only during peak season; two-night minimums year-round. $$–$$$.

Harbor Grand. 111 W. Water St., New Buffalo; (888) 605-6800; www.harborgrand.com. Done up in contemporary Prairie Style, this luxury boutique hotel on the New Buffalo harbor has lots of things to love: free beach cruiser bike rentals, complimentary beach chairs and towels, 24-hour delivery of pints of Ben & Jerry's, and splendid views from the waterfront terrace. $$$.

Kamp Across From the Dunes. 12011 Red Arrow Hwy., Sawyer; (269) 426-4971; www.kampacrossfromthedunes.com. Tooling around in an RV? This RV-only campground offers full hookup and proximity to Warren Dunes State Park. $.

Pine Garth Inn. 15790 Lakeshore Rd., Union Pier; (269) 390-0909; www.pinegarth.com. On 200 feet of private beach, this bed-and-breakfast is lauded as one of the area's most romantic and relaxing. The main house, a renovated summer estate built in 1905, offers 7 rooms of varying sizes, all variations of a charming Laura Ashley-like atmosphere, most with stellar Lake Michigan views. The guest houses come with a bit more privacy and space, like Tesi's Folly, nearly as big as my Chicago condo at 1,100 square feet. They also come with daily maid service, not typical for guest-house lodging. Or go for super-cozy in the Carriage House or super-extravagant in the 4,000-square-foot Lake Front Villa. $$$.

day trip 02

east

>>> touchdown here:
south bend, in

south bend

Famous for the University of Notre Dame and the school's beloved Fighting Irish football team (and the enthusiastic tailgating that goes with it), South Bend is also a cache of industrial history and national landmark homes—from the 1895 Copshaholm mansion, now a museum, to the tangible markers and historic tales left by Studebaker and the Oliver Chilled Plow Company, both of which provided substantial growth to this Indiana town from the mid-19th to mid-20th centuries. Like Chicago, South Bend's location along a river that flowed to Lake Michigan was crucial to its development. The city, incorporated in 1865, takes its name from its position at the southernmost bend of the St. Joseph River.

getting there

Head to I-90/I-94 east and continue on I-90 east/the Skyway toward Indiana. Stay on I-90, which merges with I-80. Take exit 77 toward South Bend/Notre Dame. Turn right at IN 933/Dixie Way (it's a major intersection; you'll know it when you see it). Take a left at North Shore Drive and veer right at Niles Avenue. Turn right onto Colfax Avenue to reach the visitor bureau.

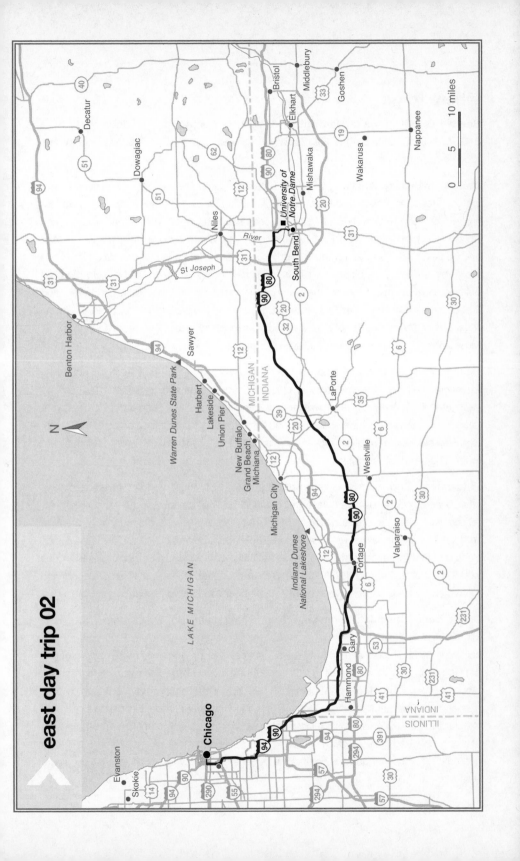

east day trip 02

where to go

South Bend/Mishawaka Convention & Visitors Bureau. 401 E. Colfax Ave., Suite 310; (800) 519-0594, (574) 232-0231; www.exploresouthbend.org. The first stop for free brochures and maps.

Center for History. 808 W. Washington St. (entrance on Thomas Street, between Washington Street and Western Avenue); (574) 235-9664; www.centerforhistory.org. Two historic homes and a main museum building comprise this center. The Romanesque Queen Anne–style Copshaholm mansion was built in 1895 for South Bend businessman J.D. Oliver and boasts a whopping 38 rooms with original furnishings. In contrast, the Worker's Home replicates the living conditions of 1930s immigrant Polish workers. At the main museum building, permanent exhibits tell the history of Notre Dame and the South Bend area, and that of the All-American Girls Professional Baseball League players who inspired the movie *A League of Their Own.* There's also a children's museum within. The Studebaker National Museum is adjacent, and tickets to both offer a discount. Open daily. Admission.

College Football Hall of Fame. 111 S. St. Joseph St.; (800) 440-FAME (3263); www.collegefootball.org. Through interactive exhibits, video, photos, and memorabilia, you'll go deep into the football field, its 140-year history, and its people and pageantry. Plus, test your passing abilities, take a trivia challenge, and, of course, browse the hundreds of inductees. See it all before the museum moves to Atlanta in 2012. Open daily; later on Notre Dame football game days. Admission.

Potawatomi Zoo. 500 S. Greenlawn Ave.; (574) 288-4639; www.potawatomizoo.org. This 23-acre zoo is Indiana's oldest, beginning in 1902 as a duck pond, then adding deer, buffalo, oxen from the Chicago stockyards in 1937, a polar bear, and sundry other animals, finally reaching today's impressive 400-some animals in modern habitats. It also features an electric train that traverses the zoo, a seasonal butterfly exhibit, a South American exhibit with a giant anteater, and the Australian Walk-a-bout that allows you to jump around with the wallaby and kangaroos. Open daily. Admission (extra charge for butterfly exhibit).

South Bend Chocolate Company Tour & Museum. 3300 W. Sample St.; (800) 301-4961, (574) 233-2577; www.sbchocolate.com. Born in 1991, the SBC now has 10 company-owned stores and 10 franchises selling everything from mint meltaways to pecan patties to variously flavored malted milk balls. But this stop is the main attraction. After all, the street name says it all, right? Samples! Take a tour to learn how cacao becomes candies and see how these beloved South Bend chocolates are made. Browse the museum featuring a 1,600-year-old Mayan chocolate pot, unique chocolate molds, and thousands of vintage tins and boxes, including—particularly sentimental for Chicago visitors—a display of Marshall Field's Frango Mint boxes. The outlet store is way too good to pass up. Tours Mon through Sat.

Studebaker National Museum. 201 S. Chapin St. (entrance on Thomas Street, between Washington Street and Western Avenue); (888) 391-5600, (574) 235-9714; www.stude bakermuseum.org. Adjacent to—and sharing an entrance and combo ticket price with—the Center for History, this 55,000-square-foot museum gets me as close as I'll probably ever come to sitting in an Avanti, one of my favorite cars. Some 100 other cars, wagons, and carriages get the spotlight here, along with a little history of the company, which began as a wagon and buggy maker in South Bend in 1852. See Studebaker military vehicles from five wars, the "Bullet Nose," Packards, the presidential carriage that took Abraham Lincoln to Ford's Theatre the night he was assassinated, and the last Studebaker made. Open daily. Admission.

University of Notre Dame. Eck Visitors Center, 100 Eck Center; (574) 631-5726; www .nd.edu. Most Chicagoans know a few rabid Fighting Irish football fans. They shirk all duties when they've got tix to a game at Knute Rockne's legendary stadium. The sprawling historic campus of Gothic buildings and religious spirit has other highlights too: The Hesburgh Library's *Touchdown Jesus* is a favorite. That's not the official name of this 132-foot-high, 65-foot-wide mural depicting Jesus with arms raised overhead (*The Word of Life* is), but it faces the football field's north end zone, so what else would it be called? The tallest building on campus, the Basilica of the Sacred Heart, offers tours of its magnificent interior, showcasing a world-renowned stained-glass collection. The Grotto of Our Lady of Lourdes bustles with candle-lighting students during finals and football games, but it's always a serene sight. Call for campus tour information.

where to eat

Fiddler's Hearth. 127 N. Main St.; (574) 232-2853; www.fiddlershearth.com. Belly up to the bar of this authentically Celtic public house for a Guinness-certified gold standard pint or one of 18 other international brews or more than 60 flavors of whiskey and scotch. Then kick back with a board game or book, cuddle up by the fireplace, watch football (the European kind) on TV, or get swept up by the live Irish music. In addition to the specialty beer-battered fish and chips, snack on soft pretzels with rarebit cheese sauce, shepherd's pie, braised lamb shank, bangers and mash, and Irish boxtys. Open daily for lunch and dinner, Wed through Sat late night. $$–$$$.

Rocco's Restaurant. 537 N. Saint Louis Blvd.; (574) 233-2464. This casual South Bend pizza parlor has been a go-to local hangout since Italy native Rocco Ameduri opened it in 1951. Though Rocco passed away in 2008, his daughter's family carries on the tradition, serving up hand-tossed thin pies to devoted diners. The garlic pizza and sausage subs are apparently Notre Dame student favorites. Also on the menu are made-to-order manicotti, mostaccioli, spaghetti, ravioli, and, on Friday and Saturday, homemade baked lasagna. Rocco's doesn't take reservations, so be prepared to wait if there's a Notre Dame game. Open for dinner Tues through Sun. $$.

Sorin's. The Morris Inn, Notre Dame Ave., Notre Dame; (574) 631-2020; www.morrisinn.nd .edu/sorins. College campus restaurants often mean mediocre food served by well-meaning students, but Sorin's—located in Notre Dame's Morris Inn and named for university founder Father Edward Sorin, C.S.C.—happens to be an exception. The decor is warm wood and white tablecloths, and the menu is a seasonally changing display of fresh ingredients, including herbs from the restaurant's garden right outside. Open daily for breakfast, lunch, and dinner; champagne brunch Sun. $$$.

Tippecanoe Place. 620 W. Washington St.; (574) 234-9077; www.tippe.com. A storied past and Richardsonian Romanesque architecture are the draws of this fine-dining destination. The Henry Cobb–designed, 26,000-square-foot National Historic Landmark was built in 1889 as a residence for Clement Studebaker, co-founder of the car company. It now offers a majestic setting for special occasions. Open for lunch and dinner Tues through Sat; brunch Sun. $$$.

Yesterday's. 12594 SR 23 (Adams Road), Granger; (574) 272-7017; www.yesterdays-granger.com. A former South Bend TV broadcaster friend tipped me off to this popular spot about 20 minutes northeast of South Bend. After Notre Dame games, fans in the know trek here for its utterly cozy atmosphere in a former house and for its massive menu. Start with shrimp cocktail or roasted garlic served with sourdough bread; move onto entrees like blue cheese-encrusted sirloin, stuffed Amish chicken breast, pistachio nut-crusted halibut, and the Bogie and Bacall surf and turf combo. End with fresh-baked desserts (more 6-inch-high peanut butter pie, please). Open Mon through Fri for dinner, Sat for lunch and dinner. $$–$$$.

where to stay

Morris Inn. 1 Notre Dame Ave.; (800) 280-7256, (574) 631-2000; www.morrisinn.nd.edu. It's a miracle to get a room at this Notre Dame campus hotel during game weekends and graduation, but at other times it's more available. In addition to a choice of 92 rooms, your rate comes with complimentary breakfast and access to the campus pools and exercise facilities. Closed during Notre Dame's winter holiday break. $$.

Oliver Inn Bed & Breakfast. 630 W. Washington St.; (574) 232-4545; www.oliverinn.com. Built in 1897 and in the wealthy Oliver family until 1987, this grand Queen Anne–style estate now welcomes guests into 9 romantic rooms—lots of bustled drapes, multi-pillowed beds, oriental rugs, fireplaces, whirlpool tubs, and eclectic antiques—as well as a private carriage house. The picture is complete with a homemade gourmet breakfast by the fire with live piano music, plus a neat green lawn, hugged by an English garden adorned with stone benches, fountains and cherub statues, and brilliant flowers. $$–$$$.

day trip 03

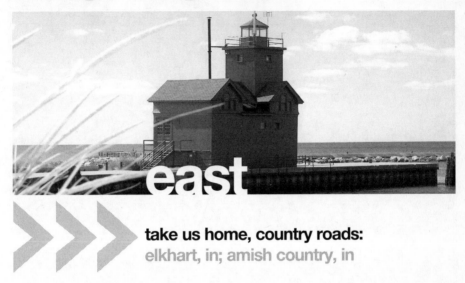

east

>>> **take us home, country roads:**
elkhart, in; amish country, in

Black horse-drawn buggies clip-clop their way along rural byways; brilliant quilt designs patterned from thousands of flowers fill the farmland from spring through early fall; RV-ers roll through the area to pay homage to the place they were produced; and two prominent rivers converge in scenic vistas. From the simple pleasures of Amish living to the contemporary amenities in downtown Elkhart, this drive gives you plenty of reasons to slow down.

elkhart

Elkhart is the largest of the Amish Country cities, so it gets a shout-out of its own. Sometimes called the "City with a Heart," laid-back Elkhart welcomes visitors with Hoosier hospitality. And, though the economy has led to a slowdown in its recreational vehicle production, the area is still famous for its nearly 1,000 RV manufacturers, along with suppliers. Fun fact: Nearly 50 percent of the RVs you see today were born in Elkhart County. There's even a museum dedicated to the rolling homes. Most records say Elkhart derives its name from the shape of Island Park, which lies at the junction of the Elkhart and St. Joseph Rivers. But stories also point to the arrival in 1800 of Shawnee Indian Chief Elkhart, cousin of renowned Chief Tecumseh. Just as famous is the name Dr. Havilah Beardsley, the noted first white settler to survey the land. The Ruthmere House Museum peeks at the life and style of Beardsley and the history of the area.

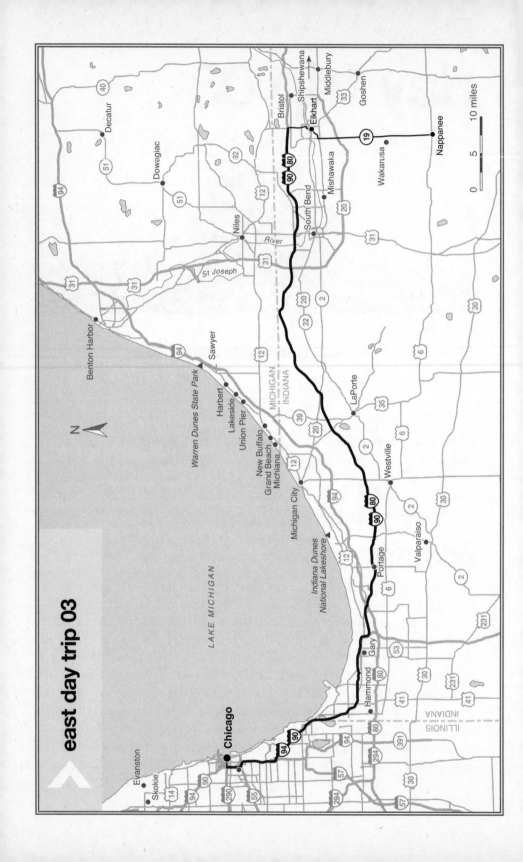

east day trip 03

getting there

Take I-90/I-94 east and continue on I-90 east/the Skyway toward Indiana. Stay left toward I-80/I-90 (Ohio). Take exit 92 toward Elkhart/IN 19. Continue straight; the road becomes North Point Boulevard. Then turn right at Interchange Drive (sign points to IN 19) and left at Caravan Drive to reach the visitor center.

where to go

Elkhart County Visitor Center. 219 Caravan Dr. (behind the Cracker Barrel at exit 92 of I-80/I-90); (800) 262-8161, (574) 262-8161; www.amishcountry.org. Pick up free brochures and maps, a free copy of the Heritage Trail Audio Tour CD, and information on the Quilt Garden Tour, and view a display of locally crafted quilts. Open Mon through Sat, along with a 24-hour vestibule.

Elkhart River Queen. Dock at 110 Bowers Court; (574) 295-1179; www.amishcountry .org/elkhartriverqueen. A two-hour cruise aboard this restored 1948 paddleboat on the St. Joseph River gives you a peek at the beautiful lawns and historic homes of Elkhart. There's a snack bar on board, or you can bring your own. If the small parking lot near the dock is full, you might need to walk just a bit from the lot at nearby American Park. Public cruises Sun, June to Sept. Fee.

Linton's Enchanted Gardens. 315 CR 17; (888) 779-9333, (574) 293-9699; www.lintons .com. Part garden store, part garden inspiration, Linton's is worth a wander through its 9 acres of themed displays featuring native and exotic flowers and plants—like the Japanese Tea House and Dutch Mill—set along the gurgling Pine Creek. Kids love the play area and petting zoo, where a pot-bellied pig, pygmy goats, a peacock, a turkey, and other friendly fauna roam. Open daily. Free.

Midwest Museum of American Art. 429 S. Main St.; (574) 293-6660; www.midwest museum.us. In a renovated neoclassical bank building, complete with a former vault as exhibit space, this museum's collection of more than 2,800 works focuses on American art of the 19th and 20th centuries. Some of its most popular works are those by folk artist Grandma Moses, the country's largest collection of Overbeck art pottery, and the most significant public display of Norman Rockwell lithograph and collotype works. Open Tues through Sun (afternoon hours Sat and Sun only). Nominal admission.

New York Central Railway Museum. 721 S. Main St.; (574) 294-3001; www.nycrr museum.org. Why New York in Indiana, you ask? Because in 1914 New York Central Railroad bought the Lake Shore and Michigan Southern Railroad, expanding Elkhart's influence as a connecting point between the country's east and west coasts. The museum, partially housed in a 100-year-old freight depot, relates rail history and displays a model train setup, along with several restored steam, diesel, and electric trains and cabooses. Plus, kids can't get enough of the real trains of the Norfolk Southern that rumble along tracks right outside every 15 minutes or so. Open Tues through Sun. Nominal admission.

Ruthmere House Museum. 302 E. Beardsley Ave.; (574) 264-0330; www.ruthmere.org. Architect Enoch Hill Turnock was quite prolific in Elkhart, but none of his buildings is as famous as this Beaux Arts- and Prairie-style combo, built in 1910 for the wealthy descendants of Elkhart's founder Havilah Beardsley (his own 1848 home is being renovated for tours as well). The ornate brick and limestone home is open for tours and includes an occasional special exhibit. During summer, take a coffee break on the elegant piazza. Check the website for podcasts about Ruthmere, Elkhart, and the Beardsley family. By the way, Chicagoans might recognize Turnock's work in the landmark 1893 Brewster Apartments at 2800 N. Pine Grove Ave. (Charlie Chaplin once stayed in the penthouse). Open for tours Tues through Sun, Apr through Dec. Admission for everyone over 5.

RV/MH Hall of Fame & Museum. 21565 Executive Pkwy.; (800) 378-8694, (574) 293-2344; www.rvmhhalloffame.org. I once slept in an RV, but it was parked in a driveway, so I don't think that counts. But I guarantee, a visit here would rev anyone's desire to hit the open road on something more than the usual four cylinders. Along with photos, videos, and a hall of fame of industry leaders and pioneers, this 80,000-square-foot mecca of motorized living and "manufactured housing" looks back through history with a display of trailers, house cars, motor homes, and more, dating from 1913 through the present. Check out the 1931 "lounge car" made for Mae West. Inspired? Elkhart is considered the RV Capital of the World, and there are more than a dozen dealers in the area. Open Mon through Sat. Admission.

Wellfield Botanic Gardens. 1011 N. Main St; (574) 266-2006; www.wellfieldgardens.org. These 36 acres of calming lush greenery, serene ponds, and vibrant perennial gardens were conceived as a way to celebrate Rotary International's centennial anniversary in 2005. Built on the site of Elkhart's historic well field just north of downtown, the gardens still host 13 wells on the site, providing much of the city's drinking water. Thus, part of its mission: to educate visitors on the importance of sustainable water resources. Wellfield is so new that gardens and learning centers are still being added. Open daily. Free.

where to eat

DaVinci's Italian Family Restaurant. 2720 Cassopolis St.; (574) 264-6248; www.davincis restaurant.biz. Joe and Rosa Siciliano, a couple of immigrants from southern Italy, have operated this low-fuss Italian eatery since 1992. They're known for their hand-tossed pizza (regular, thin, thick, or stuffed), and also their homemade garlic sticks served with entrees like chicken Marsala, baked mostaccioli, veal parmigiana, and linguini tossed with shrimp, scallops, calamari, and mussels. Hearty sandwiches like steak, meatball, and Italian beef too. Open Tues through Fri for lunch and dinner; Sat and Sun for dinner. $$.

El Maguey Grill. 56028 Parkway Ave. (along CR 17 and CR 14); (574) 522-1100. It's a fiesta of brightly colored walls, chairs, paintings, and piñatas at this bustling Mexican joint. The hot sauce flows, as do the Coronas and frozen margaritas. The extensive menu runs the gamut of tried-and-true tacos and sizzling pans of fajitas and quesadillas to "gringo" dishes like burgers and tuna melts (at least order them with Spanish rice). Open daily for lunch and dinner. $–$$.

Lucchese's Italian Restaurant. 655 CR 17; (574) 522-4137; www.lucchesesitalian restaurant.com. John and Kathy Lucchese (pronounced Lou-casey) began their business as a deli in 1982. It outgrew that a long time ago, and with three generations of Luccheses running the place, it's now a rocking restaurant and bar that typically sees a wait for tables on weekends. If you can make it past the fresh bread and olive oil on the table, try the filet mignon topped with sautéed mushrooms, the spinach and mushroom lasagna, baked tortellini, shrimp sautéed in sweet-spicy Limoncello butter sauce, or linguini in red clam sauce. Open Mon through Sat for lunch and dinner, Sun for dinner. $$.

McCarthy's on the Riverwalk. 333 Nibco Pkwy.; (574) 293-2830; www.mccarthysonthe riverwalk.com. It's more than just the scenic locale along Elkhart River that brings people here. It's the friendly service, comfy leather booths, and well-rounded menu of seafood, steaks, chicken, sandwiches, and burgers, plus a section of traditional Irish fare—corned beef and cabbage, fish and chips, shepherd's pie—that ranks among the most popular dishes served. A creative cocktail menu includes the caramel appletini, espresso martini, and "Tootsietini," garnished with a Tootsie Roll, of course. If that's not sweet enough, then save room for dessert. My pick? Bread pudding with bourbon sauce. Open Mon through Fri for lunch and dinner, Sat for dinner, Sun for brunch. $$.

Stirred. 115 E. Lexington Ave.; (574) 522-4914. Owner Tanya Bleiler is known around Elkhart for being its first female firefighter and for introducing Elkhart to creative coffee concoctions in her adjacent **Daily Grind** (113 E. Lexington, 574-293-4864). So it's no surprise this trendy nightspot is a hot spot. Located in what's known as the historic Green Block, it tempts with innovative appetizers and sushi, a changing menu of delicious desserts made by an on-site pastry chef (like flourless chocolate cake and crème brûlée), and a long list of dessert-y martinis. Open Tues through Sat for dinner. $$$.

Sweet Creams Soda Shop. 700 S. Main St.; (574) 970-5568. Refurbished vintage soda shop chairs and a 1940s soda fountain add authenticity to this old-timey ice cream shop. The building has history too, built as a saloon in 1900 by Sweet Creams owner Deb Rowe's grandfather. Rich, creamy creations are made with Valpo Velvet ice cream, made since 1947 by the Brown family in Valparaiso. Need something more substantial than a blueberry cheesecake or Neapolitan ice cream sundae? They have Vienna beefs and soup too. Open Mon through Sat. $.

The Vine. 214 S. Main St.; (574) 970-5006; www.thevinesb.com. Located in a 111-year-old downtown former bank building—the vault serves as a dining enclave, perfect for small get-togethers—this cozy restaurant specializes in upscale eclectic with Italian influences. Start with the signature hot crab and cheddar dip with oven-toasted garlic bread. Entrée standouts include bowtie pasta with sun-dried tomatoes and tomato basil chicken, Cajun-marinated salmon, and lobster ravioli. Also gourmet pizzas, salads, and sandwiches. Open Mon through Sat for lunch and dinner. $$.

amish country

Tune out technology for a change, and experience the Amish way of life as you travel through the rural countryside of Elkhart and LaGrange counties, North America's third-largest Amish settlement with 20,000 calling the area home. Taste their home cooking, tour an Amish farm, brake for horse and buggies, and pop into the many artisan Amish shops scattered throughout the seven northern Indiana communities that comprise Amish Country: Bristol, Elkhart, Goshen, Middlebury, Nappanee, Shipshewana, and Wakarusa. OK, you can turn your cell phone back on now—if you want to.

getting there

If you start your Amish excursion at Amish Acres, take IN 19 (called Bristol Street in town) about 20 miles south into Nappanee (IN 19 changes local names to Nappanee Street). Turn right at Market Street (US 6) and travel about a mile to Amish Acres.

where to go

Amish Acres. 1600 W. Market St., Nappanee; (800) 800-4942, (574) 773-4188; www .amishacres.com. This 80-acre living museum of sorts offers narrated tours, taking you to the original 1873 home and the restored Stahly-Nissley-Kuhns farmstead. You'll also see outbuildings where they dry food, bake bread, and smoke meat; a one-room schoolhouse; the blacksmith shop and weaving house; the barnyard and pasture. Hop aboard an Amish horse and buggy, taste regional wines at the Barn Loft Tasting Room, pull up a chair at a family-style threshers dinner or theme buffet, and catch a professional show at the 1911 Round Barn Theatre. Like the life? Take a little home from the bakery, gift shop, meat and cheese shop, and fudgery. Open daily Memorial Day through Sept; Tues through Sun Oct through Dec. Prices vary.

Bonneyville Mill. 53373 CR 131, Bristol; (574) 535-6458; www.elkhartcountyparks.org. Indiana's oldest continuously operating grist mill still grinds corn, wheat, rye, and buckwheat that you can purchase in the mill store. The picturesque mill along the Little Elkhart River was built in the 1830s by Edward Bonney, who was later accused of counterfeiting and fled the area. But the horizontal mill wheel kept on turning through several owners until the mill and surrounding 233 acres were donated to the Elkhart County Parks Department. Besides watching the wheel do its thing, you can hike, fish, sled, and cross-country ski. Open Wed through Sun May through Oct (visit June through Sept to avoid school-group crowds). Guided tours: nominal admission (must be scheduled two to three weeks in advance).

Heritage Trail Driving Tour. Pick up a copy of the audio tour at the Elkhart County Visitor Center, (800) 262-8161; or download the MP3 file at www.amishcountry.org. Hit all the highlights of Amish Country on this 90-mile self-guided loop. Stop along the route to chat with some of the 20,000-plus Amish who live and work here (keep that camera phone in your pocket, please) and browse their wares, from handcrafted wood furniture to one-of-a-kind quilts to locally grown produce. From Memorial Day through September, add the free Quilt Gardens Tour to your itinerary and gaze in awe at the 18 intricate quilt-themed gardens and 18 hand-painted quilt murals that create a colorful link through the seven communities.

Menno-Hof. 510 S. Van Buren (SR 5), Shipshewana; (260) 768-4117; www.mennohof .org. Did you know that Hutterites, Mennonites, and Amish are all Anabaptist? I didn't. I also didn't know that Anabaptist means "to rebaptize," describing their belief that baptism should be voluntary as an adult, not mandatory as an infant. The history of these religious sects, their persecution, their practices, and how they came to Indiana are laid out at this unique educational center. Just an FYI: There is also some encouragement to "consider becoming a follower." Open Mon through Sat year-round; closed some days in Jan and holidays. Admission.

where to shop

Countryside Shingle Shoppes Tour. Pick up a map of the shop routes at the Nappanee Area Chamber of Commerce, 302 W. Market St. (US 6), Nappanee; (877) 277-5375, (574) 773-7812; www.nappaneechamber.com. Follow the Countryside Shoppes map to find your way to all the mom-and-pops that branch off from SR 19 and US 6 in all directions. Watch live wood-carving demos at Chuppville Carving; bring home gifts and goodies from Baskets of Elegance; bag some bulk nuts, sugars, and more at Tri County Foods; get all your notions and quilt supplies at Nappanee Fabrics; and the list goes on with more than 40 stops at boutiques and workshops.

Old Bag Factory. 1100 N. Chicago Ave., Goshen; (574) 534-2502; www.oldbagfactory .com. Vintage clothing boutiques, fine art photographers, antique shops, pottery and quilts, a candle shop, artisan bakeries, and more than a dozen other intimate shops are all gathered in this revitalized 1896 former soap-turned-bag manufacturer. Open Mon through Sat.

where to eat

Das Dutchman Essenhaus. 240 US 20, Middlebury; (800) 455-9471, (574) 825-9471; www.essenhaus.com. Under a canopy of wood trusses and handmade quilts in this barnlike,

1,100-seat restaurant, you can dine either menu-style or family-style. Menu items feature comfort-food faves like hearty homemade soups, chicken pot pie, meatball stroganoff, roast turkey, and "broasted" chicken. Their famous old-fashioned all-you-can-eat family meals feature Amish specialties and include dessert, which is not to be skipped what with the 30 flavors of baked-fresh pies. If you've stuffed yourself silly, consider staying overnight at the Essenhaus Inn. Open Mon through Sat for breakfast, lunch, and dinner (dinner ends at 8 p.m., Fri and Sat at 9 p.m.). $$.

Mullet's Dining. 72800 CR 100, just north of US 6 (the first farm on the right), Nappanee; (574) 773-2140. The Amish do not have phones (no, not even cell phones), nor computers, so if you're interested in a country meal personally home-cooked for your group of 10 or more by Merlin and Mary Lou Mullet and their seven children at their farmhouse, you'll leave a message for them, and they'll let you know via community phone if they can accommodate you. If they can, you'll be treated to fresh-baked rolls and homemade jam and apple butter, mashed potatoes and gravy, lovingly cooked meatloaf, ham, chicken, roast beef, and Dutch apple pies. Available for breakfast, lunch, or dinner by reservation only Tues through Sat. $$.

where to stay

The Inn at Amish Acres. 1234 W. Market St., Nappanee; (800) 800-4942, (574) 773-2011; www.amishacres.com. With simple, country-style decor in the 64 guest rooms and complimentary continental breakfast in the Geranium Room, the inn offers a quaint place to lay your head after a busy day at Amish Acres. $$.

southeast

day trip 01

southeast

>>> **rev your engines:**
indianapolis, in

indianapolis

Although the White River lends Indy a lovely waterfront stroll today, it didn't do as well as a shipping route (too sandy for steamboats), so as the fledgling city grew in the 19th century, it relied on railway as its go-to transportation. In fact, more than a decade before New York had Grand Central Station, Indianapolis had constructed the country's first union station. In the late 19th century, the multiple rail lines gave the city its nickname "Crossroads of America." Now it could just as easily be called "crossroads of sports," boasting NFL, NBA, and WNBA teams, and the headquarters for the NCAA, USA Gymnastics, USA Diving, and other national sporting associations, along with that little thing called the Indianapolis Motor Speedway. There's an unspoken rule at the speedway not to divulge the total number of possible attendees (it's pretty much always at capacity), but it's estimated at about 300,000, meaning Indy's population increases by nearly 50 percent during racing events. The speedway is a big, raucous reason why people visit this Midwest mini-metropolis every year, but it's certainly not the only one. In fact, White River State Park is Indy's year-round top spot: a campus that encompasses 250 acres of museums, recreational paths, the scenic White River promenade, an outdoor music venue, bicycle rentals, and the restored 1871 Pumphouse. When my sister lived in Indianapolis, she took me to a baseball game at Victory Field, shopping on Broad Ripple, for a ride around Monument Circle, to the Children's Museum, and for breakfast at Café Patachou. We didn't get to the speedway, but I could almost feel its hum.

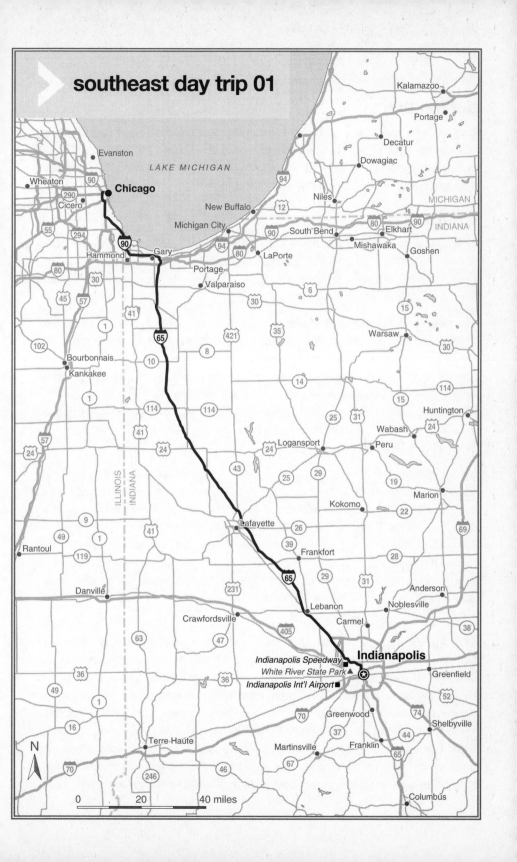

southeast day trip 01

getting there

Take I-90/I-94 east and stay toward I-90/the Skyway. Take exit 17 toward the Dunes Highway/US 12 and US 20. Off the long and winding ramp, stay right to head to I-65 south toward Indianapolis. Take exit 113 (which becomes 11th Street) toward Meridian Street. Turn right onto Meridian to get to the visitor association.

where to go

Indianapolis Convention & Visitors Association. 200 S. Capitol Ave., Suite 300; (800) 556-INDY (4639), (317) 639-4282; www.visitindy.com. The visitor center relocated to the expanded Indiana Convention Center due to road construction in preparation for Indianapolis's turn hosting the Super Bowl in 2012.

The Children's Museum of Indianapolis. 3000 N. Meridian St.; (317) 334-3322; www .childrensmuseum.org. Almost as fun without kids as with, this enormous museum features the immensely popular Dinosphere, where kids who dig dinos can dig for faux fossils and then check out a whole family of real ones. In other exhibits visit a simulated open-air market in Egypt, pretend to be earthworms, scale a climbing wall, and take a spin on a carousel. A highly anticipated archeology exhibit in partnership with National Geographic is scheduled to open June 2011. Open daily Mar through Labor Day; open Tues through Sun Labor Day through Feb. Admission.

Crown Hill Cemetery. 700 W. 38th St.; (317) 920-2644; www.crownhillhf.org. Indy's 555-acre cemetery ranks as the third largest in the country and is the final resting place of more than 200,000 people. It comes alive on more than a dozen 90-minute to 2-hour tours that focus on topics such as Civil War Women, Skeletons in the Closet, Art & Architecture, Tombstones & Trees, and Dillinger & Other Notables—yes, that would be notorious bank robber John Dillinger, who is in fact buried here. If you don't do a tour, be sure to make it up to the top of the 842-foot-tall "Crown" for a look at the final resting place of Indiana poet James Whitcomb Riley and for a panoramic view down to the city. Tour prices vary; call ahead for schedule. Open daily.

Eiteljorg Museum. White River State Park, 500 W. Washington St.; (317) 636-WEST (9378); www.eiteljorg.com. The American West and Native American culture are the focus of this 118,000-square-foot museum in White River State Park. In addition to temporary exhibits, its permanent collection includes works from the famed Taos Society of Artists, whose heyday from 1915 to 1927 resulted in a plethora of paintings depicting Taos, New Mexico. Many tribal groups of North America are represented in totem, pottery, jewelry, clothing, and more; and the Gund Gallery corrals a large collection of etchings, oils, and lithographs that depict the romantic West. Need some chow? The Sky City Café offers a Native American- and Southwestern-inspired lunch menu. Open daily. Admission.

Indiana State Museum. White River State Park, 650 W. Washington St.; (317) 232-1637; www.indianamuseum.org. Originating in 1862 as a small collection of minerals and other miscellanea stored in a cabinet, the collection grew, became a museum, moved several times, and finally in 2002 found a fitting home for its hundreds of thousands of Indiana-related scientific and cultural items. Glimpse everything from fossils and skeletons to earthquakes—see how big a seismic bump you can make—to products made in Indiana, people from Indiana (David Letterman, for example), and pioneer Indiana, where you can test your butter-churning muscles. Plus, catch an IMAX movie and hold up pinkies at the re-created L.S. Ayres Tea Room (which operated from 1905 to 1990 in the now-closed Indiana department store). Open Tues through Sun. Admission.

Indianapolis Motor Speedway & Hall of Fame Museum. 4790 W. 16th St.; (317) 481-8500; www.indianapolismotorspeedway.com. On event days you can simply follow the crowds or the roaring engines to find this world-renowned speedway. Celebrating the 100th anniversary of the first Indy 500, it's the world's largest spectator sporting facility. It also hosts two other major races, as well as Indy Racing Experience days, when speed-needing souls can push the limits of a specially designed two-seater Izod IndyCar. Also on deck: the 18-hole Brickyard Crossing Golf Course that plays four holes right inside the track's 2.5-mile oval, and the Hall of Fame Museum featuring nearly 75 cars, including the Marmon "Wasp," which won the first Indy 500 in 1911. Admission prices vary for events and attractions. Check ahead for schedule.

Indianapolis Museum of Art. 4000 Michigan Rd.; (317) 923-1331; www.imamuseum.org. From ancient art of the Americas and Mediterranean to Impressionist works by Monet, from the contemporary LED signs of Jenny Holzer to the attention-grabbing 60-foot-by-60-foot neon tube light sculpture by Robert Irwin, this world-class museum's 54,000-piece collection covers a little of a lot of things—and it's all free, no less. Also on the IMA campus and open for tours is the Oldfields-Lilly House and Gardens, including the 22-room French chateau built in the 1920s for late Indianapolis businessman J.K. Lilly Jr. And finally, adjacent to the museum is 100 Acres, an outdoor art and nature park of site-specific installations and natural beauty. Free; admission for special exhibits may apply. Museum and Lilly House open Tues through Sun; grounds open daily.

Indianapolis Zoo. White River State Park, 1200 W. Washington St.; (317) 630-2001; www .indianapoliszoo.com. You could swim with the dolphins here for an added adventure (and price), but you don't really have to, because this zoo boasts the world's only underwater dolphin viewing dome. Just stand under the glass dome and gaze up at the dolphins playfully swishing by right above you. Organized into five biomes (replica habitats), the 64-acre zoo also features the nation's largest shark touch pool, an expanded cheetah exhibit, an endangered Grand Cayman blue iguana (bred here for the first time at a zoo), elephants, zebras, and polar bears. Get up close and furry with the ponies, llamas, and pygmy goats;

> ## architecture 101

Chicago crows about its architectural history, heritage, and skyscraper superlatives—and with good reason, to be sure. But one Indiana city may have us beat, at least for its size. With a population of just under 40,000 people, quaint **Columbus** *boasts more than 60 pedigree buildings by the likes of Harry Weese, Eero Saarinen, I.M. Pei, Richard Meier, and Skidmore, Owens, and Merrill; plus more than 40 public artworks, including a 900-piece glass sculpture by Dale Chihuly in the visitor center and numerous downtown murals. Why such architectural wonder here? It was the idea of the late J. Irwin Miller, co-founder of Cummins Engine Company in Columbus. In 1957 he established a program that paid architects' fees for public buildings designed by architects chosen from a select list. It was so successful that, in 1991, the American Institute of Architects ranked Columbus sixth in a member poll that lists American cities based on architectural quality and innovation. Stop at the visitor center for a map and be sure to call ahead if you want to take a guided tour. To get to Columbus from Indianapolis, head south on I-65 and take exit 68 for IN-46 and turn left off the exit.*

__Columbus Area Visitors Center,__ 506 5th St., (800) 468-6564, (812) 378-2622; www.columbus.in.us; Open, with tours offered daily Mar through Nov (closed Sun Dec, Jan, and Feb).

and ride the zoo train, carousel, or roller coaster. Open daily year-round. Admission prices vary depending on the season; parking and special activities extra.

NCAA Hall of Champions. White River State Park, 700 W. Washington St.; (317) 916-HALL (4255); www.ncaahallofchampions.org. While you're visiting other sights within White River State Park (the zoo, the State Museum, the Eiteljorg), this small museum is worth a stop. Recently renovated, its most popular aspect is the 1930s-style gym where you can dunk, dribble, and shoot. It covers all 23 college sports with simulations, interactive exhibits, and plenty of sis-boom-bah. Open Tues through Sun. Nominal admission.

Rhythm! Discovery Center. 110 W. Washington St., lower level; (317) 275-9030; www.rhythmdiscoverycenter.org. You can bang on the drum all day at this percussion museum. It's a dream come true for little kids who love to bang (I know, I've got two of them). Besides a fascinating and extensive display of percussion instruments and artifacts collected from around the globe, there are drums, cymbals, chimes, and more, all waiting to make noise. Open daily. Admission.

Victory Field. White River State Park, 501 W. Maryland St.; (317) 269-3545; tickets (800) 745-3000; www.indyindians.com. These friendly confines of the Indianapolis Indians, Triple-A affiliate of the Pittsburgh Pirates, were once described by Bob Costas as "a miniature Camden Yards" and referred to by *Sports Illustrated* as "the best minor league ballpark in America." Victory Field is indeed cheaper and more manageable than even Wrigley Field. The most expensive tickets are $15, and lawn tickets—the ideal seat, in my opinion (though chairs are prohibited), with grass enough for 2,000 people—are under $15. Games from Apr through early Sept.

where to shop

Broad Ripple. Broad Ripple Village Association, 6311 Westfield Blvd., Suite 1; (317) 251-2782; www.discoverbroadripplevillage.com. About 6 miles north of downtown, this historic neighborhood, established in 1837, is the Bucktown/Wicker Park of Indianapolis—think indie bookshops and record stores, vintage clothing shops, funky home decor stores, and art galleries both local and national, not to mention some 85 restaurants, bars, and night-clubs. Plus, the busy 17-mile Monon Trail (constantly expanding, by the way; check www .indianatrails.org/monon_westfield.htm for more info) runs through here, as does the White River. The rippling water gives the district its name and is now a popular outdoor spot for kayaking and canoeing.

Massachusetts Avenue. (317) 637-8996; www.discovermassave.com. Billed as the "newfangled angle" because it's one of Indy's four diagonal thoroughfares, this strip was laid out in 1821 and is now listed on the National Register of Historic Places. It's also another hotbed of hip places to eat and shop. Don't miss Stout's Shoe Store, if not for the footwear selection then for its antique delivery mechanism and its claim as the oldest shoe store in the country. Several public artworks dot the avenue, including *Brick Head 3* by local artist James Tyler, complete with soundtrack.

where to eat

Bazbeaux Pizza. 811 E. Westfield Blvd.; (317) 255-5711; and 334 Massachusetts Ave.; (317) 636-7662; www.bazbeaux.com. Consistently voted among Indy's best pizza, Baz-beaux had inauspicious beginnings in 1986 in a former home of a gravedigger. But it won fast fans, moved to add outdoor seating, and has since expanded to include three locations (one more in Carmel, Indiana). On "thin or thinner" wheat or white crust, pizza toppings range from ordinary pepperoni and mushroom to adventurous Cajun chicken, snow pea pods, avocado, crab, and black bean dip (get it on the Chilopé with salsa, green peppers, onions, tomatoes, cilantro, and cheddar). Open daily for lunch and dinner. $.

Cafe Patachou. Multiple locations including 4901 N. Pennsylvania St.; (317) 925-2823; www.cafepatachou.com. When Texan Martha Hoover opened her first restaurant in 1989, she had no culinary experience whatsoever. And it's probably what made her friendly breakfast and lunch spot so successful. She relied on her passion for fresh ingredients and soon landed in *Bon Appetit* magazine's 2002 list of "Ten Favorite Places for Breakfast in the Nation." In fact, Hoover has been cooking local since before it was trendy, using three jumbo free-range eggs from Indiana farms in her omelets; humanely processed, grain-fed chickens in her chicken salad; and locally grown produce in her salads. Each cafe is uniquely decorated and features local artwork. $.

Naked Tchopstix. 6253 N. College Ave.; (317) 252-5555; and 3855 E. 96th St.; (317) 569-6444; www.tchopstix.com. The whimsical name may stem from owners David and Maggie Lee's mission to expose (get it?) Indianapolis to a wide range of Asian fusion options. What-ever it is, it's a local favorite for flown-in-fresh sushi and sashimi, teriyaki, stir-fries, noodle dishes, and sake cocktails at prices that will shock Chicagoans. Entrees range from Korean bulgoki to Japanese chicken katsu to hot and sweet shrimp. More than a dozen specialty sushi rolls include the tempura batter-fried Fire Roll with masago, cream cheese, crab, unagi, and avocado; and the Playboy Roll filled with shrimp tempura, asparagus, tempura chips, and spicy tuna and topped with cooked shrimp and spicy and sweet sauce. $–$$.

Oakleys Bistro. 1464 W. 86th St.; (317) 824-1231; www.oakleysbistro.com. Chicago native and James Beard–nominated (Best Chef Great Lakes) chef-owner Steven J. Oakley honed his skills in several of the nation's top kitchens, including Charlie Trotter's. No won-der, then, that Oakleys made a splash when it opened in 2002. Its strip mall locale belies the goodness within: a seasonally changing menu with standard starter faves like shrimp corn dogs, lobster waffle, and suckling pig, and entrees such as meatloaf, vegetable lasagna, and rainbow trout. Take a taste home with Oakleys own secret spices, rubs, stocks, and shrimp corndog mix. $$–$$$.

St. Elmo Steak House. 127 S. Illinois St.; (317) 635-0636; www.stelmos.com. Jeff Gordon, John Mahoney, the Bengals' Chad Ochocinco, Dave Grohl of the Foo Fighters. They're among the celebs who have dined at this 100-plus-year-old iconic downtown Indy des-tination. The reason? The steaks, of course—bone-in strip, filet mignon, a 24-ounce por-terhouse, and the manly 32-ounce prime rib. To start, go with the tried-and-true shrimp cocktail, served more than 70,000 times a year. An impressive and extensive wine list circles the globe. $$$.

Yats. 5363 N. College Ave.; (317) 253-8817; and 659 Massachusetts Ave.; (317) 686-6380; www.yatscajuncreole.com. My sister lived in Indy for five years, and she was a quick convert to the legendary Yats. Ask anyone in town and they'll tell you they crave it. Although a Chicago outpost did not fare so well (it wasn't operated by the same inimitable Joe Vuskovich), the originals are, well, original. Spiced beyond comprehension, the jambalaya, gumbo, and étouffée, and even simple red beans and rice and vegan white chili, are taste sensations. Open daily for lunch and dinner (Mass Avenue location closed Sun). $.

where to stay

Canterbury Hotel. 123 S. Illinois St.; (800) 538-8186, (317) 634-3000; www.canterbury hotel.com. This elegant downtown boutique hotel has roots that date back to 1858, when the first of several hotels opened on this site. Renovated and reimagined in 2010, this version is likely its best yet. The 99 sophisticated rooms feature four-poster beds and fancy Gilchrist Soames toiletries. $$–$$$.

Stone Soup Inn. 1304 N. Central Ave.; (866) 639-9550; www.stonesoupinn.com. With a feeling like you're away from it all, and yet right near downtown attractions, the Stone Soup Inn has charm written all over it. The rooms, furnished in varying Mission, Victorian, or rustic style, are comfortable and homey without being frilly. Several lofts lend a cabinlike quality and have small kitchens and sitting areas. Lounge by the living room fireplace or an outdoor porch and enjoy a complimentary continental breakfast. $–$$.

The Villa Inn & Spa. 1456 N. Delaware St.; (866) 626-8500, (317) 916-8500; www.thevilla inn.com. Owners also of the Stone Soup Inn, Ben and Elaine Life, their daughter Jeneane Life and her husband, Jordan Rifkin, bought and renovated this unusual 1906 Florentine-style villa in Indy's Old Northside Historic Area in 2001. They turned it into one of the poshest bed-and-breakfasts around, featuring 6 rooms, each with its own unique look, from a hand-carved four-poster bed in one to rattan and cherry wood furnishings in another. Treat yourself to some extra pampering at the spa; or better yet, call the massage therapist up for a treatment right in your room. The on-site Italian restaurant harks back to the inn's original owners, William J. Reid and his wife, whose trip to Italy inspired the design for their home. $$$.

south

day trip 01

south

degrees in arts & science:
champaign-urbana, il

champaign-urbana

Twin-sister cities with culture abounding, Champaign and Urbana began their synergetic relationship back in 1867 at the founding of the University of Illinois main campus. Now boasting about 43,000 students, U of I lends this major college town its bustle, its constant flow of new ideas, innovative museums, and an open-minded mentality. Surrounded by cornfields and ample Midwest land, Champaign-Urbana also features several vineyards and orchards. If you want to sound like a local, Fighting Illini fans dub the area Chambana.

getting there

This 2½-hour drive heads east (really south) on I-94. Stay right to take exit 63 heading toward I-57 S/Memphis. Take exit 237 A/74 E toward Indianapolis. To get to the visitor bureau, get off the highway at exit 182 for Neil Street in Champaign and make a right at the end of the ramp. When getting around town, there's little traffic, but be aware that driving can be tricky for outsiders. For example, there are lots of one-ways (of course, nothing new for Chicago drivers); there are Green Streets in both Champaign and Urbana, both of which have east and west designations; and there are two Washington Streets.

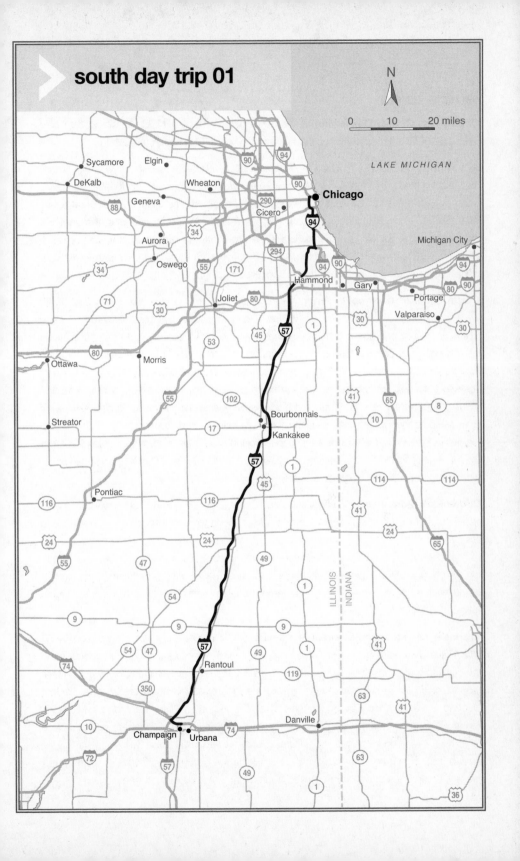

N

0   10   20 miles

LAKE MICHIGAN

Sycamore   Elgin
DeKalb   Wheaton   Chicago
Geneva
88   Cicero   94
Aurora   290
34   Michigan City
Oswego   294   94
55   171   90
Hammond   Gary
Joliet   80   Portage
30   Valparaiso
57   1   30
Ottawa   80   45   30
Morris   41   65   8
55   102   10
Streator   Bourbonnais
17   Kankakee
57   1
Pontiac   45   114   114
116   116   41
24   24
55   49
54   1
9   9
54   47   9   49   1
57
Rantoul   119   63
350   41
10   Danville   41
Champaign   74   63
Urbana
72   57   49
36

ILLINOIS   INDIANA

where to go

Champaign County Convention & Visitors Bureau. 1817 S. Neil St., Suite 201, Champaign; (800) 369-6151; www.visitchampaigncounty.org. Open Mon through Fri.

Alto Vineyards. 4210 N. Duncan Rd., Champaign; (217) 356-4784; www.altovineyards .net. Find out why this family-owned winery has won more than 750 national and international awards since its first vintage in 1988, including a gold medal in the 2009 Great Lakes Wine Competition for its Cherry Berry. I would have liked Alto to offer tours of the vineyard, located near the Shawnee National Forest, but they only do tastings. On the other hand, after a few tastes, you'll see that a tour won't be necessary—just a lift back home with your bottles. Open year-round Tues through Sun. Free tastings.

Curtis Orchard & Pumpkin Patch. 3902 S. Duncan Rd., Champaign; (217) 359-5565; www.curtisorchard.com. Do you have to travel to Champaign for apples? Why not? George Curtis grew corn and beans on his farm back in the late 19th century, but three generations later, his great-grandson Paul had visions of apples, and in 1977 planted his first 700 trees. There are now more than 5,000, producing 30 varieties of green, yellow, and red. Pick them yourself from July to October, pick them up at the country store already picked, and find them in doughnuts, pies, and fritters at the bakery. Plus, come Halloween-time, the 15-acre pumpkin patch would make Linus leap for joy. My kids gravitate toward the petting zoo and giant inflatable slides (weekends August to October) more than the trees, but we all got into the live tunes (Sunday and sometimes Saturday in September and October) and fresh apple cider. Open mid-July through mid-Dec. Fees vary.

Dodds Park Memorials. 1501 N. Mattis Ave., Champaign; (217) 398-2550; www.champaign parkdistrict.com. Besides ballparks, picnic areas, and jogging paths, this park contains two noteworthy memorials. The Laborers' Memorial Monument commemorates more than 90 men and women of Champaign County who have died on the job since 1950. The Tribute to Olympic and Paralympic Athletes honors Champaign County residents who have participated in either Olympic event; its rising-platform design symbolizes the athletes' challenging path to the top. Free.

Krannert Art Museum & Kinkead Pavilion. 500 E. Peabody Dr., Champaign; (217) 333-1861; www.kam.illinois.edu. Size-wise, this University of Illinois museum is second in the state to the Art Institute, but equally impressive. Its emphasis on temporary exhibits—it mounts close to 20 annually—leans toward the modern, thought-provoking type. Recent displays have included Chicago Imagism, and works by William Kentridge and Kabul, Afghanistan, artist Lida Abdul. Ten galleries of work from KAM's permanent collection feature artwork ranging from an ancient Peruvian drum to an 1894 Louis Sullivan elevator gate screen that once graced the Chicago Stock Exchange building to Edward Weston photographs. Open Tues through Sun (limited hours Sun). Free; suggested donation.

Krannert Center for the Performing Arts. 500 S. Goodwin Ave., Urbana; (800) KCPATIX (527-2849), (217) 333-6280; www.krannertcenter.com. This performance catch-all was designed by University of Illinois grad Max Abramovitz and opened in 1969. It now draws thousands of students, faculty, and community members to more than 300 annual music, dance, and theater events in five theaters, including its newest Stage 5, a lobby-located space next to the Stage 5 Bar. So, with two Krannert buildings, I bet you're wondering, "Who was this deep-pocketed person?" A native of Chicago, actually, a 1912 graduate of the University of Illinois, and the businessman who founded the Inland Container Corporation. Contact for schedule and pricing.

Spurlock Museum. 600 S. Gregory St., Urbana; (217) 333-2360; www.spurlock.illinois .edu. Celebrating its centennial in 2011, this U of I museum focuses on cultural heritage, covering one million years and areas of Africa, East Asia, Southeast Asia, Oceania, Europe, the Americas, and ancient Mediterranean, Egypt, and Mesopotamia. Open Tues through Sun. Free; suggested donation.

William M. Staerkel Planetarium at Parkland College. 2400 W. Bradley Ave., Champaign; (217) 351-2446; www.parkland.edu/planetarium. No exhibits here, just simulated starry nights and out-of-this-world night-sky shows projected on a 50-foot dome with a state-of-the-art machine that can illuminate 7,600 stars. A changing schedule of shows includes "Violent Universe," shining a light on comets, asteroids, and meteors; "In My Backyard," a kid-oriented look at stars through stories, poems, and songs; and the holiday-time "Santa's Secret Star." Shows take place year-round on Fri and Sat nights; reduced schedule in June and July. Admission (see two shows back-to-back and get half off the second).

where to eat

Jarlings Custard Cup. 309 W. Kirby Ave., Champaign; (217) 352-2273. I come from a family that sought out a famous ice cream shop on a trip to Cape Cod one year—and had sundaes for lunch. So this near-legendary sweet stop for U of I students is right up my alley. This second Jarlings outpost (the first opened in 1949 in Danville, Ill.) scoops straight-up vanilla, chocolate, lemon, strawberry, and orange flavors daily into cups or fresh-baked waffle cones. You can also get shakes, malts, sundaes (the cold fudge sundae doesn't melt the custard), and blends called snowstorms, with flavor sensations like strawberry shortcake, crème de menthe, and pumpkin pie. Open daily Mar through early Dec at lunch and dinner. Cash only. $.

Jim Gould. 1 E. Main St., Champaign; (217) 531-1177; www.jimgoulddining.com. Owned by Jim and Tanya Gould, who met in college working at a hotel together, this handsome downtown restaurant starts off right: with warm bread. The contemporary American menu changes periodically with everything from veggie-friendly wild mushroom and shallot ragout over cavatappi to apple amaretto chicken and the very carnivorous 24-ounce Black Angus porterhouse. Desserts in petite or regular size include brownie à la mode, tiramisu, and French-style beignets (an unexpected tasty surprise). Open daily for lunch, Mon through Sat for dinner, Sat for breakfast, Sun for brunch. $$–$$$.

Milo's. 2870 Philo Rd., Urbana; (217) 344-8946; www.milosurbana.com. Located in southeast Urbana's The Pines retail center, this is the second venture from chef Obdulio Escobar of Champaign's popular high-end Latin spot **Escobar's** (6 E. Columbia Ave., 217-352-7467). Milo's shares Escobar's upbeat vibe and vibrant color scheme, though its cuisine is Nuevo American. Raved-about dishes on the seasonally changing menu include the goat cheese and roasted red pepper strudel, the "upside-down" pizzas, and, in general, the fresh local ingredients. Open daily for lunch and dinner. $$–$$$.

Timpone's. 710 S. Goodwin Ave., Urbana; (217) 344-7619; www.timpones-urbana.com. You might seriously consider beginning your meal with dessert at this chic local Italian favorite. Made from scratch daily by pastry chef Ginger Timpone, the desserts might include chocolate hazelnut mousse cake, cinnamon-glazed peach caramel bread pudding, or thin-mint gelato. OK, fine, substance first: How about fresh-made shrimp pizza with leeks, bell peppers, broccoli, garlic, and goat cheese? Or vegetarian butternut squash ravioli? Maybe grilled hanger steak with caramelized onions? Because owner and head chef Ray Timpone is dedicated to sustainable serving, the menu changes daily, so these are just examples. The 400-plus sommelier-selected wine list includes nearly 20 by the glass. Open for lunch and dinner Mon through Fri, dinner only Sat. $$$.

Zorba's. 627 E. Green St., Champaign; (217) 344-0710. A U of I campus standard, this friendly counter-service spot is practically required eating for students. Since 1973 it's been slinging gyro sandwiches in two flavors (classic beef and lamb, and chicken) and four sizes, from the 8-ounce giant for those all-nighters to the 2-ounce small, great for a midterm snack. You can also get grilled chicken sandwiches, black bean burgers, hot dogs, and more. Sit down in the comfortably crowded little space or take it to go. Open daily for lunch and dinner. $.

where to stay

I Hotel & Conference Center. 1900 S. 1st St., Champaign; (217) 819-5000; www.stayat thei.com. High style at a low (for Chicago standards) cost brings business travelers and U of I parents alike to this contemporary-chic hotel. Located at Research Park on the University of Illinois campus, it stands out with sleek lines, luxury linens, and discount passes to the U of I rec center. $$–$$$.

Sylvia's Irish Inn. 312 W. Green St., Urbana; (217) 384-4800; www.sylviasirishinn.com. This distinguished Queen Anne–style home was designed by a University of Illinois architecture grad and built in 1895 for Urbana surgeon Austin Lindley. It went through several incarnations, including as the Lindley Bed & Breakfast. In 2003, Sylvia and Ernie Sullivan bought the historical landmark home, changed the name, and updated the interiors with European antiques Sylvia had been collecting for more than a dozen years. Sylvia was born in Dublin, and her heritage is seen, felt, and even tasted—in her fresh-baked Irish bread every morning—throughout the 4 lovingly decorated rooms and two-floor carriage house. $$–$$$.

southwest

day trip 01

southwest

>>> **riding the old route:**
joliet, il; wilmington, il; pontiac, il

Aiming for a bit of nostalgia? This trip takes you through three Illinois cities that lie along legendary Route 66. The old Mother Road's life began in Chicago, was Illinois's first paved highway by 1927, and ultimately brought drivers west to the golden lands of California. Although the multilane I-55 replaced Route 66 in the late 1970s, it had already beat a path to people's hearts, and the history of it has taken on a life of its own. You'll pass several Route 66 markers and pit stops on this drive, including at Joliet's Route 66 Welcome Center.

joliet

Most Chicagoans have seen those "Come play with us" ads about Joliet. And they ring true. There are two casinos for nearly nonstop gaming fun. There are also double plays at Silver Cross Field and theatrical plays at the historic Rialto Square Theater. Joliet was known back in the 19th century as the City of Steel and Stone because of its limestone quarry along the Des Plaines River and its belching, now-defunct Iron Works. Well, what goes around, comes around: Several of the historic limestone buildings, including the iconic Joliet Prison, are making a comeback as visitor highlights, while the Iron Works tells its story on a stroll past remnants of the factory in the Will County Forest Preserve. Route 66 takes a turn too, with a top-notch info center and its namesake raceway.

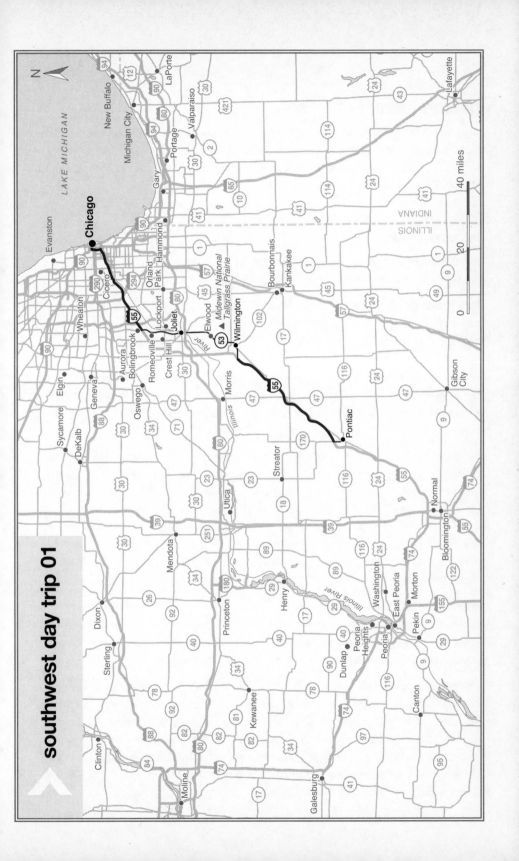

southwest day trip 01

getting there

Start on I-90/I-94 to I-55 south. Take the Joliet Road exit (IL 53). Continue south on Joliet Road through Bolingbrook and Romeoville into Joliet. Continue straight past St. Mary's Church to Bridge Street. Turn left and go over the bridge. Take the second right onto Ottawa Street. About 4 blocks down, you'll arrive at the Route 66 Welcome Center, which is the best first stop.

where to go

Joliet Visitors Bureau. 150 W. Jefferson St.; (877) 4-JOLIET, (815) 723-9045; www.visit joliet.com. Get brochures and maps of the area.

Bird Haven Greenhouse & Conservatory. 225 Gougar Rd.; (815) 741-7278; www.joliet-park.org. The name is something of a misnomer—you might see some birds as you stroll the nature trails amid the 3-acre site, but the charming glass greenhouse takes center stage. An immaculate selection of cacti (check out that crazy octopus cactus), ferns, flowers, and flow-ering plants, as well as a picturesque waterfall and seasonal displays, fill several showrooms. Outdoor gardens extend the floral arrangements and make for a spectacular background for a wedding. The 660-acre **Pilcher Park** (815-741-7277) is adjacent, offering playgrounds, picnic areas, and hiking, cycling, and cross-country skiing trails. Open daily. Free.

Chicagoland Speedway & Route 66 Raceway. 500 Speedway Blvd.; Speedway (888) 629-RACE (7223)/Raceway (815) 727-RACE; www.chicagolandspeedway.com. Together, these two sister tracks comprise 1,300 acres of racing. The 1.5-mile, D-shaped, tri-oval 69,000-seat Speedway is the place for NASCAR Sprint Cup, Nationwide, and NASCAR Camping World Truck Series events, while the Route 66 is a quarter-mile drag strip and half-mile dirt oval track. Cheer on the full-throttle action or get behind the driver's seat with the NASCAR Racing Experience or Mario Andretti Racing Experience (877-722-3527) or the Richard Petty Driving Experience (800-237-3889). Open during events; check for schedule.

Harrah's Joliet Casino. 151 N. Joliet St.; (815) 740-7800; www.harrahsjoliet.com. You can pop in almost any time to this glittering house of cards along the Des Plaines River. There are more than 1,100 slots too, with new ones added all the time, along with video poker, table games, and five dining options. Open 22 hours daily.

Hollywood Casino Joliet. 777 Hollywood Blvd.; (888) 436-7737; www.hollywoodcasino joliet.com. A spring 2009 fire led to a total renovation of this former Empress Casino. Reopened as Hollywood Casino Joliet in winter 2010, the 50,000-square-foot, two-story gambler's land is done up in Tinseltown glamour. It also has rows and rows of slots, table games, live poker daily, a high-limit area, reservation blackjack, and several restaurants, including the Hollywood Stadium sports bar, sporting a 20-by-80-foot TV wall. Casino open 22 hours daily.

Joliet Area Historical Museum/Route 66 Visitors Center. 204 N. Ottawa St.; (815) 723-5201; www.jolietmuseum.org. I say make this your first stop because it gives you such an informative and entertaining overview of the history and influence of Joliet. The free Route 66 Welcome Center in the lobby greets with lifelike statues of the Blues Brothers (good photo op) and The Route 66 Experience exhibit. Make like you're at the drive-in in the cut-out back of a replica '50s-era Corvette and view the absorbing Route 66 travel video. Then pose with various backdrops (including the Joliet Prison) in the photo booth. For a small fee, browse the small but unexpectedly top-notch museum to learn about Joliet's past. Board a replica trolley car; see vintage clothing and historic artifacts; look up at laborers working on the I & M Canal; and take the controls of a rocket ship as you discover one Joliet man's vital role in the *Apollo 11* lunar landing. Open Tues through Sun. Nominal admission for museum.

Joliet Iron Works Historic Site/Forest Preserve District of Will County. Located east of IL 53 (Scott Street) and east of the Ruby Street Bridge, on Columbia Street; (815) 727-8700; www.reconnectwithnature.org. A lesson in the industrial glory of Joliet is seen in the building foundation remnants of the old Iron Works. Opened in 1869, it operated as a foundry until the 1930s and was the source of Joliet's "City of Steel" slogan. It then lay abandoned until 1998, when the Will County Forest Preserve turned it into a 51-acre outdoor history museum, complete with 17 markers at sites along a 1-mile interpretive trail. Open daily.

Old Joliet Prison Park. 1125 Collins St.; www.visitjoliet.com/prison. This castlelike limestone structure reached legendary status in *The Blues Brothers* movie and even took on a romantic edge in the TV series *Prison Break*. Quiet and imposing, it does have a surreal mystique that, thanks to some preservation proponents, will likely avoid the wrecking ball any time soon. Not quite what I'd call a "park," the visitor area involves eight kiosk panels in the parking lot that paint a vivid picture of the infamous prison's history and its glamorous second life on the silver and small screens. In the center is an old Route 66 gas pump. Open daily. Free.

Rialto Square Theatre. 102 N. Chicago St.; (815) 726-6600; www.rialtosquare.com. Versailles, the Arc de Triomphe, the Pantheon in Rome. They all influenced the design of this 1926 vaudeville theater; its sculptor, Eugene Romeo, also worked on Chicago's Soldier Field, Merchandise Mart, and Wrigley Building. When it was built, the Rialto was considered among the top 10 most beautiful theaters in the country—and, arguably, it still is. Brought back to majestic life in 1981, the ornate performance space now plays host to musicals, comedians, musical acts, and more. Tours Tues (1:30 p.m.) and by reservation for large groups, but it's worth just a peek into the stunning lobby if you're not there when a show's in town. Box office open Mon through Fri. Tours: fee.

Silver Cross Field. 1 Mayor Art Schultz Dr.; (815) 726-BALL (2255); www.jackhammer baseball.com. If you're visiting during the summer, try to catch a JackHammers game, a team in the new independent North American Baseball League. The 2-block-big field is right downtown à la Wrigley, but on a smaller scale—including the prices. Besides kooky costumed mascot Jammer, there's Left Field Louie, a modified "muffler man" statue from the 1960s who emits smoke and lights whenever there's a home run. Antsy kids get their sillies out in the Kid's Zone with a bounce house and throwing and hitting area. Games Apr through Sept. Nominal admission.

where to eat

Ace Drive-In. 1207 Plainfield Rd.; (815) 726-7741; www.acedrivein.com. This tiny drive-in commands plenty of attention during the spring and summer, when it strains with people packed at picnic tables waiting for fast food delivered the old-fashioned way: by carhops. Opened in 1949, it's only seen three owners and has been run since 1983 by Rich and Tom Pierson, brothers who hung here when they were kids. Now, April through September, locals make a pilgrimage here for hoagies, poorboys, beef barbecue sandwiches, fish sandwiches, burgers and hot dogs, and frosty mugs of homemade root beer. Open daily for lunch and dinner in season. $.

Cemeno's Pizza/Joe's Dugout. 1630 Essington Rd.; (815) 254-2500; www.cemenos pizza.com. Since 1976, this family-friendly joint has been Joliet's go-to for thin crust pizza, though it also serves up everything from Italian sausage sandwiches to Cajun chicken to baked Florentine manicotti. The attached Joe's Dugout has a large selection of tap beers and 30 TVs for sports of all kinds all the time. Open daily for lunch and dinner. $.

The Department. 205 N. Chicago St.; (815) 714-2280; www.thedepartmentjoliet.com. Hardwood floors, rustic brick walls, black and white photos of old Joliet, and a second-floor outdoor patio make this one of Joliet's trendiest downtown spots. The building is more than a century old, and the dining is classic too, with entrees like filet mignon, grilled salmon, and lamb chops. Named in honor of Joliet's bravest and finest, the restaurant offers "department" workers a discount when they flash their badges. Open for lunch and dinner Sun through Fri; dinner on Sat. $$.

Merichka's. 604 Theodore St., Crest Hill; (815) 723-9371; www.merichkas.com. You can't miss the boomerang logo in the parking lot that has marked this family-owned Joliet area restaurant since it opened in 1933. It's meant to symbolize the fact that diners keep coming back for more. And they do—specifically, for the poorboy steak sandwich. Locals know to get it drenched in extra garlic "butterine" (though they suffer for it the next day). They also recommend the twice-baked potato with sour cream and salad with house dressing, if your arteries can handle it. Or even if they can't. There's lots more on the menu, if you want to stray: burgers, chicken plates, pork chops, broiled chopped steak, surf and turf, and fillet, to name a few. Open daily for lunch and dinner. $–$$$.

Thayer Brothers Deli & Grill. 753 Ruby St.; (815) 726-8990. Not much would tell you that this is a celebrity-owned restaurant, but it is. Former Super Bowl–winning Bears player and Joliet native Tom Thayer and his brother Rick own this totally casual eatery; mom Ann makes the soups. Hold out for homemade chocolate chip cookies. Curious about the mural? It depicts the 1923 "tent camp" in Joliet's Pilcher Park, where people used to stop on their way west. Open Mon through Sat for lunch and dinner. $–$$.

Truth Restaurant. 808 W. Jefferson St.; (815) 744-5901; www.truthrestaurant.com. This sophisticated, white-tablecloth restaurant has been a neighborhood favorite since 2003 for its spot-on contemporary American fare with a touch of Italian. The menu, which changes several times a year, features a steak of the month and mains such as chicken picatta, pork chops with sweet potato fries, pot roast and homemade mashed potatoes, and sautéed Florida grouper. Open Tues through Fri for lunch and dinner, Sat for dinner. $$–$$$.

where to stay

Harrah's Joliet Casino Hotel. 151 N. Joliet St.; (815) 740-7800; www.harrahsjoliet.com. A hotel that could stand on its own, this one happens to be connected to a casino along the Des Plaines River. Just know that guests must be 21 or over. $$–$$$.

Hollywood RV Resort. 777 Hollywood Blvd.; (888) 436-7737, (815) 744-9400; www.holly woodcasinojoliet.com. Pull up to the landscaped spaces on the grounds of the Hollywood Casino. You'll be privy to all hookups, laundry facilities, showers, and restrooms. Open mid-Apr through Oct. $.

wilmington

Wilmington might seem like a blip on the map (OK, maybe it is, with just 5,000 or so residents), but it has a big draw: the first national tallgrass prairie. And even within the prairie, there's more to see than just prairie.

getting there

A straight shot south on IL 53 will take you through the Midewin National Tallgrass Prairie.

where to go

Abraham Lincoln National Cemetery. 20953 W. Hoff Rd., Elwood; (815) 423-9958. Located on the site of the former Joliet Army Ammunition Plant (aka the Joliet Arsenal), about 8 miles north of Wilmington, this was declared the 117th national cemetery. The 982-acre cemetery is named for Illinois's honorary hometown boy, the 16th US President, who was the founder of the National Cemetery System. Open daily.

Gemini Giant. Launching Pad restaurant, 810 E. Baltimore St.; (815) 476-6535. I remember standing next to this odd 30-foot-tall "muffler man" space guy on a bike ride years back.

Stationed outside the Launching Pad drive-in restaurant, it really is the giant who gets credit for attracting people to dine there. Free photo-ops daily.

Midewin National Tallgrass Prairie. 30239 S. IL 53; (815) 423-6370; www.fs.fed.us/mntp. Not too many natural hiking and scenic areas can boast a WWII-era ammunition bunker. But Midewin, like the Abe Lincoln cemetery, took over land of the former Joliet Arsenal. It even allows hunting at certain times and places, though it's mostly visited for its 22 hiking, biking, and horseback-riding trails amid 7,200 sprawling acres. A welcome center begins your exploration with info about the area and interpretive exhibits. Various tours are offered from spring through fall. Open daily. Most activities are free.

pontiac

Thanks to an international contingent of walldog artists (who paint ads on the exterior of buildings), 19 historic wall-size murals now dot this Illinois town that's surrounded mostly by corn. The murals mark a Pontiac revitalization and a new look at an old city that experienced its first boom in the 1850s when the Chicago and Alton rail line stopped there. It got its next boost from transportation when Route 66 (then called Route 4) trucked on through, bringing people with it. The city of about 12,000 is now a favorite Mother Road pit stop for its museum dedicated to the "hard road."

getting there

About an hour south of Wilmington, Pontiac is easily accessed on I-55. Get to I-55 from Coal City Road. Take exit 201 off I-55 and turn left at the end of the ramp (IL 23). In about 2.5 miles this road will end—turn right here. After the First Baptist Church, take a left onto Howard Street to reach the visitor center.

where to go

Pontiac Visitor Center. 120 W. Howard St.; (815) 844-5847; www.visitpontiac.org. Located in the heart of downtown and adjacent to the Route 66 museum.

Illinois Route 66 Hall of Fame & Museum. 110 W. Howard St.; (815) 844-4566; www.il66assoc.org. Get your kicks at this homage to the Mother Road and to its faithful road warriors. First thing you do here is pull your car up to what they claim is the largest Route 66 mural around and snap your own commemorative photo. Then head inside this former firehouse for a trip down memory lane and down the Mother Road, its history, its people, and its places. Open daily. Donations.

International Walldog Mural & Sign Art Museum. 217 N. Mill St.; (815) 842-1848; www.muralmuseum.com. Painting ads on the exterior walls of buildings is a walldog's craft, and it's been around for ages. In fact, during the construction of this museum, a faded sign from an old clothing company, called a "ghost mural," was uncovered on one of the walls. Celebrating the artistry of the past and the growing walldog movement of the present, the museum displays examples, videos, and historic photos, some of which are for sale. It has also been instrumental in adding numerous murals around town, painted by walldogs from around the world. Open daily. Donations.

Livingston County War Museum. 321 N. Main St.; (815) 842-0301; www.warmuseum .blogspot.com. Weapons, uniforms, medals and patches, letters, photos, and more portray the triumphs, trials, and tales of the people who have fought in wars since World War I through today's battles in Iraq and Afghanistan. Have any questions? Just ask a volunteer staff member: Many of them are vets themselves and have plenty more stories to tell. Open Tues through Sun. Free.

Looking for Lincoln Story Trail Stops. Pick up information at the Pontiac Visitor Center. Among dozens of trail stops around the state and beyond, there are nine in Pontiac, including the spot where Lincoln served as attorney in 1840 at Livingston County's first trial by jury, and the Presbyterian Church where he gave a speech a few months before being nominated as the Republican candidate for president.

Murals on Main Street. Pick up a map from the Pontiac Visitor Center. If you talk to Jim Jones at the Walldog Mural and Sign Art Museum, he'll give you fascinating details about each of the 19 outdoor murals that grace downtown Pontiac. You can cruise past them easily in your car, but they're even more impressive if you do a self-guided walking tour— just follow the red footprints. While they all appear vintage—like the *Palace of Sweets, Allen Candy Co,* and *RCA Dog*—they were actually painted in 2009 by a group of 150 walldogs who landed in Pontiac for a painting marathon over four days.

where to eat

How Sweet It Is. 101 W. Madison St.; (815) 842-1377; www.howsweetitischocolatecafe .com. Let's face it, with a name like How Sweet It Is, you're probably not thinking "lunch," but owner Kristy Finkenbinder does make some delicious paninis, soups, and fresh salads. Still, I'm concentrating on the sign in this divine cafe that reads, REMEMBER: STRESSED SPELLED BACKWARDS IS DESSERTS. Of course it is, and so, what better way to *de*-stress than with a box of caramel pecan patties, chocolate creams, toffee bars, popular popcorn peanut brittle, one of Finkenbinder's 20 flavors of secret-recipe fudge, or caramel-dipped chocolate on a stick. The delightfully homey decor of mismatched tables, chairs, and rugs beckons you to stay, so get a cup of coffee and don't worry about bringing home any sweets. Open Mon through Sat (hours vary). $.

The Old Log Cabin. 18700 N. Aurora St.; (815) 842-2908; www.route66oldlogcabin.com. You'd be hard-pressed to find a less expensive meal in town, at least one served in a place with so much history embedded in its wooden walls. Joe and Victor "Babe" Selotti built a gas station and this restaurant in 1926 right along the newly paved Route 66 (then called Route 4). When Route 66 was widened and jumped to the other side of the restaurant, the Selottis simply picked up their restaurant and turned it around. Locals and Route 66 buffs still flock here for breakfast skillets, short stacks, biscuits and gravy, and fried mush (really). For lunch, stacked roast beef sandwiches, patty melts, and "gourmet" grilled cheese (with tomato), and dinners of country fried steak, rib eye, shrimp baskets, and baked cod. Homemade pies for dessert. Open Mon through Sat for breakfast, lunch, and dinner. $.

where to stay

Three Roses Bed & Breakfast. 209 E. Howard St.; (815) 844-3404; www.threerosesbed andbreakfast.com. You're in hospitable hands with innkeepers David and Sharon Hansen (and their two Yorkies) at this 1890 historic Pontiac home that Sharon named in honor of her three grown daughters, Jennifer, Monica, and Marcia, whose names also grace 3 of the 4 floral-themed guestrooms. As one guest said, "Breakfast is an event," a candlelit feast of made-from-scratch waffles, homemade cinnamon rolls, grits, hash browns, omelets, or whatever you desire. $$.

day trip 02

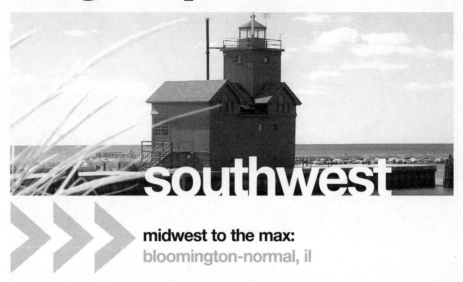

southwest

>>> **midwest to the max:**
bloomington-normal, il

bloomington-normal

When the hometown independent baseball team is named the CornBelters, you know you've reached the middle of Illinois, the heartland, Bloomington-Normal. Linked by proximity, the two cities don't mind sharing resources and recreational centers. Normal was even originally called North Bloomington. Its name followed the founding in 1857 of Illinois State Normal University—now, of course, just ISU. It was a "normal" school at the time, meaning it was set up to be a teachers' college. Along with Illinois Wesleyan University, these so-called Twin Cities bank on education to a large degree but aren't college towns like Champaign and Urbana. Besides the cornfield batters, you'll find plenty of parkland, the growing Constitution Trail bike paths, and even a few beaches at inland lakes, including the crescent-shaped, 630-plus-acre Lake Bloomington.

getting there

To reach the visitor bureau, about a 2½-hour ride, take I-55 south (toward St. Louis). Take exit 167 Veterans Parkway/Airport. Turn left on Veterans Parkway, then left on Empire Street (IL 9 west). Turn right on CIRA Drive and you'll arrive at the Central Illinois Regional Airport. The visitor bureau is inside on the second floor. You can continue into the city from there, taking Empire Street (IL 9) west.

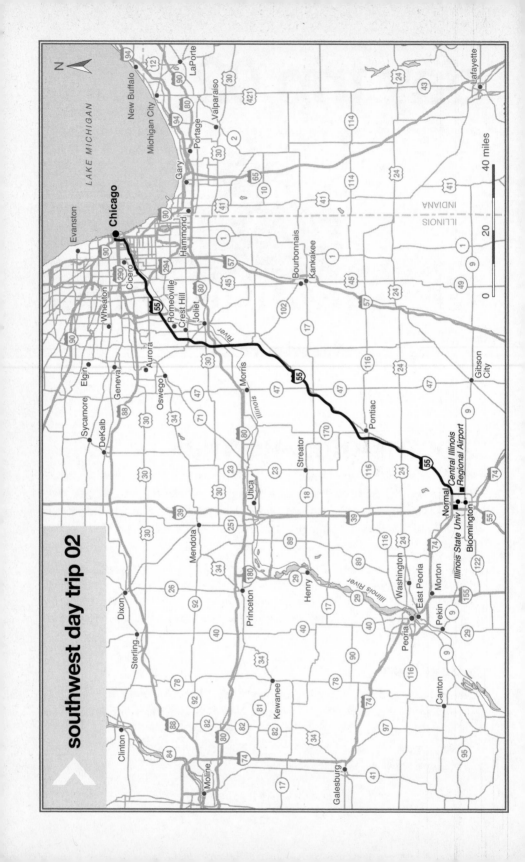

southwest day trip 02

where to go

Bloomington-Normal Area Convention & Visitors Bureau. 3201 CIRA (Central Illinois Regional Airport) Dr., Suite 201, Bloomington; (800) 433-8226, (309) 665-0033; www .bloomingtonnormalcvb.org. Learn about the area and pick up a visitor guide, calendar of events, and coupon book.

Bloomington Center for the Performing Arts. 600 N. East St., Bloomington; (309) 434-2777; www.artsblooming.org. Ira Glass. The BoDeans. Paula Poundstone. Cats. They're all making appearances at this revitalized downtown landmark venue. The massive structure was a marvel when it was built as the Scottish Rite Temple in 1921: A 1,320-seat theatre featured the largest stage west of New York. But by 2000, it was more of a mess. When it reopened in 2006, it had been given a shot in the arm with a new sound system, new seating, new ticket booth, and everything in between. Now it hosts a year-round series of music, dance, theater, musical, and comedy performances. Pricing varies.

Children's Discovery Museum. 101 E. Beaufort St., Normal; (309) 433-3444; www.chil drensdiscoverymuseum.net. Your kids will barely get past the entrance of this three-floor fun center. They'll be too busy in its crazy two-story suspended climbing maze. But there is much more to do beyond: water play, make-believe medical center, art studio, hands-on toy train table, faux cows to milk, and more. Membership reciprocity with the Chicago Children's Museum and inexpensive parking are bonuses. Open Tues through Sun. Admission.

Constitution Trail. www.constitutiontrail.org. Generally following the old Illinois Central Gulf Railroad right-of-way, these 27 miles of hard-surface trail aren't just a straight line, but offer several branches through both Bloomington and Normal. Plans continue to expand its reach. Check the website for a detailed map.

The Corn Crib. 1000 W. Raab Rd., Normal; (309) 454-2255; www.normalbaseball.com. The Normal CornBelters baseball team is a new member of the independent Frontier League, made up of 12 Midwest teams. It means affordable family outdoor entertainment and a chance for young players ages 21 to 27 to get in the game and maybe score like Ryan Sheldon and Bobby Pritchett, who were named among the Top 10 Prospects in Independent Baseball by *Baseball America*. The best part? The players emerge *Field of Dreams*–like out of, you guessed it, towering corn stalks. May through Sept. Call for seating and pricing information.

Historic David Davis Mansion. 1000 Monroe Dr., Bloomington; (309) 828-1084; www .daviddavismansion.org. As much a look at the 19th-century history of Bloomington, this 1872 National Historic Landmark is also a peek back at the life of Judge David Davis and his connection to Abraham Lincoln as his friend, campaign manager, and then appointed US Supreme Court Justice. The elegant, 36-room Victorian home was built for Davis's wife, Sarah, who wanted to stay in Bloomington rather than move to Washington, D.C., when

Davis's career took him there. She created one of the estate tour's highlights: a formal garden that still grows in basically its same form and design, including a handful of original plants. Tours Wed through Sun. Suggested donation.

Historic Normal Theater. 209 North St., Normal; (309) 454-9722; www.normaltheater .com. Not quite as grand as the Chicago Theatre sign, the vertical marquee outside this movie theater is nonetheless nearly as iconic and part of the theater's Streamline Moderne architecture (a late form of art deco that evokes Miami). It opened in 1937 with the Bing Crosby classic *Double or Nothing* and was the first theater in the area specifically designed for sound. It closed for a short time but was renovated and reopened, and now shows classics, indies, and foreign titles, an LGBT film festival, and the global Manhattan Short Film Festival. Movies shown Thurs through Sun. Ticket prices vary.

McLean County Museum of History. 200 N. Main St., Bloomington; (309) 827-0428; www.mchistory.org. It's not just the meticulously renovated 1901–03 limestone structure with its 100-foot-high domed rotunda that impresses here, but the exhibits on the Kickapoo Native Americans and European immigrants who settled on Bloomington-Normal land, the work they did, and the role they played in army battles. The Harriet Rust Pioneer Discovery Room features a re-created log cabin with hands-on elements that put you in the pioneers' shoes. Open Mon through Sat. Nominal admission.

Miller Park. 1020 S. Morris Ave., Bloomington; (309) 434-2260. Encompassing a zoo, 11-acre lake with paddleboat rentals, historic 1905 pavilion, colorful new playground, and Civil War, Vietnam War, and Korean War memorials, this 67-acre park is one of Bloomington's main public parks. Open daily.

where to eat

Biaggi's. 1501 N. Veterans Pkwy., Bloomington; (309) 661-8322; www.biaggis.com. Yes, this is a chain with 21 locations from Utah to New York (even three in the Chicago area), but the Bloomington restaurant launched it all in 1998. Their shtick: belt-busting portions of fresh Italian favorites that won't bust your budget. Entrees include a handful of pizzas made on handmade dough, rigatoni Bolognese, eggplant Parmesan, chicken Marsala, and New Zealand lamb chops. There's also a great kids' menu and an extensive gluten-free menu. Don't miss the cannelloni for dessert. Open daily for lunch and dinner. $$.

Destihl Restaurant & Brew Works. 318 S. Towanda Ave. (in The Shoppes at College Hills), Normal; (309) 862-2337; www.destihl.com. Don't mind the mall location of this brewery. The food is beyond boring bar food, the dozen-or-so beer options (including several small-batch blends) are interesting and varied, and the vibe is laid-back and social—all very Rock Bottom Brewery-ish, actually. The menu tempts with everything from beer-battered bacon as an app to bison burgers and portobello and brie sandwiches, to mussels in hefeweizen and chimi-churri sauce, skirt steak atop ancho rice and beans, and Thai fried chicken. Sweet endings too: four-layer chocolate or carrot cake, sour cherry bread pudding, and the intriguing stout ice cream sandwiches. Open daily for lunch and dinner, Sat and Sun brunch. $$.

Medici. 120 W. North St., Normal; (309) 452-6334; www.medicinormal.com. The name is no coincidence; this is, indeed, an offshoot of Chicago's Hyde Park mainstay owned by Hans Morsbach since 1962. The look here is completely different, though, and somewhat hard to describe. The eye-catching focus is the debarked mulberry tree that divides a dual staircase leading to balcony bar seating. Antique glass lighting, blue-stained concrete floor, back-lit onyx bar, stained glass windows, and end-grain wood tables almost compete for attention with the food. But you'll focus when your food arrives: popular Medici pizzas, salads with homemade dressing, burgers, pastas, sandwiches, and mains including steak frites and caramelized salmon; plus goodies from the adjacent Medici Bakery. Open daily for lunch and dinner. $$.

Station 220. 220 E. Front St., Bloomington; (309) 828-2323; www.station220.net. A raging 1900 fire left most of downtown Bloomington in ashes. The disaster inspired the purchase of the largest hook-and-ladder available and the construction of this firehouse. Bloomington's bravest served from this station house until 1974; after remaining vacant for a few years, a restaurant moved in called Central Station. The engine bar became the dining room; the horse house became the kitchen. New owners changed the name recently, and gave the decor and cuisine a more upscale feel. The menu of steak, pasta, chicken, and chops emphasizes fresh, local ingredients. Open Mon through Sat for lunch and dinner; Sun brunch. $$$.

where to stay

The Burr House. 210 E. Chestnut St., Bloomington; (309) 828-7686; www.burrhouse .com. Another of Abraham Lincoln's pals, lawyer Luman Burr had this Civil War–era home built in 1864 with area bricks; he later added Queen Anne–style gables and spindlework. It remained in the Burr family through Luman's great-granddaughter, until Jeffrey and Mary Ann Rhodes opened it as a bed-and-breakfast in 1997. Its 6 rooms are charmingly decorated in European country style, one with a clawfoot tub. You'll wake up to full hot breakfasts in the formal dining room. $.

Vrooman Mansion Bed & Breakfast. 701 E. Taylor St., Bloomington; (877) 346-6488, (309) 828-8816; www.vroomanmansion.com. Fair warning: You may not want to leave this beautiful estate once you've arrived, especially considering the rates are so surprisingly low compared to anything you'd ever find in Chicago. The 5 spacious rooms are graciously decorated to reflect the late-19th- and early-20th-century original furnishings, color schemes, and luxury living of the wealthy Scott and Vrooman families. Gourmet breakfasts are served on the same carved-wood dining table that Julia Scott Vrooman used to entertain the likes of Adlai Stevenson, Franklin and Eleanor Roosevelt, William Jennings Bryan, and poet Vachel Lindsay. Ask hosts Pam and Dana Kowalewski about the charismatic and influential Julia, who was born in the Safe Room and Study in 1876 and lived here until her death in 1981. $–$$.

day trip 03

southwest

>>> **beauty & bustle:**
peoria, il

peoria

The largest city on the Illinois River, Peoria boasts a growing riverfront scene of restaurants, shops, a new visitor center, and a museum that's in the works. Get the skyline perspective on a river cruise. Or sightsee down the historic, 2-mile Grandview Drive, affording scenic river vistas and glimpses of spectacular homes. The modestly sized Bradley University gives Peoria its young energy, as well as a great green space that'll make you feel like you're skipping class too.

getting there

From Chicago, take I-55 south toward St. Louis. When you reach Bloomington, merge onto I-74 west toward Peoria. After crossing the bridge into Peoria, take the Adams Street exit (exit 93). Turn right at NE Adams Street, then take the first right onto Eaton Street. Take the second left to stay on Eaton. Turn right on NE Water Street. The Riverfront Visitors Center will be on the left in a historic two-story building.

where to go

Peoria Riverfront Visitors Center. 110 NE Water St.; (309) 672-2860; www.peoria .org. This historic two-story building is a clearinghouse for area maps, guides, brochures,

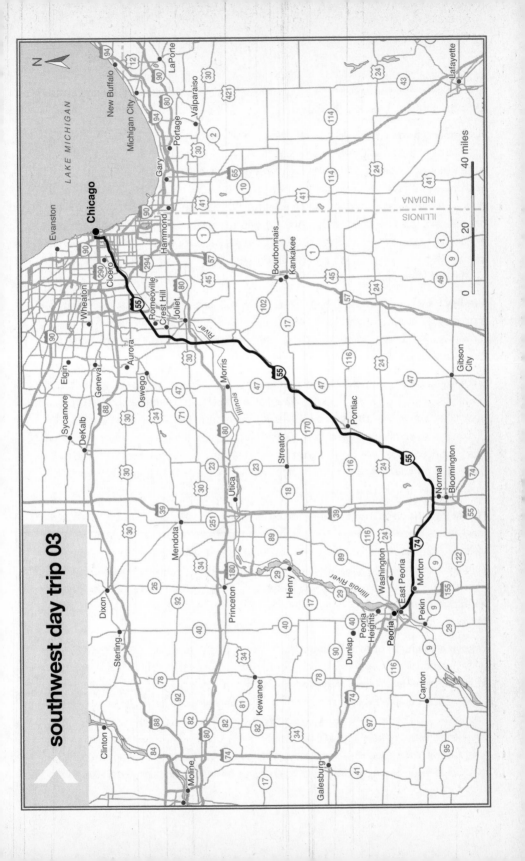

southwest day trip 03

and merchandise, plus snacks, gifts, and tickets to some local events. It's located in the developing riverfront district. Open daily.

Ackerman Farms. 27158 US 150 (Jackson Street), Morton; (309) 266-7459; www.acker manfarms.com. Just a 10-minute drive east of Peoria, you'll find this family farm that flourishes in the fall. Choose your favorite from among more than 125 varieties of pumpkins and squash—some of which are used by Libby—and 16 flavors of U-pick apples, plus Indian corn, corn stalks, straw bales, and 30 types of chrysanthemums. A corn maze and hay rides are in September and October. The fifth-generation farm began in 1909 with John H. Ackerman, who built the two-story home that still stands. Get garden gifts and decor here or at the shop in downtown Morton (122 S. Main St.). Open daily mid-Aug through Oct and during Christmas. Free admission.

Bradley Park. 1314 Park Rd.; (309) 682-1200; www.peoriaparks.org. For some loafing like the locals do, head to this 100-year-old park, adjacent to Bradley University. It's popular for its disc golf course, picturesque picnic spots, new dog park, and peaceful woodlands. Open daily. Free.

Contemporary Art Center. 305 Water St.; (309) 674-6822; www.peoriacac.org. No dead poets here: Works by living artists fill wall space at this innovative arts center. Repurposed from its days in the late 1870s as a coffee-bean warehouse, the 14,000-square-foot facility boasts two floors of studios and three display galleries. Join the dance party of Live at the Five Spot every Friday evening and grab a bite at the attached Rhythm Kitchen Music Café, creating its own culinary masterpieces of fresh-made soups, salads, and sandwiches. Gallery open Tues through Sat. Free.

Forest Park Nature Center. 5809 Forest Park Dr., Peoria Heights; (309) 686-3360; www .peoriaparks.org. You're out of the city, so get in touch with nature for a change. Hike the trails through this 540-acre preserve. Do some bird-watching from the viewing room or from amid the prairie and forest. Listen to live monthly concerts featuring singer-songwriters and folk musicians. And support the center at the Trailhead Nature store, peddling nature-related gifts like birdfeeders, organic chocolates, jewelry, and tree-free note cards. Open daily. Free (fees for concerts).

Lakeview Museum of Arts & Sciences. 1125 W. Lake Ave.; (309) 686-7000; www.lake view-museum.org. Having art and science exhibits both in one location makes a trip here multidimensional and always interesting. The collection encompasses fine art paintings and sculptures, decorative furniture and ceramics, Midwestern folk art, Native American art, and mineralogy. One of the highlights is the display of Illinois River duck decoys, with fascinating detail and artistry. There's also a Children's Discovery Center as well as a planetarium with nearly a dozen different shows. My favorite part, though, has to be the community solar system. Listed in the Guinness World Records book as the largest, it spans across five towns, using a 42-foot-to-1-million-mile scale and labeling the planetarium as the sun; now, see if you can find all the planets. Open Tues through Sun. Admission.

O'Brien Field. 730 SW Jefferson Ave.; (309) 680-4000; www.peoriachiefs.com. Attending a game here is sort of like going to a Cubs game. O'Brien's home team is the Peoria Chiefs, the Midwest League's Class A Minor League baseball team, affiliated with the Cubs. Chances are, though, the Chiefs have more wins than the Cubs: In 2009, the team won a record 48 home games. A fairly impressive list of Chiefs have even gone on to the Majors: Darwin Barney to the 2010 Cubs, Jose Ceda to the 2010 Marlins, Matt Pagnozzi to the 2009 Cardinals. Kids love Homer, the mascot dalmatian. Schedule Apr through Sept. Admission.

Peoria Zoo at Glen Oak Park. 2218 N. Prospect Rd.; (309) 686-3365; www.peoriazoo .org. A herd of elks donated to the Peoria Park District back in the 1800s were the forerunners of this now fully accredited zoo featuring more than 100 species. The newest exhibit houses animals from Africa, including two grand white rhinos and a pair of friendly giraffes, along with the endangered Grevy's zebra and strikingly colorful mandrill monkeys. Along with the Asia and Australia habitats, you might spot spotted turtles, green frogs, ring-tailed lemur and red-necked wallaby, Norway rats, and Nigerian goats. Guided tours are available. Open daily. Admission.

Spirit of Peoria. 100 NE Water St.; (800) 676-8988, (309) 637-8000; www.spiritofpeoria .com. If there's a river, there's a riverboat, and Peoria has a beautiful one. In turn-of-the-20th-century style, it boasts an eye-catchingly red paddlewheel that churns through the water as you cruise an hour and a half along the Illinois and Mississippi Rivers, with commentary along the way. Fall foliage and holiday tours get booked up fast. Regular sightseeing cruises run Wed, Fri, Sat, and Sun from June through Sept. Admission varies.

Tower Park. 1222 E. Kingman, Peoria Heights (off 4901 N. Prospect & Grandview Drive); (309) 682-8732; www.villageofpeoriaheights.com. About 5 miles north of downtown Peoria is the village of Peoria Heights. It's worth the visit to take an elevator ride up its 200-foot-tall red water tower, where observation decks afford sometimes 20-mile panoramic views of the Illinois River Valley. Open early Apr through Oct. Nominal admission for observation decks.

Wheels O' Time Museum. 1710 W. Woodside Dr., Dunlap; (309) 243-9020; www.wheels otime.org. (Note: Official address is 11923 N. Knoxville Ave., Peoria, but due to major construction in the area, the museum has temporarily relocated; call ahead to check its current location). Time to turn back the . . . well, you know. This quirky museum's three large buildings burst at the seams with antique autos and artifacts. Fifty vehicles span in age from 1915 through the 1980s, including fire trucks and farm tractors, along with a bunch of two-wheelers. Nostalgia for gram and gramps, and curiosities for kids, there are also musical instruments; early tools, toys, and clocks; a faux life-size barbershop quartet of former presidents; a miniature circus and a calliope; and, displayed outdoors, several old rail cars. Open May through Oct, Wed through Sun. Admission.

where to eat

Kelleher's Irish Pub & Eatery. 619 SW Water St.; (309) 673-6000; www.kellehersirish pub.com. Housed in a 19th-century structure, Kelleher's gets its Irish authenticity—and its name—from co-owner Pat Sullivan's mother, whose family immigrated from Ireland to America in the 1700s. Some of the decor comes from items Sullivan's daughter picked up while studying in Ireland and others from old buildings in the area. The tap pours traditional Guinness and Harp, plus a globally representative assortment of others, and more than 60 in bottles. On the menu: the Emerald Isle's best fish and chips, corned beef, and Irish stew, but also burgers and salads. If you can, catch the St. Practice Day celebration, the third Saturday of every month, with drink specials, dancers, and music. Open Mon through Sat for lunch, dinner, and late night. $.

One World Eats & Drinks. 1245 W. Main St.; (309) 672-1522; www.oneworld-cafe.com. A trio of brothers from the South Side of Chicago opened One World in 1993 as a small coffee shop in a less-than-desirable part of town. It's now a hugely expanded, beloved destination for Peoria's Bradley University students, professors, and parents, and a hip, young crowd from the neighborhood. Its walls are decked with local artwork, and its very veggie-friendly global menu achieves, as they say, a "delicate balance of health and decadence." Try eggplant Parmesan, a gluten-free Thai noodle salad, or basil pesto chicken pizza. And pizza for breakfast? They're all over it, along with bagel sandwiches and Belgian waffles. I wish those guys would bring some of that back to Chicago! Open daily for breakfast, lunch, and dinner. $$.

Rhythm Kitchen Music Café. 305 SW Water St.; (309) 676-9668; www.rhythmkitchen musiccafe.biz. Located in the Contemporary Arts Center, this upbeat cafe fits right in: artsy decor and regular live music sessions Wednesday through Saturday. There's no cover and no Wi-Fi, just down-to-earth eating, tunes, and conversation. Menu items start cleverly with the "Tuning Up" section of choices like chips and homemade salsa and move on to "Main Choruses" of anything from Jamaican jerk chicken to the gourmet meatloaf of the day. Be sure to check the blackboard for "Special Performances." Hours change seasonally; call ahead. $.

Ulrich's Rebellion Room. 631 Main St.; (309) 676-1423; www.peoriairishpub.com. I'm not sure what owner Joey Ulrich is rebelling from, but he certainly has a happy crowd at this great, classic Irish pub and restaurant. Dark wood, stained glass, plenty of booths and room at the bar, a big beer selection (Guinness on draught, of course), and a hearty bar menu—burgers, chicken sandwiches, wings, pizza—make for a convivial atmosphere and plenty of reasons not to rebel. Open Sat through Wed dinner and late night, Thurs and Fri lunch, dinner, and late night. $.

where to stay

Mark Twain Hotel. 225 NE Adams St.; (866) 325-6351, (309) 676-3600; www.marktwain hotel.com. This recently renovated downtown hotel features an invitingly sophisticated, contemporary feel. All 109 rooms, some with picturesque views of the Illinois River, come with a complimentary hot breakfast buffet. $$.

day trip 04

southwest

>>> **rocks to river:**
utica, il; davenport & quad cities, ia

As far as rocks go, Chicagoans know them either as the ice in our drinks or the boulders strategically placed at the lakefront at Belmont Harbor. Well, news flash: The rocks outside the city are usually of the naturally occurring kind—and Starved Rock in Utica is the big daddy of them. At 125 feet tall, Starved Rock lends its name to an entire state park, the first in Illinois, established in 1911. Its trails lead you to awe-inspiring scenery where stones and trees tell of Native American history and legend. The Illinois River is your first river on this trip, seen from scenic Starved Rock overlooks (couples, be sure to get some corny-cute pictures at "Lover's Leap") and open to fishing and boating. The next river is on your drive to the Quad Cities—the big momma of them, the Mississippi.

utica

Utica is truly a tiny town, with fewer than 1,000 residents. Its claim to fame is its natural resources (clay, sand, and limestone) and its nature. Starved Rock makes Utica a destination. If you're interested in learning more about the city itself, check out the **LaSalle County Historical Society & Museum** (101 E. Canal St., 815-667-4861). Otherwise, just wave to the good folks who welcome the multitude of Starved Rock–bound visitors every year.

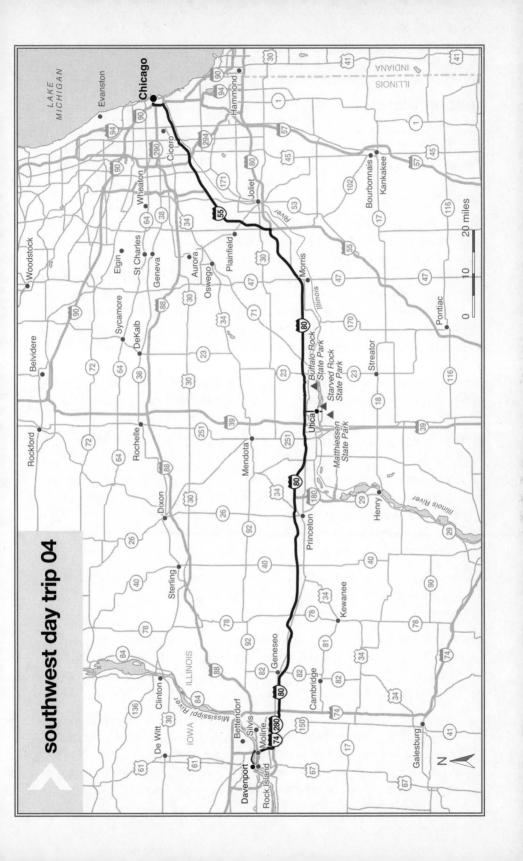

southwest day trip 04

getting there

Take I-55 south (toward St. Louis). Take exit 250B toward Iowa and I-80 west. In about 45 miles, take exit 81 IL 178/Utica/LaSalle. Turn left at IL 178/East 8th Road and follow signs to the park (keep following IL 178 south until IL 71; then turn left and then right at 950th Road).

where to go

Starved Rock State Park. Visitor center near I-80 and I-39 intersection and IL 178 in Utica, technically 2568 E. 950th Rd. (beware: entering the address into your GPS device does not work to get you here), Oglesby; (800) 868-7625, (815) 667-4726; www.starved rockstatepark.org. Start at the visitor center to pick up trail maps to Starved Rock as well as the other nearby parks. There are also several orientation videos, along with snacks and souvenirs. Carved out by glaciers and erosion along the south bank of the Illinois River, Starved Rock attracts a whopping 2 million people each year, and for good reason. The 13 miles of hiking trails traverse some of the park's 2,630 acres of varying rock formations and lush forests and vegetation, 18 canyons, sandstone bluffs, impressive waterfalls (or ice falls depending on the season), and scenic vistas of the Illinois River that follows the park's outline. You can see more than 200 species of wildflowers and might spot red fox, musk-rats, white-tailed deer, gophers, rabbits, or other wildlife; just wear long pants to avoid nasty chigger bites, which I suffered from the first time I visited. Below are a handful of Starved Rock activities. You can also go horseback riding and canoeing. Open daily.

Bird Watching: The feathered star here is the mighty bald eagle. With some luck, you could spot up to 30 in one visit, but they may last longer than you do, because they're most detectable in winter when they're looking for fish in closer-to-shore parts of the Illinois River that aren't frozen. Didn't bring your own binoculars? Exchange your driver's license for a pair from the visitor center.

Camping: While my own camping experience was a rather soggy one, Starved Rock is a mega-popular spot for families, couples, and groups wanting to pitch a tent. Reserve your plot at www.reserveamerica.com.

Fishing: The Illinois River swims with catfish, bullhead, sauger, carp, and more. If you don't have your own boat, check with the visitor center for the best spots to fish from land. Applebee's Bait Shop provides the tools to catch them (2956 N. State Route 178, 815-667-7036).

Hiking Trails: The biggest draw of this spectacular gift from Mother Nature is the hiking—13 miles of connecting and inter-looping trails. Plan your hike to pass through at least one of the 18 canyons with the most impressive waterfalls—St. Louis, French, Wildcat, Tonty, Ottawa, and Kaskaskia canyons. Trails also take you to the actual "Starved Rock" rock, named for a Native American legend about a group of Illiniwek who hoped to escape attack from Ottawa and Potawatomi, but who instead starved to death atop the 125-foot sandstone butte.

Trolley Tours: Trolley tours take you through the village of Utica, providing info, history, and legends of Starved Rock, the area, and the Illinois and Michigan Canal. Mar through Dec daily. Nominal ticket price. Call (815) 220-7386 for details.

Buffalo Rock State Park. 1300 N. 27th Rd. (also called McKinley Road), 5 miles east of Starved Rock; (815) 433-2224; www.stateparks.com/buffalo_rock.htm. Just down the road from Starved Rock is this 298-acre park along the north bank of the Illinois River. Two observation decks along the River Bluff Trail provide scenic views of the river. A fascinating example of landscape artwork is spaced throughout 1.5 miles of the park as well. Created in 1983 by Michael Heizer, the *Effigy Tumuli* consists of five animal-shaped mounds, including a 770-foot-long catfish and a 650-foot-long turtle. Though difficult to discern standing right at the sculptures—and because some have been eroded or overgrown—you can see them better from afar and consult interpretive signs that describe what they are. Open daily. Free.

Matthiessen State Park. Off IL 178, 5 miles south of Starved Rock. (815) 667-4868; www.dnr.state.il.us. Just south of Starved Rock State Park, Matthiessen is considered a hidden gem in the shadow of its more famous bigger sister park. But detouring beyond Starved Rock's beaten path will reward you with 5 miles of quieter trails, scenic picnicking spots, lush wildlife, a playground, and two deep canyons (called dells) separated by a 40-foot waterfall. In winter, 6 miles of cross-country ski trails are available. Open daily except during hunting season.

US Army Corps of Engineers Illinois Waterway Visitors Center. 950 N. 27th Rd. (aka Dee Bennett Road); (815) 667-4054. Watch hefty towboats make their way through the Starved Rock Lock, one of eight lock and dam systems along the 300-mile Illinois Waterway (which encompasses the Illinois River and parts of the Des Plaines, Chicago, and Calumet Rivers). The visitor center also features exhibits about the waterway. Open daily (closed major holidays). Free.

where to stay

Grizzly Jack's Grand Bear Resort. 2643 N. IL 178; (866) 399-FUNN (3866); www.grizzlyjacksresort.com. Say, "Wheeee!" The 92 rooms in a variety of styles (whirlpool suites, bunk-bed suites, deluxe family suites with fireplace) all include free passes to both a 24,000-square-foot indoor water park and separate 36,000-square-foot indoor amusement park. There are also large (try 1,800 square feet) villas and even larger (2,800 square feet) cabins that sleep up to 18 people. $$$.

Starved Rock Inn. Intersection of US 6 and IL 178; (815) 667-4211; www.starvedrock statepark.org. Rustic lodging just outside Starved Rock State Park, this 8-room inn includes access to amenities at Starved Rock Lodge (book rooms here through the Lodge). $.

Starved Rock Lodge. IL 178 and IL 71; (815) 667-4211; www.starvedrocklodge.com. If you want to wake up at dawn and hit the trails—or hike, then hit the hay—this on-property hotel, a historic landmark, fits the bill. There are three ways to do the Lodge: East Wing rooms that are part of the original 1939-built log structure; West Wing rooms that were added in the late 1980s; or cabins, some of which have fireplaces. All options offer use of the indoor pool and the historic Great Hall, which features a massive double-sided stone fireplace, perfect for lounging. $$.

davenport & quad cities

The Quad Cities straddle Iowa (Davenport and Bettendorf) and Illinois (Rock Island and Moline/East Moline) and combine to make up one of the largest metropolitan areas along the Mississippi River. Davenport boasts an active riverfront and downtown, while Moline's engine is the John Deere headquarters. Rock Island is famous for its island arsenal, and although I didn't specifically direct you to any Bettendorf attractions, it made a little history when it opened the first modern-day riverboat gambling (**Isle Casino,** 1777 Isle Pkwy., 800-724-5825). So do like Mark Twain did and explore the mighty river and its river towns.

getting there

Take I-80 west toward Des Moines. Continue straight on I-280/I-74 west toward Moline/ Rock Island. Take exit 5A to stay on I-74 west toward Moline. You'll cross Rock River, then continue about 5 miles to the Mississippi River. When you cross the Illinois-Iowa Memorial Bridge into Iowa, take the first exit, exit 4, for US 67 toward Grant Street/State Street/Riverfront. Turn left on US 67 (Grant Street). Follow it as it curves and changes names to River Drive. In downtown Davenport, turn left on Harrison Street. The visitor center is in Union Station on the corner. FYI: Here, as in Madison, Wisconsin, parking garages are called "ramps."

where to go

Quad Cities Visitors Center. The Visitor Center at Union Station, 102 S. Harrison St., Davenport; (563) 322-3911; www.visitquadcities.com. Find out about the area and rent bikes here to explore it. Open daily.

Credit Island Park. 2500 W. River Dr., Davenport; (563) 326-7812. You've seen Georges Seurat's Impressionist favorite *A Sunday on La Grande Jatte* at the Art Institute of Chicago; now meet some of the people who make up the scene. Or life-size artistic versions of them, at least. In this 420-acre park in the Mississippi River stand 10 wood statues of characters inspired by Seurat's colorful painting and carved from downed trees by local artist Thom Gleich. There are also typical recreational activities on this island, whose name is derived from its use as a French trading post with the Native Americans. Do some biking, fishing, birdwatching (bald eagles, in particular), strolling, and picnicking. You can rent bikes here at **Credit Island Adventure Rentals** (563-289-5445). Open daily. Free.

Figge Art Museum. 225 W. 2nd St., Davenport; (563) 326-7804; www.figgeart.org. A vision of glass blocks and towers that change their mood with the sky, the Figge Art Museum does its job to anchor a developing downtown Davenport. Views inside the 114,000-square-foot architectural marvel are equally impressive: the nearly 20-foot-wide *Mural* by Jackson Pollack; samples of Frank Lloyd Wright's leaded glass, furniture, and decorative textiles; a collection of Teco vases; and the only self-portrait Grant Wood ever made. The permanent collection numbers more than 4,000 and spans the 16th century to the present. The museum also hosts temporary exhibits. Open Tues through Sun. Admission.

German American Heritage Center. 712 W. 2nd St., Davenport; (563) 322-8844; www.gahc.org. Originally a hotel for immigrants who crossed the Mississippi River into Iowa in the 1860s, the forest green–crowned building now houses a museum that tells the story of the many German people who settled in the area during that time. Along with two exhibit spaces for rotating displays are the award-winning permanent exhibit "The German Immigrant Experience" and two restored hotel rooms—which make you appreciate modern hotel amenities a bit more. Ever want to know what a zither sounds like? Come on down every Saturday for a performance of the ancient instrument. Open Tues through Sun. Admission.

John Deere Pavilion. 1400 River Dr., Moline; (309) 765-1000; www.johndeereattractions.com. Tractors, combines, and other agriculture big boys make city slickers say "Wow" at this temple to the farming giant. Considered one of the world's largest agricultural exhibits, the 12,000-square-foot John Deere Pavilion is also one of the top attractions in Illinois. Exhibits trace the company's early innovations that began in 1848 when Deere moved his manufacturing business to Moline, then continue through today and end with a peek into the future of farming. The best part, of course, is the display of all those antique and sparkling new farming machines. Bring home a miniature version from the retail store. Open daily. Free.

Putnam Museum & IMAX Theatre. 1717 W. 12th St., Davenport; (563) 324-1933; www.putnam.org. At 115,000 square feet, the Putnam is the largest museum in the Quad Cities and houses Iowa's only 3-D IMAX. Founded in 1867, the history and natural science center now boasts more than 170,000 artifacts and specimens. Crowd favorite? The two mummies, now even cooler with an interactive computer station that uses CT imagery to peel back the wrappings. Prefer living things? Head to the Black Earth/Big River exhibit, where a 718-gallon aquarium bustles with Mississippi River fish. Stars shine daily in the ViewSpace gallery, a self-updating display that features recent images, movies, and animations from the Hubble Space Telescope and other NASA observatories. Open daily. Admission varies; check website (extra fee for 3-D IMAX).

Rock Island Arsenal Museum. Entrance at north side of Building 60, corner of Rodman and Gillespie Avenues, Rock Island; (309) 782-5021. Established in 1905, this museum is the second oldest US Army museum in the country. The arsenal began production in 1862 and manufactured everything from leather horse equipment to canteens to artillery recoil. It presents a unique look at Civil War history with photographs and documents from the Rock Island Prison Barracks that held Confederate prisoners of war. In fact, there are two cemeteries on the island as well—a Confederate cemetery for POWs who died while there and a national cemetery for Union soldiers who died guarding them (call 309-782-2094 for more cemetery information). Small arms weaponry on display include five weapons used by Native Americans during the Battle of the Little Bighorn. Open Tues through Sun (closed Mon and federal and major holidays). Free. U.S citizenship and photo I.D. required to enter Rock Island for all visitors over 16 years old (foreign nationals may enter with pre-approval and registration).

Schwiebert Riverfront Park. On the riverfront between 17th and 20th Streets (main entrance at 18th Street), Rock Island; (309) 732-PARK (7275); www.rigov.org. Like Chicago's river, the Mississippi is becoming more user-friendly in the Quad Cities. A tear-down of an obsolete national armory resulted in a beautiful new park along the Mississippi, complete with an open-air music venue, interactive fountain, landscaped grounds, and, oh yes, spectacular, up-close river views from along a waterfront promenade and an observation shelter. Two playgrounds feature the latest and greatest of playground technology with fancy digital play elements. Named for former Rock Island mayor Mark Schwiebert, the park is also part of the Great River Trail bike path that runs from Rock Island for 62 miles north to Savanna. Open daily. Free.

TPC Deere Run. 3100 Heather Knoll, Silvis; (309) 796-6000; www.tpc.com/TPCDeereRun .aspx. Bogie, birdie, and eagle where the champions of the John Deere Classic play. With elevations up to 75 feet and the Rock River flowing along one side, this 18-hole course is as scenic as it is challenging. Open seasonally. Fees.

where to shop

Bucktown Center for the Arts. 225 E. 2nd St., Davenport; (309) 230-1594; www .bucktownarts.com. If you've ever been to Andersonville's Galleria in Chicago, you get the idea of this arts consortium in Davenport's historic Bucktown neighborhood (known in the 1920s for its red light district): More than a dozen galleries of locally created artwork including hand-painted batiks, jewelry, feminist-focused works, found-art sculptures, handmade candles, glass beads, and fine art photography. You may even catch some of the artists in action. Open Wed through Sat.

Freight House Farmers Market. 421 W. River Rd., Davenport; (309) 764-0062; www .freighthousefarmersmarket.com. This twice-weekly, year-round market boasts a scenic waterfront locale and a spread of more than 200 of Davenport's finest locally grown, baked, and made foods, flowers, and artwork. Open Sat mornings and Tues afternoons.

Riverbend Antiques. 419 Brady St., Davenport; (563) 323-8622; www.riverbendantiques .wordpress.com. Practically doubling as a museum, this 39-year-old antiques store is located in seven historic brick buildings that span a half-block of Davenport's original main street. Owner Ron Bellomy named the famous shop after the Mississippi's only east-west bend. Where there were once stables, an 1862 home, a buggy works, and the first Christian church built west of the Mississippi (in 1830; Davenport's oldest standing building), there are now antique dolls, furniture, stained glass, movie props, musical instruments, and more. Open daily.

where to eat

The Boat House. 1201 E. River Dr., Davenport; (563) 326-FOOD (3663); www.boathouse davenport.com. As it should be, this American restaurant is located along the river and, as it should, focuses much of its menu on fish. Grilled salmon, catfish platters, shrimp platters, mahimahi, crab legs, and even a dish I'd never seen before: fried lobster tail. Carnivores, never fear, there's enough here for you too: sirloin, prime rib, chicken, ribs, and more. In warm weather, take a seat on the outdoor patio and watch the river come to life. Open daily for lunch and dinner. $$.

Front Street Brewery. 208 E. River Dr., Davenport; (563) 322-1569; www.frontstreetbrew .com. Two century-old buildings in the Bucktown area combine to make up this locally owned brewery. Along with the history, its exposed brick walls and wood floor and furnishings create a warm and comfortable ambiance. Accompany one of the half-dozen brews— the light Cherry Ale and hoppy Raging River Ale score tops with suds lovers—with fish and chips, burgers, the lemon hefeweizen-marinated chicken, Cajun ahi tuna, barbecue pork ribs, or the regular Friday night prime rib special. Open daily for lunch and dinner. $–$$.

Lagomarcino's. 1422 5th Ave., Moline; (309) 764-1814; www.lagomarcinos.com. Much like Margie's in Chicago, Lagomarcino's is a legend of chocolate fantasies and ice cream scrumptiousness. Italian immigrant Angelo Lagomarcino began the business in 1908, and it has remained family-run ever since. Now in its fourth generation of confectionary wizards, Lagomarcino's won the James Beard America's Classic Award in 2006. It still serves up the famous Green River sodas Lagomarcino's introduced to the area more than 80 years ago (students come for a sample when they're studying 1920s, '30s, and '40s history), plus cherry cokes, boxes of pecan dainties with homemade caramel, chocolate truffles, English toffee, sponge candy, and dish after dish of homemade ice cream topped with what locals argue is the best hot fudge in the world (the recipe is closely kept, of course). Custom-made booths, Tiffany lamps, metal ceilings, and original candy cases complete the nostalgic picture. Open Mon through Sat from 9 a.m. to 5:30 p.m. $.

The Machine Shed. 7250 Northwest Blvd., Davenport; (563) 391-2427; www.machineshed .com. This small Midwest chain first opened here in 1978, and though perhaps the farm theme is a bit of an overkill, it has since been featured for its breakfasts on the Travel Channel and for its chocolate-covered bacon (really) on the *Tonight Show*. But in general this place is known for its hearty, down-home-style meals. From pecan pancakes to steak and eggs, country-fried steak to famous skillets and cinnamon rolls, you may just need one meal all day. Just in case, though, you can add an extra egg to any breakfast entree for free. Open daily for breakfast, lunch, and dinner. $–$$.

where to stay

Beiderbecke Inn. 532 W. 7th St., Davenport; (866) 300-8858, (563) 323-0047; www.bb online.com/ia/beiderbecke. Beiderbecke may sound familiar to jazz aficionados, and indeed this 1880 4-room bed-and-breakfast was originally built for the wealthy grandparents of Davenport native and 1920s jazz great Bix Beiderbecke. Its authentic Stick Style Victorian architecture—with steep gabled roof, turrets, and towers—gives the 5,000-square-foot house a distinct appearance. Its elegant outfitting, detailed woodwork, 11-foot ceilings, and grand staircase make it a charming place to spend a night or two. Lounge on the veranda and take in the scenery from your vantage atop a bluff overlooking the Mississippi River, shoot a game of pool, or just cozy up by the fireplace in your room. $.

Hotel Blackhawk. 200 E. 3rd St., Davenport; (888) 525-4455, (563) 322-5000; www .hotelblackhawk.com. Sometimes it's OK when history repeats itself, like when it comes to multimillion-dollar renovations of glorious historic hotels. Which is the case with this one, first opened in 1915 and in its heyday played host to Cary Grant, Jack Dempsey, and President Nixon, among other notable guests. The room redo brought sleek designs in warm earthy tones and artwork by local artists. Luxury can't be without amenities like an indoor heated pool and full-service spa, so those are here too. Make the most of your location by requesting a river-view room. $$–$$$.

day trip 05

southwest

springfield

The Land of Lincoln takes shape in this hub of Abraham Lincoln lore, historic locations, and modern commemorations. It was actually ol' Honest Abe and his collaborators "The Long Nine" (all men over 6 feet tall) who argued that Springfield should be the capital of Illinois; so in 1837, it moved here from Vandalia (it started out in Kaskaskia). Lincoln lived here for nearly 25 years before heading off to Washington. And while "honest" is not a nickname you hear these days to describe politicians in the capital, the place itself exceeds expectations as an honest-to-goodness travel destination.

getting there

This 3½-hour trip starts on I-55 south for about the first 200 miles. Then take exit 98B toward I-97 west/Clear Lake Avenue. Turn left at 7th Street, and the visitor bureau will be down a short distance on the right. Bonus once you're in town: You don't need to feed the meters on Saturday or Sunday (Chicago, are you listening?).

where to go

Springfield Convention & Visitors Bureau. 109 N. 7th St.; (800) 545-7300; www.visit springfieldillinois.com. Get the full gamut of brochures and maps. Open Mon through Fri.

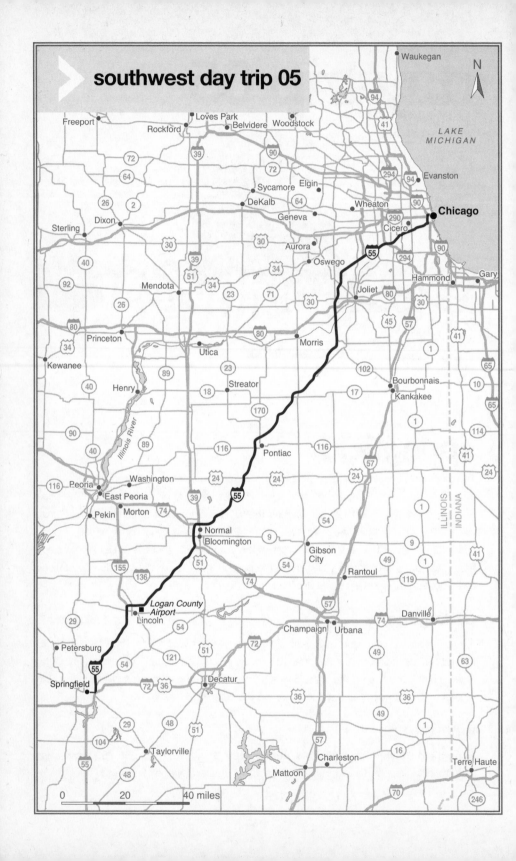

Note: The **Illinois Visitor Center at Union Station** (500 E. Madison St.) is open daily (217-557-4588).

Abraham Lincoln Presidential Library & Museum. 212 N. 6th St.; (800) 610-2094, (217) 782-5764; www.presidentlincoln.org. Put on a tall black hat and a fake beard, utter something about "four score and seven years ago," and you're instantly Abraham Lincoln. But behind our 16th President's iconic visage, there's a complex personal story of love and loss, hard work and hard decisions, courage, fear, triumph, and, of course, tragedy. This 100,000-square-foot museum, divided into two "journeys," paints an intimate picture of Lincoln from boyhood to presidency, and puts it in the broader context of the Civil War, slavery, and Lincoln's legacy. It does an amazing job of educating, intriguing, inspiring, and even entertaining visitors with multimedia wizardry; a hands-on kids space; realistic life-size models of people such as Lincoln and his family (take a photo standing next to them) and John Wilkes Booth; scaled replicas of key places like Lincoln's log cabin home and the White House; and dozens of artifacts from Lincoln's life including family photos, the clock from his law office, and, yes, his famous stovepipe hat. To end your journey, you file past a re-creation of Lincoln's closed casket and into the Gateway where you can learn even more about Lincoln. Open daily. Call ahead for admission prices, as they sometimes change.

Illinois State Capitol. 301 S. 2nd St.; (217) 782-2099; www.visit-springfieldillinois.com, www.ilstatehouse.com. So, maybe politics in Illinois don't present the shining example of democracy that we'd like them to, but the action at the State Capitol (during legislative session) still entertains. The current capitol building is the sixth since Illinois achieved statehood in 1818. It was built between 1868 and 1888, measuring 379 by 268 feet and topped off by a dome that reaches 361 feet—be sure to gaze up at the stained glass and plaster frieze on its interior. Flanking the southern corners of the capitol are the Illinois Firefighter and Illinois Officers memorials. Open daily. Free (don't forget your ID).

Lincoln Home National Historic Site. Visitor center at 426 S. 7th St.; (217) 391-3226; www.nps.gov/mwr/liho. Of all the places that claim "Lincoln slept here," this is the most reliable, not to mention the most captivating. Abraham Lincoln and Mary Todd bought the house in 1844 from Reverend Charles Dresser, who married the couple in 1842. After several remodelings and additions, the five-room 1839 Greek Revival home grew to the 12-room, 3,000-square-foot home the Lincolns lived in for 17 years. Tour the home, then stroll the surrounding 4-block neighborhood, which boasts 12 additional historic homes, two of which (the Arnold House and the Dean House) have small museum exhibits. Open daily. Free (tickets required from the visitor center; during summer, early arrival is suggested).

Lincoln's New Salem. 15588 History Lane, Petersburg; (217) 632-4000; www.lincolns newsalem.com. See how Lincoln lived at this re-creation of the village where he grew up, circa 1830s. Log buildings, a tavern, workshops, stores, mills, and a school contain collected artifacts including wheat cradles, candle molds, cord beds, and more. During the

more than lincoln

*There's no question that Abraham Lincoln–related sites star in this trip, but there are other things to see in the area too. Like Frank Lloyd Wright's 1902 **Dana Thomas House** (301 E. Lawrence Ave.; 217-782-6776), a stunning example of Wright's signature architecture and the largest collection of his site-specific art glass and furniture. It's a whopping 35 rooms in 12,000 square feet on 16 varying levels. It's a must-see for architecture fans and open Wed through Sun for tours. On the other end of the fun spectrum is **Knights Action Park** (1700 Knight's Recreation Dr.; 217-546-8881, www.knightsactionpark.com), a one-stop fun shop with driving range, mini golf, water park, batting cages, bumper boats, and drive-in movie theater. It even has some history, launched in 1952 as a driving range by golf pro George Knight. And maybe somewhere in the middle of history and kitsch is **Shea's Route 66 Gas Station Museum** (2075 Peoria Rd.; 217-522-0475), a tribute to the days of pumps and signs with character. Owner Bill Shea adds his own character, regaling visitors with stories of his life on the Mother Road for more than five decades.*

summer, get a seat at the outdoor amphitheater for a live performance. Open days and hours change seasonally. Donation suggested.

Lincoln Tomb. Oak Ridge Cemetery, 1500 Monument Ave.; (217) 782-2717; www.il.gov, www.state.il.us/hpa/hs/lincoln_tomb.htm. Pay respects to the late US President where he, Mary Todd Lincoln, and three of their sons lay entombed (their eldest son is buried at Arlington National Cemetery). Besides the 117-foot granite tomb with obelisk, the site features four large war-themed bronze statues around the 72-foot-square base and numerous statues inside the tomb's marble and bronze interior. One is a replica of Daniel Chester French's famous marble monument of Lincoln in Washington, D.C. Another, Chicagoans will recognize as a replica of the "Standing Lincoln" near North Avenue and Clark Street in Chicago. Perhaps most popular, though, is the one by Gutzon Borglum (famous for Mount Rushmore): a large bronze bust of Lincoln whose nose visitors rub for luck. Open daily May through Labor Day, then Tues through Sat until May (times vary). Free.

where to eat

Caitie Girls. 400 E. Jefferson St.; (217) 528-1294; www.caitiegirls.com. Whimsical decor and Van Gogh–inspired murals make a perfect backdrop to the creative comfort food here. The mac and cheese is made with pepperjack and pulled pork; the pot pie is stuffed with lobster and Brie (traditionalists can get chicken too); the meatloaf is wrapped in sourdough and drizzled with béarnaise sauce; and the chicken salad comes as a casserole with pulled chicken topped with buttery crumb topping. Better come hungry. Open Tues through Fri for lunch and dinner, Sat for dinner. $$$.

Charlie Parker's Diner. 700 North St.; (217) 241-2104; www.charlieparkersdiner.net. Black-and-white checkered tile floor. Counter with chrome swivel stools. Breakfast all day. All the ingredients are in place here for a fabulous 1950s-style diner experience. Once a well-kept Springfield secret, Charlie Parker's achieved destination status when it appeared on the Food Network's *Diners, Drive-Ins and Dives.* Now people line up out the door for its 16-inch pancakes, omelets, steak and eggs, and local horseshoe sandwiches (topped with fries or Tater Tots). Its location in a Quonset hut (those metal half-cylinder-shaped structures) adds a bit of quirk and WWII-era character. By the way, don't trust your GPS to get here—get directions from a local if you tend to get lost. Open daily for breakfast and lunch. $.

Cozy Dog Drive In. 2935 S. 6th St.; (217) 525-1992; www.cozydogdrivein.com. Whatever you do, do not ask for a "corn dog" at this Route 66 stop. It's a Cozy Dog, thank you very much. And whether or not it was the first hot dog served on a stick, it was the first Cozy Dog, introduced in 1946 at the Illinois State Fair by Ed Waldmire Jr. The drive-in opened in 1949, and the rest is Mother Road history. There are, in fact, other items on the menu where everything is under 5 bucks, from French toast to bacon sandwiches, burgers to barbecue. But you're here for the Cozy Dogs, so don't stray. Open Mon through Sat for breakfast, lunch, and early dinner. $.

Maldaner's. 222 S. 6th St.; (217) 522-4313; www.maldaners.com. A fixture in Springfield since John Maldaner opened his Confectioneries and Bakers in 1884, this contemporary American restaurant with a twist is the oldest restaurant in the city. Popular with politicos (President Obama occasionally dined here), it features white-tablecloth appeal and a second-floor dining area adorned with stained-glass windows from the 1890s. When chef-owner Michael Higgins bought the business in 1994, he introduced a strong sustainable component to the menu, but maintained its historic roots. The horseshoe sandwiches—open-faced burger (or other meat choice or just veggies) topped with fries and a beer-cheddar sauce—are still a lunchtime hit, along with beef Wellington and homemade lemon sherbet that locals say was inspired by Mary Todd Lincoln's favorite dessert. Much of the meats, dairies, and produce are now locally grown and seasonally selected, and the sherbet is low fat. Open Mon through Fri for lunch, Tues through Sat for dinner. $$$.

Osaka Japanese Restaurant. 1665 Wabash Ave.; (217) 726-8037; www.osakaspring field.com. While Chicago has sushi on nearly every block these days, Springfield is a little less inundated with raw fish. Osaka could hold its own to any one of Chicago's spots, with food presentation as stunning and sophisticated as the setting. Besides more than two dozen fancy rolls and a creative bar menu where liquor is infused with various fruits and veggies, Osaka also serves up Thai curry and noodle specialties, and showman-like hibachi dining. Open daily for lunch and dinner. $–$$.

Sebastian's Hideout. 221 S. 5th St.; (217) 789-8988; www.sebastianshideout.com. Dramatic red drapes make booth seating extra intimate in this upscale-casual eatery. The menu doesn't commit to any particular cuisine, instead offering everything from thinly sliced duck breast with roasted candied cashews to New York strip with Lyonnaise sauce to sesame seed–encrusted yellow fin tuna. Customize your steak with optional toppings like horseradish crust and caramelized onions. Open Mon through Fri for lunch and dinner, Sat for dinner. $$$.

where to stay

Inn at 835. 835 S. 2nd St.; (217) 523-4466; www.innat835.com. This renovated Classical Revival structure was built as luxury apartments in 1909 by Bell Miller, florist to the society set during the early 20th century. Now on the National Register of Historic Places, its second life as a graceful inn offers 10 elegant guest rooms, some with antique canopy beds, double-size Jacuzzis, private verandas, and fireplaces. After touring the town, relax in the sitting room with a glass of wine, gratis, and fresh-baked cookies. The new La Vita Grand spa adds to the pampering. $$–$$$.

President Abraham Lincoln Hotel. 701 E. Adams St.; (866) 788-1860, (217) 544-8800; www.presidentabrahamlincolnhotel.com. If you're looking for affordable lodging within walking distance of attractions, this 316-room hotel makes the cut. $–$$.

State House Inn. 101 E. Adams; (217) 528-5100; www.thestatehouseinn.com. Though a bit younger than some of Springfield's notable attractions and accommodations, the State House Inn is historic in its own right. A celebrated relic of 1960s design, it underwent a total renovation in 2003, but retained the color schemes and styles that made it such a fashionable hit when it originally opened and makes it a retro success today. Complimentary full breakfast, shuttle service to area attractions, fitness center, and cocktail lounge too. $$.

west

day trip 01

west

from malls to mom-and-pops:
schaumburg, il; rockford, il

Schaumburg might be the butt of some city-centric jokes, but once there, you'll be duly smitten with its shopping extravaganza and surprised by its more natural features. Rockford's main drag may seem ubiquitous, but a closer look reveals charming historic homes, woodsy settings, the pretty Rock River, and a downtown making a comeback with its renovated museum complex.

schaumburg

This western suburb was named by and for the German population that put it on the map beginning in the 1830s. Not long after, Schaumburg saw the inklings of its future mall-dom with the opening in 1858 of Schaumburg Centre, a market with general stores, cheese factories, a cobbler, a blacksmith, and other sundry services. Now, of course, it's a shopaholic's dream come true: 275 stores at Woodfield Mall, strip malls full of every chain store you can possibly think of, and a 458,000-square-foot IKEA store that could suck you in for an entire day if you let it (just stay on target and don't let the impulse-buy bins hypnotize you). But there's a softer side of Schaumburg too, so go discovering. By the way, I didn't include the endless chain restaurants here, because you know what they are.

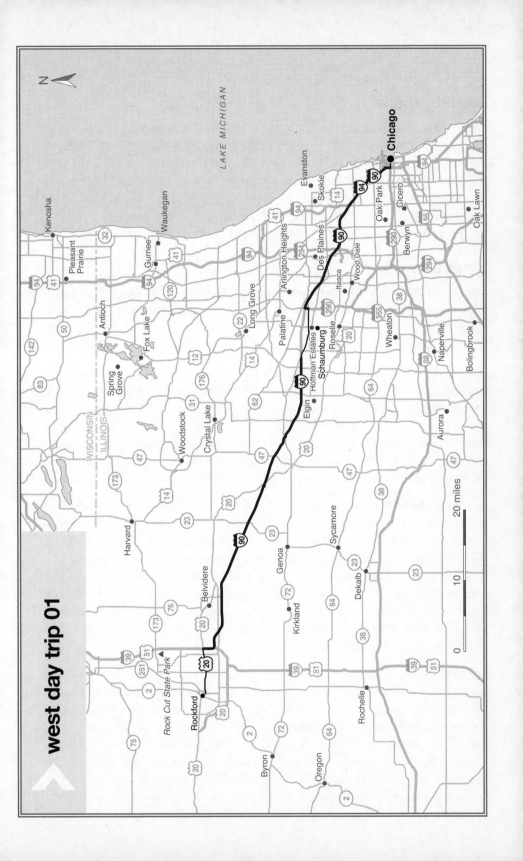

getting there

Take I-90/I-94 west and continue following I-90 west. Follow the signs to I-290 east/IL 53 south. Keep right as you approach signs for Golf Road via Woodfield Road. Exit to the frontage road and merge to make a right onto Woodfield Road heading west. Continue on Woodfield Road past Woodfield Mall and get into the left lane. Cross Meacham Road and turn left into the visitor bureau parking lot. Once you're in town, you can also park in one major destination (like Ikea), hop the free Schaumburg Trolley (Fri through Sun; daily during Christmas shopping), and travel to 11 other locations; call (847) 923-3880 for details.

where to go

Woodfield Chicago Northwest Convention Bureau. 1375 E. Woodfield Rd., Suite 120; (847) 490-1010; www.chicagonorthwest.com. This is your one-stop shop for coupons, guides, maps, and package-deal info. Online and on your smart phone, you'll also find numerous podcasts about the area, as well as coupons and a complete visitor guide.

Alexian Field & Flyers Baseball. 1999 Springinsguth Rd.; (847) 891-2255; www.flyers baseball.com. Major points for this unaffiliated Minor League team. They've got a success-ful team, with shortstop Travis Brown earning the Northern League's top defensive player award two years running, and a successful recipe for family fun on the cheap—try 5 bucks for lawn seats (remember to pack a blanket). Bearon, the enthusiastic mascot, peps up the fans and is eager to pose for photos, shake little kids' hands, and give out prizes. The field even has a full bar and a decent restaurant. Games May through Sept. Prices vary.

Legoland Discovery Center. Streets of Woodfield, 601 N. Martingale Rd.; (847) 592-9700; www.legolanddiscoverycenter.com. Enter under the giant Lego giraffe into a 30,000-square-foot world of Legos, the first one in the United States. Even more than an impressive showcase of Legos and Duplos—there are elaborate structures throughout—Legoland boasts an indoor amusement park of rides, 4-D movies, a mini factory tour, and, yes, bins brimming with building pieces and even giant rubberized Legos for the littlest ones. My daughter said she was scared on the Dragon Ride, but then we did it twice. Forewarning on two things here: The staff is strict about ride height limits, and the exit takes you through the tantalizing gift shop. Admission. Open daily.

Lynfred Winery. 15 S. Roselle Rd., Roselle; (630) 529-WINE (9463); www.lynfredwinery .com. Less than 10 minutes south of Schaumburg on Roselle Road lies this well-known Midwest wine-making superstar. Fred Koehler, now considered the grandfather of Illinois wineries, turned his hobby into his business in 1979 and has raised it into an award-winning winery. Named for Fred and his wife, Lynn, it's now considered the oldest and largest continuously operating winery in the state, producing more than 50 varietals, including an award-winning plum wine, Seyval Blanc, and Cabernet Shiraz, among many others. Take a tour and enjoy the tastings—you get seven, which change each month, and on Saturday and Sunday include cheese pairings at an additional charge. Then relax with a glass at the gazebo, porch, or heated benches, or stay the night at the Lynfred Bed and Breakfast, a luxurious experience that caps off the visit quite wonderfully. Fee.

Medieval Times Dinner & Theater. 2001 N. Roselle Rd.; (888) WE-JOUST (935-6878), (847) 882-1496; www.medievaltimes.com. This grand castle whose turrets peek over I-90 has been a longtime family and birthday party destination for a reason. Its live show set in 11th-century Spain leaves audiences (the under-12 set, especially) wide-eyed, with its long-haired knights riding handsomely decorated horses, its beautiful princess, and its spectacular lighting and musical score. Carefully choreographed duels incorporate authentic swords, lances, battle-axes, and fearsome bolas—you can't help but hoot and holler for your hero. If that's not all, everyone gets to eat the dinner feast with their hands because, much to kids' delight (and parents' chagrin), there weren't eating utensils back in the 11th century. Call for schedule. Admission varies depending on package.

Spring Valley Nature Center & Heritage Farm. 1111 E. Schaumburg Rd.; (847) 985-2100; www.parkfun.com. Get in touch with Schaumburg's natural side, as well as its historical German roots, on a stroll along the nature center's winding trails traversing 135 acres of fields, wildflowers, forests, marshes, and streams. At the Heritage Farm, costumed interpreters of the late 19th century tell tales of days gone by, of farming and butter-churning, cooking, and even playing. It's all very hands-on, so go ahead and stroke the sleek cheeks of the horses. The visitor center features an observation tower, natural history exhibits, a library, and a gift shop. On most Sunday afternoons, the Merkle log cabin is open for an afternoon sip of tea by the fireplace, and docents are available to answer questions. Bonus: Paths are stroller- and wheelchair-friendly. Nature center open daily; Heritage Farm closed Dec through Feb. Free.

The Streets of Woodfield. 601 N. Martingale Rd.; (888) 564-6401; www.thestreetsof woodfield.com. Right across from Woodfield Mall, but with a different feel altogether, this outdoor mall gets its character from charming street lights, fountains and ponds, wrought-iron grating, brick pavers, and street-sign-like signage. Tenants are storefront, including Crate and Barrel and Carson Pirie Scott, plus a GameWorks, the Legoland Discovery Center, and a movie multiplex.

Trickster Gallery. 190 S. Roselle Rd.; (847) 301-2090; www.trickstergallery.org. Often relegated to stereotypes and history books, Native American artists reveal the real picture in the context of the modern world in this Native American–operated and –focused arts center, the only one of its kind in the state. Breaking out of the norm, it features exhibits from contemporary artists (post-1960s) who paint a vivid and multifaceted picture of Native Americans today. Open Tues through Sat. Admission.

Woodfield Mall. 5 Woodfield Mall; (847) 330-1537; www.shopwoodfield.com. More than 275 stores, including five big-time anchors: Nordstrom, Macy's, Lord & Taylor, JCPenney, and Sears. Dining options include Texas de Brazil, Cheesecake Factory, P.F. Chang's, and Stir Crazy Café.

where to eat

Finn McCool's. 1941 E. Algonquin Rd.; (847) 303-5100; www.finnmccoolschicago.com. An offshoot of the Division Street rowdy house, this one's much the same. Named for a mythological Celtic hero, it caters to sports fans with more than 40 big flat-screens and one even bigger 50-inch screen—just tune the speakers right at your table to the game you're watching. Or compete in video game competitions with players in bars around the country using cordless satellite gadgets. On Thursday kick back with your beer and some acoustic live tunes. As for the food, It's a pretty extensive menu, heavy on steak and burgers, but also including a turkey clubhouse sandwich with brown sugar bacon, lake perch fish fry, and buffalo shrimp. Or have nearby Moretti's pizza delivered right to your table. $.

Mad Mark's Pizza & Sports. 871 E. Algonquin Rd.; (847) 397-3100; www.madmarks pizzaandsports.com. Formerly known as Mad Mark's Mystic Pizza, this place wins raves not just for its fresh-made pizza, but also for its "broasted" chicken and its huge patio that can seat more than 350 people and offers pre- and post-dining activities: sand volleyball, cornhole toss, and a basketball court. The interior decor is comfortably woody with some kooky, space-themed light fixtures. The menu is, well, huge. Besides pizza and chicken, Mad Mark's serves loaded nachos, burgers—including one with Cajun spices and another topped with a fried egg—spicy shrimp tortillas, pulled-pork fajitas, coconut shrimp, and barbecue ribs. You get the idea. Daily specials include kids-eat-free Monday. $–$$.

Westwood Tavern & Tap. 1385 N. Meacham Rd.; (847) 969-9500; www.westwoodtavern .com. This upscale-casual spot pours 16 brews from the spigot and about two dozen more in bottles. Six coveted booths are outfitted, fittingly, with individual taps that offer a choice of two draft beers to serve yourself. While the entrance doesn't scream cozy, the spacious interior is all woodsy and warm. An outside patio with couches makes a perfect spot for hanging in warmer weather. You'll find the expected burgers, sandwiches, and salads, but also maki rolls and sushi. $–$$.

where to stay

Eaglewood Resort. 1401 Nordic Rd., Itasca; (877) 285-6150, (630) 773-1400; www .eaglewoodresort.com. If you really want to give your trip a getaway feel, stay the night at this 295-room Prairie Style–influenced resort 10 minutes from Schaumburg. Stay long enough, and you'll have time to hit the greens, a par-72 18-hole golf course that plays through hills and lakes, along with a six-lane bowling alley, heated skylit indoor pool and Jacuzzi, and 10,000-square-foot salon and spa featuring treatments like a rose quartz facial, mineral spring detox, reflexology, and Reiki. $$–$$$.

four swinging places

There are more than two dozen golf courses in and around the cities on this drive, and all skill levels and price points are represented. So toss your clubs in the trunk and get on the greens. These four will get you started.

1. Aldeen Golf Club & Practice Centre. *1902 Reid Farm Rd., Rockford; (888) 425-3336, (815) 282-4653; www.aldeengolfclub.com. Named by Golf magazine as one of the top 50 courses in the country for under $50, Aldeen features water hazards on 12 of the 18 holes, along with 62 sand bunkers.*

2. Poplar Creek Country Club. *1400 Poplar Creek Dr., Hoffman Estates; (847) 781-3682; www.poplarcreekcc.com. Considered one of the area's best public greens, this 18-hole, par-70 course is just west of Schaumburg. It also has a 55-tee lighted driving range.*

3. Schaumburg Golf Club. *401 N. Roselle Rd., Schaumburg; (847) 885-9000; www.parkfun.com, www.schaumburggolf.com. This park district course has 27 holes, a driving range, two practice greens, a pro shop, and a clubhouse.*

4. TopGolf Chicago. *699 W. Thorndale, Wood Dale; (630) 595-GOLF (4653); www.topgolfusa.com. About 10 miles from Schaumburg, this isn't straight golf, but rather high-tech tee-up competition. Microchips in every ball track your shot as you aim for targets from 20 to 250 yards away. Mini-golf course too.*

Lynfred Winery Bed & Breakfast. 15 S. Roselle Rd., Roselle; (630) 529-WINE (9463); www.lynfredwinery.com. The Lynfred Winery doesn't stop at simply welcoming visitors to their winery; they invite people to stay the night in superior style and luxury. Suites decorated to reflect wine countries around the globe—America, Italy, France, and Germany—do not skimp on comforts. They treat you to heated floors, heated towel racks, and wood-burning fireplaces. Take full advantage of your situation with a private wine cellar tour (included); a premium wine-tasting with fruit, cheese, and homemade chocolate truffles; and a gourmet breakfast. $$$.

rockford

When I visited Rockford, I got a T-shirt that touts the city's new motto: "Real. Original." And they've got it right. It's not a glamorous or glitzy city, but simply a midsize Midwestern community that has gone through some ups and downs and has made a commitment to self-improvement. Even on its snowiest, bitterest days (the city gets about 35 inches of snow on average annually), there's a warm spot at the CoCo Key Water Resort, along with warm welcomes at area restaurants and fascinating and fun museums.

getting there

Take I-90 to the Rockford Business 20/State Street exit (not US 20, which comes up first). Stay right as you exit and merge onto E. State Street heading west. Stay on State Street for about 7 miles. The Rockford Area visitor bureau is located at the second intersection after you cross the bridge at State and Main Streets (it's the intersection directly after you cross Wyman Street). If you're staying at the Clock Tower Resort, just continue straight off the State Street exit, and you'll find a community information center inside.

where to go

Rockford Area Convention & Visitors Bureau. 102 N. Main St.; (800) 521-0849, (815) 963-8111; www.gorockford.com. Get guides, city and walking tour maps, and suggested itineraries. There are also visitor kiosks filled with informational brochures in the museums and some hotels. Open Mon through Fri.

Anderson Japanese Gardens. 318 Spring Creek Rd.; (815) 229-9390; www.anderson gardens.org. Anderson isn't the first name you'd associate with a Japanese garden, but it was local resident John Anderson's vision, determination, enchantment with Japanese culture—and the swampy land near his home—that led to the formation of this serene 12th-century-style space. Since 1978, renowned Portland-based landscape designer Hoichi Kurisu has developed, enhanced, and tended to Anderson's 12 acres of quiet paths, calm pools, hidden waterfalls, and trickling streams, replete with lanterns, pagodas, gazebo, a teahouse, and more. Open daily May 1 through Oct; off-season hours are weather-dependent. Nominal admission (Thurs is a donation day).

CoCo Key Water Resort. 7801 E. State St.; (866) 754-6958, (815) 398-6000; www.coco keywaterresort.com. Splish-splash like a kid at this tropical-themed indoor water park, the largest in the state. Scream down a spiraling water slide (you go shockingly fast), bob around in the huge indoor-outdoor whirlpool, take a fast-paced tube ride or a leisurely one along the lazy river. A huge suspended bucket dumps hundreds of gallons of water every few minutes—a bell alerts the crowd to its imminent drenching, and some kids race to it, while others (mostly grown-ups) dash out of its way. The diaper set is not neglected here: There's a zero-depth wading pool with tame slides too, although my youngest liked dipping her toes into the hot tub best. And parents, never fear: A diligent staff of lifeguards patrols the entire 60,000-square-foot space. You can include this in an overnight stay at the attached Clock Tower hotel or purchase first-come, first-served day passes. Open daily. Admission varies by season (if you're not planning to get wet, there's just a $5 charge to enter).

Lockwood Park Trailside Equestrian Centre & Children's Farm. 5201 Safford Rd.; (815) 987-8809; www.rockfordparkdistrict.org. Millie, a 21-by-19-foot cow sculpture, welcomes visitors to the children's farm at this 94-acre park district facility. For kids ages 1 to 7, pony rides are a favorite; kids 8 and up can take trail rides. Plus, there are hiking and biking paths, playgrounds, tractor-pulled hayrides, and more. Open daily. Free.

Riverfront Museum Park. Three museums along the Rock River plus a radical wooden play structure make up this must-do.

Burpee Museum of Natural History. 737 N. Main St.; (815) 965-3433; www .burpee.org. Did you know that Rockford was under water millions of years ago? This tidy, four-floor museum takes you back to the town's sea years, displaying fossils from the era and a 3-D build-out of what it might have looked like then. Browse beautiful geological finds from the area and discover Rockford's Native American heritage. The museum's newest resident, and the hands-down highlight, is Jane the 21-foot juvenile T. rex skeleton. She's joined by Homer, a young triceratops whose bones you can see being prepared by the pros in the downstairs viewing lab. Open daily. Admission.

Discovery Center Museum. 711 N. Main St.; (815) 963-6769; www.discoverycenter museum.org. If you think you can quickly pop in and out of this children's museum, think again. There are 250 hands-on exhibits on two floors. The recently enhanced and expanded Tot Spot alone kept my two little ones entertained for almost an hour in its pretend pizza parlor, kid-size house, train, car mechanic's station, dollhouse, and more. The Ag-Zibit lets kids climb aboard a real tractor, hook up cows to be milked, gather eggs, and send soybeans down a conveyor belt. In the sports area they can measure the speed of their pitch and snowboard in virtual reality. *Child* magazine listed the museum fourth in a top-10 list of best children's museums in the country (ahem, Chicago's museum wasn't included). Your kids might just rank it number one. Open daily. Admission.

Rockford Art Museum. 711 N. Main St.; (815) 968-2787; www.rockfordartmuseum .org. Starting in 1913 as a local arts group, the RAM collection now includes more than 1,600 pieces focusing on 20th-century American art, American Impressionist paintings, photography, works by self-taught African-American artists, and contemporary glass. The 17,000-square-foot, multi-gallery museum stages exhibits from the permanent collection as well as rotating temporary shows. Open daily. Admission (children under 12 free; Tues is donation day).

Rock Cut State Park. 7318 Harlem Rd., Loves Park; (815) 885-3311; www.dnr.illinois .gov. Just 10 minutes north of Rockford you'll find this dreamland for outdoorsy types. Within its 3,092 acres lie a 162-acre lake for fishing, canoeing, and kayaking; a 50-acre swimming lake; 13 miles of horseback riding (no rentals), 23 miles of mountain biking, 40 miles of hiking; and the list goes on. Be on the lookout for wild critters and wildflowers, along with remnants of the railroad that gave this park its name—rock-blasting left lasting marks. Stay the night in the fully equipped campgrounds and start all over the next day. Open daily. Free.

Tinker Swiss Cottage Museum & Gardens. 411 Kent St.; (815) 964-2424; www.tinker cottage.com. Not a cottage by any stretch of the imagination, this unique 1865 Swiss-style home was built for Rockford businessman and mayor Robert Tinker, who lived here for 75 years, then donated it to the Rockford Park District along with all his family's belongings. In 1943 it opened as a museum, showcasing the ornate woodwork, murals, sculptures, spiral staircase, and the Tinkers' own furnishings and even clothing. Ongoing restoration efforts have included rebuilding a suspension bridge across Kent Creek and re-creating a rose garden in front of the home. Open Mar through Dec (closed Jan and Feb). Tours Tues through Sun. Admission (Tues free).

where to eat

Bandana's Bar-B-Q. 5494 E. State St.; (815) 226-2444; www.bandanasbbq.com. Lasso your posse and high-tail it over to this outstanding barbecue restaurant. The meats are hand-rubbed and smoked in-house, but the house isn't smoky; everything comes sauce-less, but nothing is dry. The company cred comes from its Missouri headquarters (24 of its 32 locations are also in the Show Me State), and it certainly lives up to Kansas City's best barbecue. Four sauces in squeeze bottles on the table add sweet and smoky, spicy, hot, or mustard-tangy to your chicken, ribs, pork, beef, or turkey. Sides like sweet corn, crunchy coleslaw, and buttery garlic bread are equally mouthwatering. Extra napkins, please. $–$$.

Chocolat by Daniel. 211 E. State St.; (815) 969-7990; www.chocolatbydaniel.com. Chicago has loads of sweet shops for chocoholics, but it's OK, you can get your fix here too. Daniel Nelson hand-makes his confections, which are melt-in-your-mouth delicious without containing any artificial flavors, corn syrup, wax, or preservatives. From the dark 70 percent pure Venezuelan chocolate in the Rugged Adventurer truffle to the Swiss milk chocolate in the Swiss Pecan Torte to the white Belgian chocolate in the white chocolate raspberry cheesecake, Nelson finds the finest ingredients from around the world and creates truly addictive treats. Open Mon through Sat. $.

HearthRock Café. Benson Stone Co., 1100 11th St., 1st Floor; (815) 227-2000; www.bensonstone.com. Want some landscape brick or a barbecue grill along with that waffle or Caesar salad? Tucked into the first floor of a stonework showroom and shop—housed in a century-old historic building of hardwood floors, post-and-beam construction, and multiple working fireplaces—this breakfast and lunch spot serves up a light menu in a unique location. Open Mon through Sat for breakfast and lunch. $.

JMK Nippon. 2551 N. Perryville Rd.; (815) 877-0505. One side sushi, the other Japanese steakhouse, plus a cocktail lounge and karaoke room, this is one of the area's largest and most popular Asian eateries. For fresh-rolled sushi hit the cafe; for a performance of knife-wielding skill and artistry, sit at a *teppan* table where your chicken, shrimp, beef, and veggies are cooked up in front of your eyes. Open for lunch and dinner Tues through Sat, dinner only Sun and Mon. $$.

Lino's Restaurant. 5611 E. State St.; (815) 397-2077; www.linosrockford.com. Prepare to kick it Old World style at this family-run favorite since 1972. Opened by Italian immigrants Michaelino (thus, the name) and Pasqua Battista, Lino's is now run by sons Joe and Jim. The big, bustling space is divided into several distinct dining areas, including one raised and under a replica Leaning Tower of Pisa. Lots of trompe l'oeil and faux finishes make for an Italian piazza-like setting, and friendly, career servers make for comfortable dining. With a group, ordering from the Festa Dinner menu gets you loaded platters for sharing. The house salad comes topped with Romano-laden vinaigrette and slices of Italian sausage (never seen that before); steaks are cooked just right; the lasagna (a small is more than enough for one) is some of the best around; and ice cream comes with all entrees. Can't beat that. Open daily for dinner. $–$$.

Stockholm Inn. 2420 Charles St.; (815) 397-3534; www.stockholminn.com. Honoring the Swedish part of Rockford's history, this cheerfully decorated multiroom, 750-seat restaurant dates back to the 1940s. It has changed ownership and even locations several times, but has maintained its top-notch reputation for scrumptious renditions of Swedish pancakes and meatballs, pot roast, herring, and cabbage rolls. The extensive full menu also drifts to everything from hamburgers to chicken Parmesan to turkey sandwiches and Denver omelets. During football season, Swedish colors give way to shades of Bears, Packers, and other rival team jerseys and banners. Open Mon through Sat for breakfast, lunch, and early dinner; open Sun for breakfast. $.

where to stay

Clock Tower Resort & Conference Center. 7801 E. State St.; (877) 875-4697; www .clocktowerresort.com. The big attraction for staying at this Best Western is that it's connected to the CoCo Key Indoor Water Resort and day passes are an inexpensive upgrade to your room. Plus, there are a racquet club and indoor and outdoor pools, a restaurant, a pub, and a hair salon too. $$–$$$.

Copperstone Inn. 6702 Yale Bridge Rd.; (815) 629-9999; www.copperstoneinn.com. Sophisticated luxury comes in spades when you stay at this majestic 9,000-square-foot limestone home. Built in 1858 on 130 acres of countryside with gardens, ponds, and trails, its 6 richly decorated rooms feature private baths, some with fireplaces and private balconies. A small spa offers massage therapies. $$$.

day trip 02

west

charmed, we're sure:
galena, il; dubuque, ia

Glaciers took a detour around Jo Daviess County, meaning Galena was saved from typical Midwestern flattening and now greets visitors with actual hills, even some big enough for skiing—and no, not just cross-country. Nearby Dubuque draws its beauty largely from the Mississippi River. They both offer outdoor activity, some romance, and, yes, plenty of charm.

galena

The first time I visited Galena, I was in the heady beginnings of a relationship with my now-husband. Maybe my pitter-pattering heart had something to do with it, but I could swear that Galena had scented the air with romance. Probably more likely is the fact that more than 85 percent of the city's 19th-century buildings are listed on the National Register of Historic Places, and they still beat with the energy of shop and restaurant owners who care about their town and the people who care to visit.

getting there

This three-hour trip starts on I-90 west toward Wisconsin. From there, take the I-39/US 20 exit toward Rockford. Follow US 20 west. Through the small town of Elizabeth, US 20 changes names and curves to the left to Main Street, then Madison Street. When you reach Galena, veer right onto Bouthillier Street (signage will indicate to turn for "Visitor

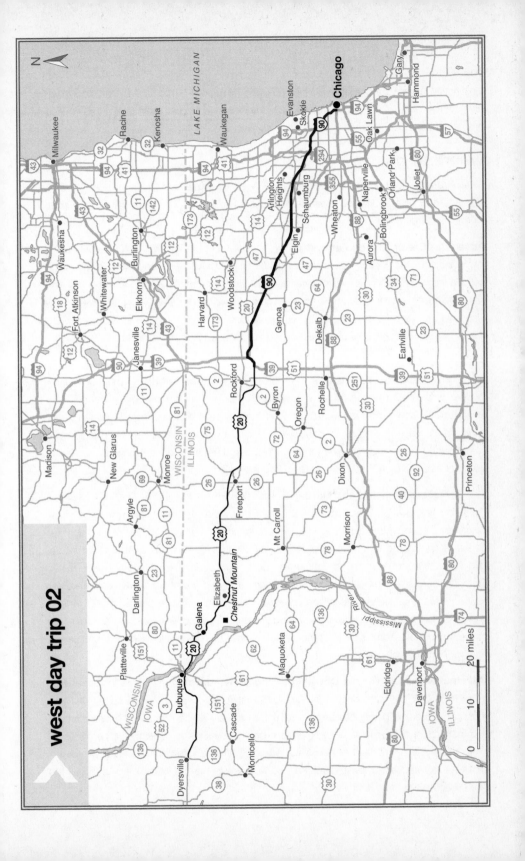

west day trip 02

Information"); there's a cemetery on the right here. At the bottom of the hill, take the first left onto Park Avenue. The visitor center is on the first floor of the Old Train Depot immediately on the right after turning.

where to go

Galena/Jo Daviess County Convention & Visitors Bureau. 101 Bouthillier St.; (877) GO GALENA (464-2536); www.galena.org. Get travel tips and resources about the area. Open Mon through Fri.

Adventure Creek Alpaca Farm. 9401 W. Hart John Rd.; (815) 777-4200; www.galena logcabins.com. Call out to Quincy, and he'll come right up to you, eager for attention. He and his fellow alpacas greet visitors warmly here, and, as guardians Ruth and Frank Netzel say, "We dare you to find a cuter animal"—you can take one for a walk for a small fee. They also own the site's Galena Log Cabin Getaway lodging. Their gift shop sells alpaca items that boast a fleece that's lanolin-free and warmer than wool. Open daily. Free.

Apple River Fort. 311 E. Myrtle, Elizabeth; (815) 858-2028; www.appleriverfort.org. About a 15-minute drive east of Galena is this replica of the fort erected during the Black Hawk War in 1832. The fort and cabins were rebuilt on their original footprint by volunteers, who toiled with the same tools and materials used in the original construction. Exhibits, a video, an interpretive center, and a trail now tell the story of the Native Americans and early white settlers who fought here. Once a month, guided stargazing and Native American storytelling take place here. Open Wed through Sun. Suggested donation.

The Belvedere Mansion and Garden Tour. 1008 Park Ave.; (815) 777-0747; www.bel vederemansionandgardens.com. In 1857 the *Galena Gazette* newspaper devoted some space to describing this extravagant, 22-room Italianate mansion, the home of J. Russell Jones, a steamboat magnate who befriended Ulysses S. Grant and Abraham Lincoln, and was later ambassador to Belgium. Crystal and stained-glass chandeliers, gilded Victorian mirrors and other decor, ornate woodwork, and a story of the Civil War era still fill the space. Plus, take note of the emerald velvet drapes made famous in *Gone With the Wind,* bought in an auction and displayed here. Tours and gardens open mid-May through mid-Nov. Admission (a combo ticket to tour the historic Dowling House is available for purchase as well).

Chestnut Mountain Resort Downhill Skiing/Snowboarding. 8700 W. Chestnut Rd.; (800) 798-0098; www.chestnutmtn.com. Don't let your ski-snob friends rip on Midwest mountains; there is plenty of downhill adventure to be had right here in Galena. Rentals and instruction are available. Plus, there are barely any lines for Chestnut Mountain's 19 runs across 220 acres built for all levels. A snowboard park features half-pipes, quarter-pipes, table tops, and rails. Exhausted? Bunk down in the 120-room hotel and call it a night. Prices vary.

Galena Cellars Vineyard & Winery. 4746 N. Ford Rd. (just off Stagecoach Trail), main office at 515 S. Main St.; (800) 397-WINE (9463); www.galenacellars.com. With the twice-named Illinois Winemaker of the Year Christine Lawlor-White at the helm of this family-owned winery, it's no wonder that since it first produced 500 gallons of cherry wine in 1976, Galena Cellars keeps getting better—and bigger. They now bottle 60,000 gallons of 40 varieties of dry red, semidry, fruit, dry white, semisweet, dessert, and sparkling wines. Tours let you in on the vineyard operations and tastings. You can even have your bottles custom-labeled. Open daily May through Oct, Sat and Sun in Nov. Fee for tours.

Galena Trolley Tours. 314 S. Main St.; (815) 777-1248; www.galenatrolleys.com. The quaint way to tour the town, this trolley operation offers four tours, the most time-efficient one being the one-hour narrated Non-Stop Tour that rolls you past nearly all of Galena's historic district. A 2½-hour Tour of Homes lets you off at three historic mansions, including the Dowling House, the Belvedere, and Grant's Home. Trolleys also go out at night for a Haunted Tour and out of downtown for a Wine and Country tour. Daily Apr through Nov, seasonal hours Feb through Mar. Admission varies.

charm to go

Nary a mall in site, Galena does it small scale, homegrown, and one-of-a-kind. Check out these local favorites along the Main Street that Midwest Living *magazine voted one of the country's best.*

1. The Atomic Toy Co. *211 S. Main St.; (815) 777-8697; www.theatomictoyco .com. Recall the good old days with new toys replicated from the 1930s to 1970, like tin robots, wooden ABC blocks, harmonicas, Chinese finger traps, and more.*

2. Galena Candle & Bath Company. *114 N. Main St.; (815) 777-3060; www .galenacandle.com. Breathe in the deliciousness of natural soy candles, bath beads, scented bubble bath, lotions, and other doze-inducing products.*

3. Galena Canning Company. *106 S. Main St.; (815) 777-2882; www.galena canning.com. More than 200 award-winning jams, jellies, salsas, sauces, and more, packaged in-house by chef Ivo Puidak.*

4. Galena Garlic Company. *311 S. Main St.; (815) 777-9625; www.galenagarlic .com. More yummy stuff, including the title fave, naturally grown gourmet garlic, plus blends, rubs, seasonings, olive oils, balsamic vinegars, and cookbooks to use with all your new ingredients.*

Old Blacksmith Shop. 245 N. Commerce St.; (815) 777-9129; www.galenahistory museum.org. In the mid-19th century, blacksmiths kept very busy shoeing horses, but as cars took over the streets, they put most blacksmiths out of business. Considered Galena's last remaining blacksmith shop, this renovated 1897 structure was owned by Willard Richardson, who worked here from 1929 to 1979. His original tools and equipment are on display, and contemporary blacksmiths regularly visit to work so you can watch the tools in action too. Open Fri through Mon May through Oct. Suggested donation.

Ulysses S. Grant's Home. 500 Bouthillier St.; (815) 777-3310; www.granthome.com. You get the sense that the Civil War hero and 18th US President could walk right into his former Galena home, a stunning example of an 1860 Italianate structure. Much of the furnishings and decor actually did belong to the Grant family, as Grant's children donated the house in 1904 as a museum and tribute to Grant. Both a National Historic Landmark and on the National Register of Historic Places, the home is open for tours. Open May through Oct. Free.

where to eat

The Flying Horse. 216 S. Commerce St.; (815) 777-4800; www.theflyinghorse.com. A relative newcomer to the Galena dining scene, The Flying Horse takes an upscale-but-comfortable approach to its decor and its menu. Tin ceilings, hardwood floors, dim lighting, and white tablecloths complement the menu of fresh seafood and grilled steaks. The crab cake appetizer scores high, as does the "A to Z martinis" list, which literally offers 26 creative libations. Open for dinner Tues through Sun. $$–$$$.

Fried Green Tomatoes. 213 N. Main St.; (815) 777-3938; www.friedgreen.com. Nothing to do with the movie, this downtown spot in the 1838 stone Dowling building serves up contemporary takes on Italian favorites (Italians were eating fried green tomatoes long before the American South, don't you know) and boasts a big bite of history. In fact, Ulysses S. Grant's father once owned a leather shop here. It also housed the county court, a saloon, a grocery store, and a theater; the curly wall stencils, part original and part copied, are relics of the theater. Entrees include lobster ravioli, tortalloni, seared scallops, pork osso bucco, duck breast, and an espresso-encrusted fillet. Of course, the must-try is the eponymous fried green tomatoes appetizer. Open daily for dinner. $$–$$$.

Galena Beer Company. 227 N. Main St.; (815) 776-9917; www.galenabrewery.com. Once a small town with a whopping nine breweries, Galena hadn't seen a home-turf beer for more than 80 years. After learning that their new home had once operated as the Illinois Brewery and still had two fermenting cellars, Galena residents Warren and Kathy Bell decided to bring back the town's brewery roots. Their first beer was produced in Wisconsin, but since the revitalization of an old WWII munitions battery factory in 2010 as the Galena Beer Company, they now brew it right in town, viewable through glass walls from the brewpub. Along with Miner's Treasure Amber Ale, Anna Belle's India Pale, and other craft brews, they offer an enticing tapas menu, plus fancy sandwiches and salads. Open Mon, Wed through Sun (closed Tues); during winter, also closed Wed. $–$$.

Little Tokyo. 300 N. Main St.; (815) 777-8883; www.littletokyoofgalena.com. Being the first traditional Japanese restaurant in Galena, Little Tokyo could have just been mediocre. After all, a lot of area residents had never tried sushi. But owner Amy Chen made it superb. The fish is fresh, the saki is artisanal, and the raves (even from seasoned sushi eaters) are consistent. $$.

where to stay

DeSoto House Hotel. 230 S. Main St.; (800) 343-6562, (815) 777-0090; www.desoto house.com. Abraham Lincoln once spoke from the balcony of this 1855 hotel, the oldest operating hotel in Illinois. Named for Hernando DeSoto, the first European to discover the Mississippi River, its 55 Victorian-style rooms are also named for people important to Galena's history. $$$.

Eagle Ridge Resort & Spa. 444 Eagle Ridge Dr.; (800) 892-2269, (815) 777-5000; www .eagleridge.com. You'll want for nothing at this upscale resort sheltered among 6,800 acres of gorgeous rolling countryside. Stay in one of its 80 guest rooms in the main inn or one of the 300-plus 1- to 8-bedroom villas, most with wood-burning fireplaces. Tee off at one of the 4 championship golf courses, float around the 220-acre Lake Galena in a canoe or pontoon, book a massage at the Stonedrift Spa, lounge at the heated indoor pool, or rent a bike and tool around the 20 miles of surrounding trails. There are even hot-air balloon rides at sunrise and sunset. $$$.

Goldmoor Inn. 9001 W. Sand Hill Rd.; (800) 255-3925, (815) 777-3925; www.goldmoor .com. It doesn't get much better than this. Situated for ultimate views on a bluff above the Mississippi River, 3 cottages, 2 authentic log cabins, and 12 suites all immerse you in the lap of luxury. Each is lavishingly and lovingly furnished in varying themes, such as the Mississippi suite with its breathtaking views of the mighty river, and the Irish cottage with greens and purples and a fireplace made with river boulders. Every option pampers with top-level amenities like terry robes and heated towel bars. Honeymoons, baby-moons, and anniversaries are extra special here. $$$.

dubuque

This Mississippi River city at the intersection of Iowa, Illinois, and Wisconsin (the Tri-Cities) got quite a pat on the back recently when *Forbes* listed it among "The Best Small Cities to Raise a Family." The distinction takes into account things like education level, median household income, rate of home ownership, housing affordability, and average commute time. I bet it doesn't hurt either that there's been a concerted effort since the late 1990s to revitalize the riverfront, which now bustles with activity from casinos to a winery. The city still keeps its history intact too, claiming the first permanent white settler in the area, Julien Dubuque; check out where he was buried, now amid an outdoor scenic area.

getting there

Take US 20 west. When you cross the Julien Dubuque Bridge into Iowa, take a right onto Locust Street. Take another right onto 4th Street and then a right onto Main Street. This will take you to the Dubuque Chamber of Commerce office, about a 20-minute drive.

where to go

Dubuque Area Chamber of Commerce. 300 Main St., Suite 200; (800) 798-4748, (563) 557-9200, welcome center direct line: (800) 798-8844; www.dubuquechamber.com.

Diamond Jo Casino. 301 Bell St.; (563) 690-4800; www.diamondjo.com. Located along the riverfront, this land-based casino has all the expected games and slots, plus a bowling alley, a dueling piano bar, and a comedy club. Open daily.

Dubuque River Rides. 500 E. 3rd St.; (563) 583-8093; www.dubuqueriverrides.com. Experience the Mississippi River on the *Spirit of Dubuque,* Iowa's only authentic paddle wheeler, or the *Miss Dubuque,* a modern yacht. Besides sightseeing, lunch, and dinner cruises, there are private charters, murder mystery cruises, and fall color lunch cruises. Operates May through Oct. Ticket prices vary.

Mines of Spain Recreation Area & E.B. Lyons Interpretive Center. 8991 Bellevue Heights Rd., access from US 52 South on the southern edge of Dubuque; (563) 556-0620; www.minesofspain.org, www.iowadnr.gov. Why Spain? Because Spain once owned this land, and in 1796, the first European to settle here, Julien Dubuque, received a land grant from Spain to work a 189-square-mile swath of land. Thus, it was dubbed the Mines of Spain. Dubuque is actually buried here, under a stone monument built in 1897. It's visible along one of the 11 trails in this 1,380-acre recreation area. The newly expanded E.B. Lyons Interpretive Center features exhibits about its history, flora, and fauna, as well as a bird and butterfly garden and a historic farm site. On the 21 miles of hiking trails, from a quarter-mile jaunt to some challenging 2- and 3-milers, there are numerous educational signs as you pass limestone bluffs, scenic overlooks, prairies, wetlands, and creeks. You might even spot some of the rare species here, including flying squirrels, bald eagles, and bobcats. In winter there are 5 miles of cross-country skiing paths. Interpretive center open daily mid-Apr through mid-Oct, then Mon through Fri; Mines of Spain park open daily.

Mystique Casino & Dubuque Greyhound Park. 1855 Greyhound Park Dr.; (800) 373-3647; www.dgpc.com. This Port of Dubuque facility began as the nation's first nonprofit greyhound racetrack and expanded to include casino games, then got a renovation and renaming in 2009 to feature a French theme, a steakhouse, and an entertainment and events center. Open daily.

National Mississippi River Museum & Aquarium. 350 E. 3rd St.; (800) 226-3369, (563) 557-9545; www.mississippirivermuseum.com. The river runs alongside this two-for-your-money museum dedicated to river history, people, and wildlife. The highlight? A 40,000-gallon tank that holds sharks, rays, and schooling fish that are native to the mouth of the Mississippi. This water wonder also boasts six aquariums filled with river fish, turtles, ducks, and more. Interactive exhibits feature a touch tank and a 1934 dredge boat used during WWII that welcomes you to walk its decks. Plus, check out the 4-D movie theater and a floating dock with steamboat artifacts. Open daily. Admission (extra fees for movies).

Stone Cliff Winery. Star Brewery Building, 700 Bell St.; (563) 583-6100; www.stonecliff winery.com. In 1996 Nan and Bob Smith decided to transform their traditional farm into a vineyard, and in 2001 they sold their first bottles to much acclaim. Sample some of the fruits of their labor at the tasting room, where five tastes get you a take-home engraved souvenir glass. Check out where the wine is made, stroll the adjacent Mississippi Riverwalk, and return in the evening (Thurs through Sat) for free live entertainment. Open daily. Free tours; fee for tastings.

where to eat

Catfish Charlie's River Club. 1630 E. 16th St.; (563) 582-8600; www.catfishcharlies dubuque.com. From the butter-brushed bread sticks to the salad dressing to the giant onion rings, even the pre-entrée part of your meal here is top-notch. The menu, divided into Fin Fish, Shell Fish, and Steaks and Such, has some standouts, including the bourbon salmon and the hickory-smoked pork ribs. Every seat in the house has a view of the river here, and the "Bikini Deck" is the hot spot in summer, especially for the popular Sunday brunch that wows diners with a feast of made-to-order omelets, biscuits and gravy, sausage, salads, beef, chicken, French toast, desserts, and the famous "Bloody Dozen" of Bloody Marys. Open daily for lunch and dinner, Sun brunch too. $–$$.

L. May Eatery. 1072 Main St.; (563) 556-0505; www.lmayeatery.com. This warm, welcoming bistro owned by sibling team Lea and EJ Droessler gets high marks for its delectable gourmet pizzas (try the Fig-tastic with a creamy Sauvignon Blanc sauce topped with figs, spicy Italian sausage, shallots, toasted pecans, mozzarella, goat cheese crumbles, and balsamic glaze). The seasonally changing menu also features other creative Italian dishes that have fresh written all over them, like vodka chicken and portobello and Parmesan ravioli. Or just go for drinks: An extensive beverage menu includes nearly 30 beers (most under 4 bucks, if you can believe it), a carefully edited wine list, and martinis like the Mississippi River—as the menu says, "dirty." Open Mon and Thurs through Sun for dinner. $$$.

Star Restaurant & Ultra Lounge. 600 Star Brewery Dr.; (563) 556-4800; www.dbq star.com. While Chicago shines pretty darn bright when it comes to steak, when you're in Galena, you go to the Star for stellar, hand-cut steaks. Dress them up peppercorn-encrusted with a blue cheese cream, Cajun style with maitre d' butter, or teriyaki-style. Other favorites in this sophisticated bilevel loft space include the burgers and barbecue pork ribs. In summer dine on the spacious patio overlooking the Mississippi and Dubuque Riverwalk. Or get cozy in the Ultra Lounge, with its trippy glowing bar top. Open daily for lunch and dinner. $–$$$.

where to stay

Hotel Julien. 200 Main St.; (800) 798-7098, (563) 556-4200; www.hoteljuliendubuque .com. Named for Dubuque's first European settler, this first-class downtown hotel began its life in 1839, seeing guests as illustrious as Abraham Lincoln, Buffalo Bill Cody, Mark Twain, and Al Capone. A sparkling renovation returned the hotel to its elegant glory, featuring 133 rooms and suites, an upscale restaurant, a lounge, an indoor pool, and an outdoor terrace. $–$$$.

worth the drive

Field of Dreams **Movie Site.** 28995 Lansing Rd., Dyersville; (888) 875-8404; www.fieldof dreamsmoviesite.com. About 25 miles west of Dubuque, you'll reach the field that Universal Studios literally built out of farmland owned by the Lansing family for over a century. The 1989 Kevin Costner movie has inspired tens of thousands of fans to "go the distance" and see for themselves where Shoeless Joe and his teammates appeared out of the cornstalks. Bring your own bat, ball, and glove and play catch with your kids, hit a few into the corn, or just take a seat on those famous bleachers, snap photos, and dream a little dream of your own. Get an "If you build it" souvenir T-shirt while you're there too. Don and Becky Lansing will continue to welcome thousands of visitors every year until they sell it and take their turn on the bleachers for a change. Open Apr through Nov. Free.

northwest

day trip 01

northwest

lake geneva

One of those gorgeous glacier-formed areas, Lake Geneva, Wisconsin (whose area also wraps in Fontana and Williams Bay), added its own man-made beauty when wealthy Chicagoans started building massive summer retreats around Geneva Lake—much like Newport, Rhode Island, resulting in its nickname the Newport of the West. Take a boat cruise or a walk around the lake to gawk at many of these mansions, like the 1901 Italianate, 18,000-square-foot Stone Manor, and the House in the Woods, built in 1906 under a circus tent as a surprise for the owner's wife. The lake itself is massive too, the second-deepest in Wisconsin at 152 feet at its deepest point, but small enough that if you wanted to, you could walk around the entire 21 miles. Or just lounge at the beach, on a chartered yacht, or with a cocktail at a waterfront eatery.

getting there

The easiest way to get up and over to Lake Geneva (and to skip the tristate tolls), about an hour and 45 minutes away, is to take I-90/I-94 west. Continue straight on US 41 toward Waukegan when I-94 splits off. Then merge back onto I-94 west. Take exit 344 toward WI 50/Kenosha/Lake Geneva. Turn left off the ramp at WI 50/75th Street. Turn left on Broad Street, which takes you to the corner of Wrigley Drive, where you'll find the visitor bureau.

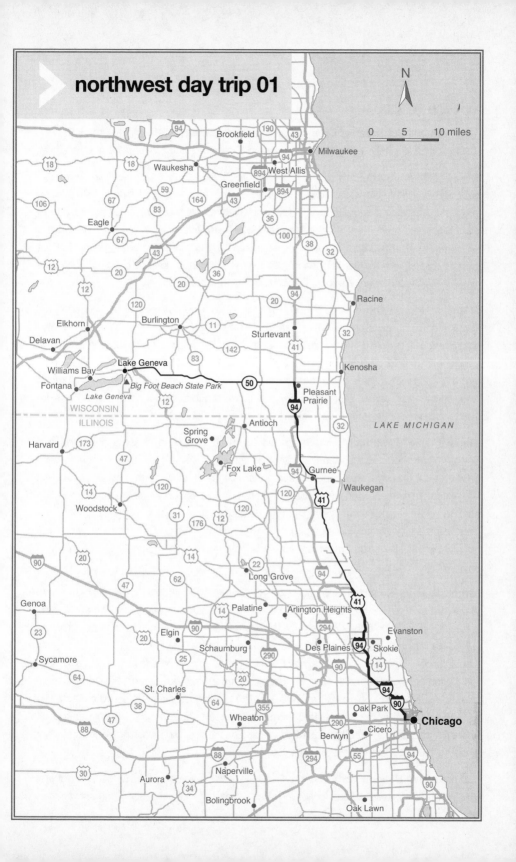

northwest day trip 01

N

0   5   10 miles

Brookfield

94

190

43

Milwaukee

18

18

Waukesha

West Allis

894

59

Greenfield

894

106

67

83

164

43

Eagle

67

36

36

12

20

36

100

38

32

20

20

94

Racine

Elkhorn

120

Burlington

11

Sturtevant

32

Delavan

142

41

Williams Bay

83

Lake Geneva

50

Kenosha

Fontana

Big Foot Beach State Park

Pleasant Prairie

Lake Geneva

12

94

WISCONSIN

LAKE MICHIGAN

ILLINOIS

Antioch

32

Harvard

173

Spring Grove

47

Fox Lake

94

Gurnee

Waukegan

14

120

41

120

Woodstock

31

12

120

176

90

20

14

22

Long Grove

94

47

62

Genoa

Palatine

Arlington Heights

41

23

14

294

Evanston

Elgin

90

Des Plaines

94

Skokie

Sycamore

20

Schaumburg

290

14

64

25

20

94

St. Charles

64

90

38

355

94

Wheaton

Oak Park

Chicago

47

290

88

Berwyn

Cicero

55

Naperville

88

294

30

34

90

Aurora

Bolingbrook

Oak Lawn

where to go

Lake Geneva Chamber of Commerce & Visitors Bureau. 201 Wrigley Dr.; (800) 345-1020, (262) 248-4416; www.lakegenevawi.com. Get info on the lake and town. Open daily.

Big Foot Beach State Park. 1550 S. Lake Shore Dr. (entrance); (262) 248-2528; www.dnr.wi.gov, www.wiparks.net. Not always rated super-high for camping, this park is still a lovely place for picnicking and hiking the 6.5 miles of leisurely trails, including a self-guided nature tour. Right next to the park is **Lake Geneva Boat Rentals** (262-249-9647) where you can rent a pontoon, speed boat or wave runner. Just across from the campgrounds is Big Foot Beach, a small non-lifeguarded beach. Call for rental pricing. Beaches have entrance fees per vehicle. Beach open Memorial Day through Labor Day.

Dancing Horses Show. 5065 WI 50, Delavan; (262) 728-8200; www.thedancinghorses.com. Hoofing it takes on new meaning at this razzle-dazzle show in a 300-seat climate-controlled theater amid a 40-acre woodland setting. Complete with elaborate costume changes for the four-legged performers, the 90-minute show highlights the pony prowess and skilled trainers. There are also an exotic bird show and water and light show; petting zoo; and wagon, camel, and pony rides. Open year-round; call for schedule. Admission; lunch and dinner shows offer special package pricing.

Geneva Lake Museum. 255 Mill St.; (262) 248-6060; www.genevalakemuseum.org. Take a walk back through Lake Geneva history on the brick Main Street exhibit of this quaint museum. On one side see a replica creamery, trading post, blacksmith, post office, general store, fire department, and more. On the other see four residential facades, representing the Georgian, Greek Revival, Italianate, and Second Empire styles of historic homes in the area. Kids will get a kick out of trying on helmets in the Military Room and checking out an old-fashioned schoolroom. Hours vary seasonally (closed from early Dec through early Mar). Admission.

Grand Geneva Resort & Spa. 7036 Grand Geneva Way; (800) 558-3417; www.grandgeneva.com. You don't have to get a room at this posh resort to partake in its many amenities. Four-season fun begins in winter at The Mountain Top for skiing and snowboarding. Its 18 downhill slopes feature a quarter-mile run and 211-foot vertical drop. Prefer to maintain your altitude? Go cross-country skiing or snowshoeing. There are also ice-skating and sledding (Mon through Thurs only for non-guests). When the snow melts, golf season starts on the 36 championship holes at The Brute and The Highlands courses. Year-round activities include trail rides from the on-site Dan Patch Stables (262-215-5303), body treatments, indoor tennis and a climbing wall at the Well Spa, and splish-splashing at the adjacent Moose Mountain Falls water park. Fees vary.

Lake Geneva Balloon Co. Meet at Lake Geneva Pie Company, 150 E. Geneva Square; (262) 206-3975; www.lakegenevaballoon.com. See the lake, the land, and the famous mansions from a sky-high perspective in these beautiful balloons at sunrise or sunset. To ensure a spot aboard the basket, purchase a certificate for one of the two packages in advance from the website. Notice the meeting place? An added bonus for sure. Age restriction is 8 and up, and pregnant women are not permitted. Runs May through Oct. Individual or couples rates.

Lake Geneva Beach. Wrigley Drive at Center Street (near Flatiron Park); (262) 248-3673. Popular with families, this public beach has a lifeguard on duty every day during the summer. Entrance fee.

Mail Boat Tour. Lake Geneva Cruise Line, Riviera Docks, 812 Wrigley Dr.; (800) 558-5911, (262) 248-6206; www.cruiselakegeneva.com. A Geneva Lake cruise is a must-do while you're in town, affording views of stunning lakefront estates. And for a one-of-a-kind waterway excursion, hitch a ride on the Mail Boat Tour, a tradition that began back in 1870. On the 150-passenger *Walworth*, you ride along as an agile mail carrier leaps off the moving boat, delivers and collects mail to some 60 homes around the lake, then swiftly jumps back on board. Talk about working under pressure! Operates June 15 through Sept 15. Reservations strongly recommended.

The Shore Path. Various entry points from Fontana to Lake Geneva; call the Geneva Lake Conservancy for more information, (262) 275-5700. Also simply called the "lake path," this 21-mile loop around Geneva Lake might not garner you an invitation into the majestic mansions you'll pass, but it does allow you to hike right across their private shoreline property and snap a few pics. Also along the route are several camps, a boatyard, the 60-building Lake Geneva campus of Aurora University, Yerkes Observatory, and even an old family tombstone. If 21 miles seems a bit much for one day, go as far as you'd like, then call the Geneva Lake Water Taxi (262-749-0882) for a lift back to your starting point. Free.

Watson's Wild West Museum. W4865 Potter Rd., Elkhorn; (262) 723-7505; www.watsons wildwestmuseum.com. Strap on your chaps, yank up your boots, don your 10-gallon, and mosey on over. About 10 minutes north on US 12, this quirky, kitschy attraction presents an OK Corral of a bygone era. Pan for gold in the faux mine, see some good ol' rope-twirling, sip a sarsaparilla in the saloon, and browse a bonanza of historic cowboy paraphernalia from the 1880s, including hundreds of antique tins, spurs, holsters, firearms, saddles, bear traps, and more than 2,000 branding irons. You don't actually have to dress up, but you'd blend in if you did. Open daily May through Oct (call ahead, as the museum closes to the public for bus tours and private outings). Free.

Yerkes Observatory. 373 W. Geneva St., Williams Bay; (262) 245-5555; astro.uchicago .edu/yerkes. If you attended a Chicago-area school like I did, it's likely you field-tripped to this astronomical icon. It's claim to fame? Built in 1897, the University of Chicago's Yerkes Observatory is the largest lens-type telescope in the world. In a lush, tree-filled 73-acre parklike setting, it rises to glorious stature, capped by a 90-foot dome, one of the largest ever built. You'll leave with stars in your eyes. Free tours every Sat at 10 a.m.; walk-in tours available daily (except Wed) for a donation; monthly evening observation sessions (fee) for visitors 8 years old and up. Tours free; donation suggested.

where to shop

The Cheese Box. 801 S. Wells St.; (800) 345-6105; www.cheesebox.com. Get your delicious Dairyland variety pack at this 60-plus-year-old institution. Carefully selected flavors include cheddars, blues, smoked, Gouda, brick, and Brie. Open daily.

Cornerstone Shop & Gallery. 214 Broad St.; (262) 248-6988; www.cornerstoneshoppe .com. A perennial local favorite, this spacious boutique gives you plenty of reasons to stop in. From its Hartmont and Beanstock soy candles to its paintings and pottery by Wisconsin artists to its spectacular holiday displays and gemstone jewelry, there's a broad range of home accent pieces, gifts, and souvenir ideas. Open daily.

where to eat

Popeye's. 811 Wrigley Dr.; (262) 248-4381; www.popeyeslkg.com. No, not the chain Popeyes, but a Lake Geneva classic, opened in 1972 by Nick and Veronica Anagnos as Popeye's Galley & Grog. Famous for its unbeatable lake views and its famous rotisserie meats—chicken, ribs, pork—slow-roasted on the enormous outdoor spit, Popeye's is often packed on summer weekends. Other mouthwatering, heart-wrecking plates include the "ultimate cheeseburger," two 6-ounce patties stacked with smoked bacon, cheese, lettuce, tomatoes, grilled onions, and mushrooms; roast prime rib; meal-worthy nachos; and French dip sandwiches. No fear, though, there are also a few lighter options, like smoked salmon spinach salad and whitefish. Open daily for lunch and dinner. $–$$.

Ryan Braun's Tavern & Grill. 430 Broad St.; (262) 248-0888; www.ryanbraunslg.com. Beware Cubs and Sox fans, this is Brewers land. So it makes sense that Milwaukee Brewers 2007 National League Rookie of the Year and two-time Silver Slugger–winner Ryan Braun lent his name to this Lake Geneva newcomer, soon after opening his Waterfront Grill in Milwaukee. It scores with an accessible menu of Italian-style dishes including angel hair pasta with steamed mussels, chicken or veal picatta, gnocchi with sweet Italian sausage, and artisan pizzas with fresh toppings like fontina cheese, torn basil, and artichoke hearts. Plus, tiramisu and gelato for a home-run finish. Open daily for lunch and dinner. $$.

Simple Café. 525 Broad St.; (262) 248-3556; www.simplecafelakegeneva.com. Chartreuse chairs and apricot-colored accent walls, light fixtures fashioned from found objects such as vintage market baskets, old milk bottles, and tin cookie cutters and lunch boxes. They all make for a cheerfully eclectic atmosphere that reflects the heart of this adorable cafe owned by neighborhood locals Lori and Tom Hartz. From mushrooms to apples, sausage to soda, nearly every ingredient in the omelets, pancakes, wraps, salads, and sandwiches travels just a short distance from a Wisconsin farm. Open daily for breakfast and lunch. $.

Sopra—An American Bistro. 724 W. Main St.; (262) 249-0800; www.soprabistro.com. An elegant choice for a leisurely meal, this downtown restaurant beckons with warm wood-framed storefront windows. Beautifully presented dishes change seasonally and might feature chef-owner Simon Cumming's creative takes on bistro dishes: pappardelle with braised beef shoulder, pork chop with chili marinade, and spicy seafood linguini. Open daily (except closed Wed) for lunch and dinner; during fall/winter season, open for dinner only. $$$.

where to stay

Abbey Resort & Avani Spa. 269 Fontana Blvd.; (800) 709-1323, (262) 275-9000; www.theabbeyresort.com. Totally renovated in 2005, with the 35,000-square-foot Avani Spa debuting in 2008, this resort has been a Lake Geneva fixture for more than 45 years. Its iconic 80-foot A-frame reception building serves as the nucleus for its 90 landscaped acres and pleasant guest rooms, all with patio or balcony. Don't want to spend a sunny day inside for a full spa treatment? Get a poolside chair massage. Dining options offer traditional fare, quick coffees and muffins, clubby lounging, and live music. No bored kids here, what with the bike rentals, board games, summer programming, year-round s'mores nights, indoor pool, and arcade. $$–$$$.

Diplomat Motel. 1060 Wells St.; (800) 264-5678, (262) 248-1809; www.budgethost-lake geneva.com. No frilly soaps, no triple-sheeted beds, no nonsense. That's what you get at this friendly and budget-friendly motel. An outdoor heated pool (feels good at over 80 degrees all the time) is a bonus. $.

Grand Geneva Resort & Spa. 7036 Grand Geneva Way; (800) 558-3417; www.grand geneva.com. In addition to all of the recreation and relaxation noted above, there are also actual guest rooms at this resort opened originally by Hugh Hefner in 1968 as a Playboy Club. In fact, 355 of them, all recently updated to include cool extras like TVs embedded in the bathroom mirrors. Looking for more? The premiere suites satisfy with fireplaces, wet bar, and oversize jet tubs. Six restaurants, plus live piano entertainment in the lobby every night and live DJ in the nightclub six nights a week. $$–$$$.

SevenOaks. 682 Wells St.; (262) 248-4006; www.sevenoakslakegeneva.com. Hosts Leon and Amanda Lavallin grew up in England and styled their posh bed-and-breakfast after gracious inns from across the pond, even naming the 9 suites after some of their favorite places, like Ascot and Canterbury. All rooms boast fireplaces and two-person tubs, perfect for a grown-up getaway—i.e., no kids allowed here—within walking distance of downtown Lake Geneva. $$$.

day trip 02

northwest

>>>

college cool:
madison, wi

madison

Between my sophomore and junior years at college, I spent nearly the whole summer laz-ing around the University of Wisconsin–Madison campus with my best friend who was a student there. We sun-worshipped at Lake Mendota. . . . Or was it Monona? The city is at the isthmus of both. We saw the Indigo Girls perform at the student union. We window-shopped along the State Street pedestrian mall that links Capitol Square with the university. And we drank more beer than I care to remember. Seeing it now, it surprised me to realize that there's a whole world of culture here too. And how did I miss the amazing farmers' market? With more than 40,000 students at UW-Madison, the city pulses year-round with activity. Although, like Chicago, Madison's winters are brutal, they're also beautiful, with steam floating off the area's five frozen lakes.

getting there

Start out on I-90/I-94 west toward Wisconsin. At the split between I-90 and I-94, stay left on I-90 W/the Kennedy. Take exit 142A toward US 12/US 18 W/Madison. Take exit 263 and continue along John Nolen Drive; then turn left at Blair Street. Stay right, and turn right at Washington Avenue to the visitor bureau.

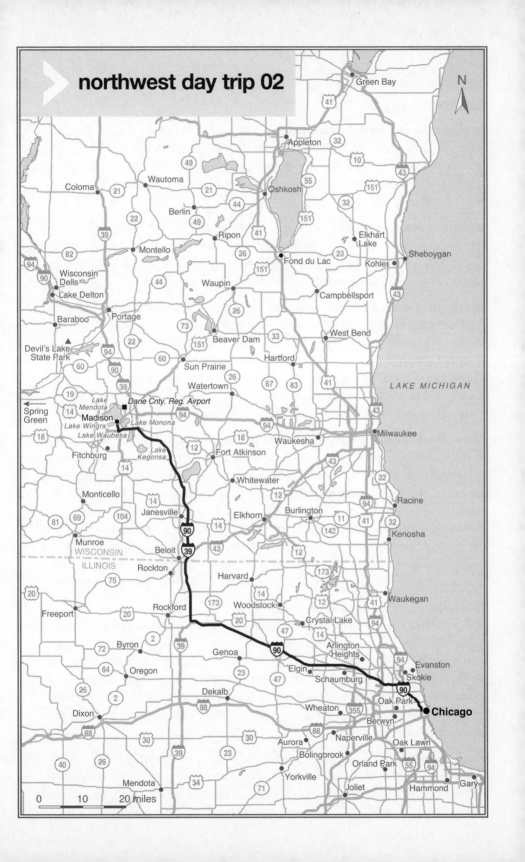

where to go

Madison Convention & Visitors Bureau. 615 E. Washington Ave.; (608) 255-2537; www.visitmadison.com. Pick up brochures and maps of attractions, bike paths, and dining destinations. There is also a Welcome Center at 21 N. Park St. (608-262-4636), which is a partnership between the CVB and the University of Wisconsin–Madison. The centers are both open Mon through Fri.

Downtown Madison Visitor Center. 452 State St.; (608) 512-1342; www.visitdowntown madison.com. This new center is located in the renovated Elizabeth Link Peace Park. It's staffed by downtown ambassadors, who share sightseeing and dining information and tips to navigating downtown. There's also a public restroom, a rare commodity. Open daily.

Budget Bicycle Center. 1230 Regent St.; (608) 251-8413; www.budgetbicyclectr.com. Madison claims to have more bicycles than cars, and they take full advantage of the nearly 100 miles of paths. So join the cycling scene and rent a bike to pedal around town or beyond. Mountain bikers can head over to Kettle Moraine State Forest, Devil's Lake, Blue Mound State Park, and other areas, while road riders can do flatter Glacial Drumline State Trail, Badger State Trail, and Ice Age National Scenic Trail. Get a bike path map from the visitor bureau or the welcome center.

Dane County Farmers' Market. Locations change seasonally: Early Jan through mid-Apr: at the Madison Senior Center, 330 W. Mifflin St.; mid-Apr through early Nov: at Capitol Square; mid-Nov through mid-Dec: at Monona Terrace, 1 John Nolen Dr.; (608) 455-1999; www.dcfm.org. Ask any local what the best things about Madison are, and this farmers' market inevitably tops the list. Started back in 1972 with a handful of farmers, it now bustles year-round with 160 to 180 strictly producer-only vendors who bring their local fruits and vegetables, cheeses, meats, baked goods, flowers, pastas, preserves, and more. From January through April, start your market day at the Madison Senior Center with a full breakfast made from farmers' ingredients. Sat; call or visit the website for specific hours. Free.

Eplegaarden. 2227 Fitchburg Rd., Fitchburg; (608) 845-5966; www.eplegaarden.com. About 10 miles south of Madison are a grouping of picture-perfect red barns and white picket fences and the welcoming duo of Vern and Betty Forest, who own this "selv plukk" farm with a Norwegian accent. Depending on the time of year, you can pick raspberries, an amazing number of apple varieties, and pumpkins, gourds, and squash. Of course, Halloween brings haunted things, hayrides, and music. While you're out picking, keep a lookout for the family of carved trolls in the orchard. Open July through Nov; call for specific days and hours. Prices vary.

Henry Vilas Zoo. 606 S. Randall Ave.; (608) 258-9490; www.vilaszoo.org. From 1904 to 1910, Col. William Vilas and his wife, Anna, donated land and money to create a park near Lake Wingra and named it in memory of their son Henry, who died at a young age. Their only requirement: that the park remain free. When animal exhibits appeared in 1911, thus launching the zoo, it was decided they would also be free. Like Lincoln Park Zoo, this free city zoo is an extraordinary asset to such a large urban environment. Besides big cats, black swans, snakes, goats, colobus monkeys, and more, the newest addition is the children's zoo featuring an electric train, a carousel, and a tree house climbing structure. Open year-round. Donations encouraged (free parking).

Madison Children's Museum. 100 N. Hamilton St.; (608) 256-6445; www.madisonchildrens museum.org. Madison moms and dads were decidedly giddy with the recent opening of this new and improved kid corral. It tripled the old museum's public space to 28,000 square feet, added on-site parking and two extra floors for future growth, and expanded the reach to entertain kids up to 12 years old. Pint-size Picassos go to town in the art studio; the Possible-opolis exhibit is tricked out with interactive, electronic, hands-on, brain-, and brawn-challenging exhibits. Up on the Rooftop Ramble, kids coo over the homing pigeons and

rock out

*Creepy. Bizarre. Amazing. Weird. They're all descriptions that have been bestowed on the **House on the Rock,** an ultimately indescribable architectural marvel-slash-museum of curiosities. It began in 1945 as Alex Jordan's Prairie Style take on a Japanese house built atop a 60-foot outcropping of rock. Over the years it swelled into a sprawling complex of buildings and gardens. Self-guided tours today take you on a surreal journey of more than 2 miles (it can take three hours), often through low-ceilinged and musty-smelling rooms jammed with odd collections that are at times whimsical—the largest carousel in the world (it's indoors and not rideable)—and at other times bordering on vulgar—above the carousel hang half-naked mannequins dressed with angel wings. Coin-operated music machines (some with robotic animation) pop up throughout and veer from quaint to disquieting. Other assortments include replica suits of armor, paperweights, Burma Shave signs, dolls and dollhouses, a three-story stacked bookcase, a scrimshaw, model airplane replicas, antique guns, and the world's largest cannon. Or take a death-defying stroll out into the Infinity Room, essentially a glassed-in 218-foot-long passage cantilevered over the valley below. During the winter holidays, more than 6,000 Santas of varying degrees of kitsch and craziness are scattered throughout. People debate whether the late reclusive and eccentric Jordan was brilliant or insane; but there's no arguing that his house is one-of-a-kind. Open year-round. Call or check online for schedule, which changes seasonally. Admission. House on the Rock, 5754 SR 23, Spring Green; (608) 935-3639; www.thehouseontherock.com.*

chicken coop. The Wildernest exhibit is specifically aimed at infants to 5-year-olds. Besides all the playful opportunities, the museum even hits the green mark by its repurposing of a former Montgomery Ward department store. Find out more about its eco-friendly factors on a monthly Green Building Tour (third Thurs of the month at 5 p.m.). Open daily. Admission.

Madison Lakes. Call the visitor bureau for more information, (608) 255-2537. Sometimes more is better. Case in point: Chicago has one oceanlike lake that we all adore, but the Madison area is home to five smaller glacially created lakes—Mendota, Monona, Waubesa, Kegonsa, and Wingra—which means more aquatic diversity and, unlike the Windy City, about a half-dozen lakefront restaurants. The two largest lakes are Mendota, measuring almost 10,000 acres, and Monona, at about 3,200 acres. From either one you can hop aboard one of the popular **Betty Lou Cruises** (608-246-3138) for lunch, brunch, dinner, or cocktail cruising. All the lakes come with bordering parks and offer fishing opportunities and swimming—there are 13 beaches, 10 of which have lifeguards. Petite Lake Wingra is a peaceful spot for boating too. Rent canoes, kayaks, and paddleboats at **Wingra Boats** (608-233-5332). Along Wingra's banks lie the University of Wisconsin Arboretum, the Henry Vilas Zoo, and a children's playground where kids get a kick out of the city's famous Old Woman in a Shoe slide. Open year-round.

Madison Museum of Contemporary Art. 227 State St.; (608) 257-0158; www.mmoca .org. Designed by internationally renowned architect Cesar Pelli, Madison's contemporary art museum is an eye-catching sensation of gleaming geometric glass. In its galleries is even more to scintillate the senses. Art from the 20th and 21st centuries runs the gamut of media, from photography to drawings to sculptures to paintings. Highlights include works by Frida Kahlo and Diego Rivera. Temporary exhibits have focused on contemporary powerhouses like Chuck Close, Sol LeWitt, Georgia O'Keeffe, and Claes Oldenburg. Topping it all off, a 7,100-square-foot rooftop sculpture garden that can be viewed up close or from the confines of the museum restaurant, Fresco. Open Tues through Sun. Free.

Madison Union/the Terrace. 800 Langdon St., University of Wisconsin–Madison Memorial Union Terrace; (608) 265-3000; www.union.wisc.edu. Its motto, "The heart and soul of UW-Madison," suits this gathering ground along Lake Mendota just fine. Designed by then–campus architect Arthur Peabody, "the Union" opened in 1928 and a year later gained its famous adjoining outdoor stone seating area, "the Terrace" (designed by Peabody's architect daughter Charlotte). Besides socializing, sipping beer at der Rathskeller, and doing some incomparable people-watching, you can enjoy live bands, lectures, films, classes, and other programming. If you're college shopping, the Union puts UW-Madison's best foot forward; if you're way beyond college years, it'll make you feel like you're back again. Though the Union is not technically open to the public (it's a membership thing for the university community), the school doesn't mind if you visit, and you can get a free daily guest pass to enter.

Olbrich Botanical Gardens & Bolz Conservatory. 3330 Atwood Ave.; (608) 246-4550; www.olbrich.org. This 16-acre natural paradise along Lake Monona is here thanks to the passion and funding of Michael Balthazar Olbrich, a UW alum, Madison attorney, and nature preservationist. It began when Olbrich purchased property for parkland in 1916. Though he died unexpectedly in 1929, plans continued into the 1950s, finally resulting in the lush, landscaped gardens he had envisioned. In 1991 the 50-foot-tall Bolz Conservatory opened. A tropical paradise of 650 plants and flowers and 20-foot waterfall, it's particularly appealing in frigid winter months. From mid-July to mid-August, the conservatory's Olbrich's Blooming Butterflies event sees free-flying butterflies emerge from their chrysalises every day. The gardens also include the only Thai Pavilion and Garden in the continental US. Open daily. Gardens: free; conservatory: nominal admission.

Wisconsin Historical Museum. 30 N. Carroll St.; (608) 264-6555; www.wisconsinhistory .org. A little history, a little archaeology, a little quirkiness, and all Wisconsin. A portion of the state museum's 510,000-item collection is on display, documenting industry, life, struggles, and triumphs dating from prehistoric times to the present. Explore a replica mine, see historic bank documents, examine a Wisconsin farm family's trash to learn about their lives, and discover what happened to the Native Americans who once inhabited this land. Open Tues through Sat. Suggested donation.

Wisconsin State Capitol. 2 E. Main St.; (608) 266-0382; www.wisconsin.gov. Anchoring Madison on an isthmus of Lake Mendota and Lake Monona, this impressive capitol building was built between 1906 and 1917. Surrounding its granite dome and four equal wings are 13.5 acres of manicured grounds. Before entering, crane your neck upward at the 200-foot-high dome—it's the largest by volume in the country and is capped with a gilded bronze statue by Daniel Chester French (of D.C.'s Lincoln Monument fame). Look up when you step inside as well, to glimpse the Edwin Blashfield mural *Resources of Wisconsin.* More lavish artwork, hand-carved furniture, Italian marble, 12-foot-tall glass mosaics, and other decorative details make a visit to this governmental seat nearly as artistic as a museum. Open daily for tours. Free.

where to shop

Shops on State Street. While Chicago's pedestrian-only State Street experiment failed miserably, Madison's has been a rousing success. Along these blocks that connect the Capitol Building with the University of Wisconsin–Madison campus, you'll find more than 200 beloved locally owned bookstores, gift shops, bath and body shops, record stores and, OK, some chains too. There are also dozens of restaurants and 20 outdoor cafes. In October, the strip goes spooky with the annual Freakfest, a crazy scene of tens of thousands of Halloween revelers.

where to eat

Babcock Hall Dairy Store & Plant. 1605 Linden Dr.; (608) 262-3045, (608) 265-4039; www.babcockhalldairystore.wisc.edu. I scream, you scream, UW students all scream for Babcock ice cream. Here's the scoop: This campus institution was built in 1951 as part of the university's department of food science and is considered the oldest university dairy plant building in the country. See the ice cream–making process from the second-floor observation deck (tours are available by calling one week in advance with 10-person minimum), then taste the creamy concoctions for yourself. Standard flavors of vanilla, chocolate, and strawberry are crowd-pleasers, but fancier flavors like Union Utopia (vanilla with peanut butter, caramel, and fudge) and the super-premium (read: high-fat) Badger Blast, a chocolate-lover's dream, fill plenty of cups and cones too. You're in Wisconsin, of course, so the plant also gets kudos for its cheese—try master cheesemaker Gary Grossen's award-winning aged Gouda. Babcock ice cream is also sold at the Union. Open Mon through Fri at breakfast and lunch, Sat for ice cream only. $.

Essen Haus. 514 E. Wilson St.; (608) 255-4674; www.essen-haus.com. The decor here consists primarily of beer steins dangling from the ceiling, hinting at what lures people to this kitschy German mainstay. Completing the *gemuetilchkeit:* servers in lederhosen; oompah bands; a menu of sauerbraten, schnitzel, and rouladen; and, to fill your own stein, more than 250 brews. The question is: Can you down that bootful of beer? It's the thing to do here, so give it your best glug. Open Tues through Sat for dinner and late-night drinks, Sun for dinner. $$–$$$.

Harvest. 21 N. Pinckney St.; (608) 255-6075; www.harvest-restaurant.com. It's no coincidence that Harvest is planted right across from Capitol Square's famous farmers' market. It embodies what this place is all about: sustainable, seasonal, farm-to-table dining. A lovely, glowing ambiance from the candlelit tables and large picture windows that face the capitol add to accolades for the restaurant and executive chef Derek Rowe—*Organic Style, Gourmet Magazine, The New York Times,* and *Madison Magazine* have all lavished praise. With an emphasis on fresh instead of frou-frou, dishes change frequently and might include house-made tagliatelle pasta with pork sausage, arugula, and garlic; Wisconsin grass-fed beef co-op's porcini salt-rubbed tenderloin; or Lange Family Farm roasted pork loin with Lancinato kale and Anson Mills polenta. Open Mon through Sat for dinner; themed dinners one Sun a month. $$$.

Himal Chuli. 318 State St.; (608) 251-9225. Students swarm this place, former students crave it, locals love it, and newcomers are immediately notified: This little storefront with its red awning is a must-visit. The Nepalese menu, a vegetarian heaven, includes powerfully flavorful plates of spicy chili chicken, lamb sikar, tofu palungo, bhutti, seitan kebab, beef buff, and the divine momocha (steamed vegetable dumplings). Open daily for lunch and dinner. $–$$.

State Street Brats. 603 State St.; (608) 255-5544; www.statestreetbrats.com. UW-Madison Badger football fans go wild for this brat house, which many red-clad fans also argue is the best bar in town. It certainly packs 'em in for traditional beer brats or signature red brats—opened and grilled—plus chargrilled burgers, salads, sandwiches, flat bread pizzas that are far from boring (pesto, sweet red chili, buffalo chicken), and, of course, beer. The heated beer garden gets high marks and big crowds on game days. Open daily for lunch, dinner, and late night (post-party snacking, perhaps?). $.

Velobahn. 120 E. Wilson St.; (608) 258-8787; www.velobahn.com. The buzz surrounding this brand-new restaurant was loud enough to get a mention on this trip. After two years serving New Scandinavian cuisine as Restaurant Magnus, James Beard–nominated chef Nick Johnson redesigned the space and menu, paving a new path to Madison's first bicycle-themed bistro. Roll in with your own bike or just soak up the two-wheelin' vibe as you dine on international comfort cuisine like grilled cave-aged cheddar sandwiches with fried tomato, Dr. Pepper pork shoulder with Swiss cheese, Moroccan chicken pot stickers, or Asian meatballs. Live music Fri and Sat evenings, DJs late-night Sun through Thurs. Open daily for lunch, dinner, and late-night dining. $–$$.

where to stay

Arbor House, an Environmental Inn. 3402 Monroe St.; (608) 238-2981; www.arborhouse.com. Considering you've probably driven here, your carbon footprint is smaller than if you'd flown, so shrink it even further while being treated like gold at this 8-room, eco-friendly inn on the city's near-west side. The hospitality of innkeepers John and Cathie Imes goes hand-in-hand with their commitment to sustainability: recycled flooring, organic cotton and wool mattresses, low-flow showerheads, toiletries in refillable containers, recycled wood sauna decks, and more. Five of the tastefully decorated rooms are located in the historic 1853 national landmark Plough House, and 3 others in a newly built annex. $$–$$$.

Hotel Ruby Marie Bed & Breakfast. 524 E. Wilson St.; (877) 690-7829, (608) 327-7829; www.rubymarie.com. Like a visit to grandma's house, a stay at this beloved inn exudes hominess, features eclectic antiques, and has colorful stories to share. Used as a hotel as far back as 1873, the historic Victorian across from Lake Monona also boasts a former railroad saloon on its first floor, the Up North Pub, where winter happy hours get guests two free drinks. Some rooms include fireplaces, whirlpool tubs, and private balconies. On the weekend, a full breakfast is served; continental during the week. $$–$$$.

Madison Concourse Hotel. 1 W. Dayton St.; (800) 356-8293; www.concoursehotel.com. If you can swing a room in the updated Governor's Club, do it—great views, complimentary eats, some rooms with double-size Jacuzzis, huge flat-screens—but either way, this conveniently located 365-room hotel scores with super-friendly service, noteworthy restaurant and cozy bar, indoor pool and whirlpool, and ultra-comfortable beds. $$–$$$.

day trip 03

northwest

>>> **splash down to fun:**
wisconsin dells, wi

wisconsin dells

If you think the Wisconsin Dells is over-the-top touristy; if you think it's a total cheese-fest; if you think water parks rule the world here, you're absolutely right. And you're 100 percent wrong too. While the water parks get most of the glory, the nature-made attractions were what first drew tourists in the 1850s. A flood from a glacial lake about 15,000 years ago was gracious enough to carve out a magnificent terrain of gorges, canyons, bluffs, and sandstone sculptures. Historic photos by celebrated landscape photographer H.H. Bennett and current-day boat tours give you an idea of why 19th-century visitors were so taken by it all. Yes, fast-moving water gave this area its unique look, and fast-moving water gives the Dells its claim to fame today. In fact, more than 200 waterslides, tube rides, speed slides, water roller coasters, lazy rivers, and indoor surf machines help attract up to 55,000 guests every day in a community—comprising the City of Wisconsin Dells and the Village of Lake Delton—of barely more than 5,000 residents. And lest you think you have to do the Dells with kids, statistics show that nearly a quarter of visitors are adults traveling without children. If you haven't tied the knot yet, there's even a Las Vegas–style wedding chapel (**Dells Bells,** 43 LaCrosse St., 608-393-4228).

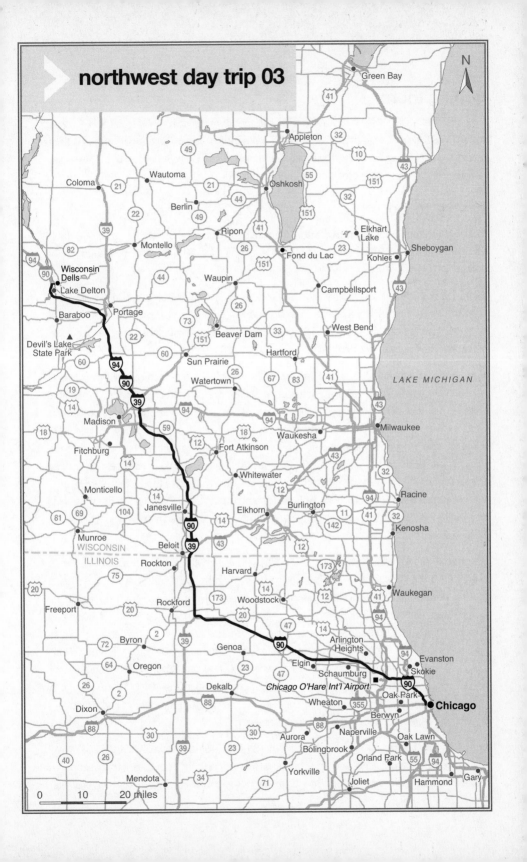

N

getting there

You could take US 41/I-94 and avoid tolls, but the more direct route is to follow I-90 west toward Wisconsin. Take exit 87 (toward WI 13/Wisconsin Dells). There's only one way to go off the exit. Go through the fourth stoplight and take a right onto Superior Street. The visitor center is at the end of the block on the right-hand side.

where to go

Wisconsin Dells Visitor Information Center. 701 Superior St.; (800) 223-3557, (608) 254-4636; www.wisdells.com. Your official launchpad for "The Waterpark Capital of the World!"

Dells Duck Rides. 1550 Wisconsin Dells Pkwy.; (608) 254-6080; www.dellsducks.com. Amphibious former army vehicles splash from land to water and afford views of the phenomenal scenery of Dell Creek and Dells Glacial Park rock formations, grottoes, and forestry. Apr to Nov (weather permitting). Fee (children 30 pounds and under ride free).

H.H. Bennett Studio. 215 Broadway; (608) 253-3523; hhbennettstudio.wisconsinhistory .org. Before the Dells became a water park wonderland, it attracted visitors for Mother Nature's handiwork. And Henry Hamilton Bennett was largely responsible for getting the word (or picture) out there. The studio Bennett built in 1875 is considered the longest continuously operating photography studio in the US; it is now run by the Wisconsin Historical Society and open to the public. Bennett himself is touted as one of the best landscape photographers of the 19th century and is credited with pioneering the instantaneous shutter, promoting the Wisconsin Dells with his stereographic (dual-image) photos, introducing stop-action photography, and documenting the Native American Ho-Chunk tribe of the Dells area. Open May through Oct. Admission.

Kalahari Resort. 1305 Kalahari Dr.; (877) 525-2427; www.kalahariresorts.com. Surf's up every day at this African safari–themed indoor-outdoor adventure park. Catch the waves of the Kalahari's FlowRider—50,000 gallons of water and 5-foot waves. The Leopard's Lair keeps things wet and wild with water guns, various slides (dare you to try the 400-foot-long Rippling Rhino), a 3,000-square-foot zero-depth pool, lazy river, whirlpool, and more. Oh, and that's just what's *inside*. The outdoor water park features the Dells' only Extreme Rush Slalom Racers, another lazy river, another whirlpool, and the 40-mph Zimbabwe Zipper spiral flume ride. When you've become fully prune-y, dry off in the 100,000 square feet of indoor amusements, from bowling to mini golf, a Ferris wheel to a ropes course. Hang ten, dude. Open daily. Admission (free for resort guests).

Lost Canyon Tours. 720 Canyon Rd.; (608) 254-8757, off-season (608) 253-2781; www .lostcanyontour.com. Climb aboard a horse-drawn carriage for a journey into Wisconsin's deepest and longest land canyon. Bring a jacket for the cool spots (which feel heavenly after

embrace the devil

*The most-visited state park in Wisconsin, **Devil's Lake State Park** is a worthwhile extra 15 miles south of the Wisconsin Dells in Baraboo (you can also do the Devil from Madison, which is about 40 miles southeast of the park). Go with your camera and you'll come away with postcard-perfect images of the 360-acre spring-fed lake, quartzite bluffs, kettle ponds, shady woods, 880-odd plant species, and likely some of the 100 species of birds. The 29-plus miles of the 14 different trails cover varied terrain and scenery. Want a workout with your fresh air and natural beauty? Follow one of the more strenuous of the 14 hiking trails, like the 0.3-mile Potholes trail; the steep climbs and stone steps can take about a half-hour one way to complete. Or take it a bit easier with the popular Tumbled Rocks trail, less than a mile and lain with asphalt. Give those knobby tires a beating on the 5 miles of off-road bike trails. Catch stocked brown trout, walleye and northern pike, bass, and panfish from the shore or a boat (fishing permit required for 16 and over). Dip into the lake for a cooldown at one of two beaches—bask in the sun on the north shore side (which gets understandably full faster) or keep away from the rays at the shadier south side beach. In winter, snowshoeing is available and there are two loops for cross-country skiing marked by level, while a hill behind the nature center turns into unofficial sledding central. Camping is also available (call 888-947-2757). S5975 Park Rd., Baraboo; (608) 356-8301; www.devilslakewisconsin.com.*

a day in the summer sun) and be prepared for a stop to purchase trinkets and a solicitation for tips (which, of course, if you feel are merited, go ahead and give). Open mid-Apr through Oct. Tours start approximately every 15 minutes. Admission.

Noah's Ark Waterpark. 1410 Wisconsin Dells Pkwy.; (608) 254-6351; www.noahsark waterpark.com. Not sure what Noah would think of this, but it sure attracts a lot of wild animals. And the wildest head straight for the park's newest ride, the Scorpion's Tail, the country's first near-vertical looping waterslide (yes, I said looping; it doesn't quite go upside-down, but close enough to scare *me* away). That shrieking you hear? It could be coming from the brave folks spiraling through the Black Anaconda, a quarter-mile-long "watercoaster," or perhaps the Black Thunder, a waterslide through total darkness and special effects, or the Point of No Return that racks you 10 stories up, then plummets you practically straight down. Don't worry, there are tamer parts too, like the mini-golf, wave pool, spray park, mini coaster, bumper boats, and more. Just hope for drier weather than in Noah's day. Open Memorial Day weekend through Labor Day. Admission.

Tommy Bartlett Show & Exploratory. 560 Wisconsin Dells Pkwy.; (608) 254-2525; www .tommybartlett.com. Practically synonymous with the Wisconsin Dells, Tommy Bartlett made a splash heard 'round the world when he brought his Chicago-based traveling water show here in 1952. Though the late Bartlett himself only water-skied once, his show became a legendary must-see. Acts change every year for the 90-minute display of won-drous water and stage skills along Lake Delton. There are also a nighttime laser-light and water show and plenty of amazing water-skiing moments. The Exploratory, open since 1982, is a year-round attraction that puts science and astronomy in the spotlight. Check out one of just three authentic Russian Space Station MIR core modules, a hands-on—or in this case, feet-on—high-wire bicycle exhibit, high-tech gadgets, and virtual reality computer games. Water show twice daily Memorial Day through Labor Day; admission. Exploratory open daily year-round; admission.

where to eat

Cheese Factory Restaurant. 521 Wisconsin Dells Pkwy. S.; (608) 253-6065; www.cooking vegetarian.com. No, not cheese*cake* (though, they have a mouthwateringly good one), just cheese—so named because the landmark building used to be a cheese factory. Now a vegetarian restaurant, it also happens to be one of the most unanimously raved-about res-taurants in the area, by meat-eaters and non alike. The sweet country-ish decor and friendly staff make dining here a 180-degree departure from a typical Dells experience. If the name has you craving dairy, go for the Big Cheese, a grilled double-decker of cheddar and Swiss on sourdough; ravioli sacre bleu; or Wisconsin beer cheese soup. Non-cheese-focused plates on the globally inspired menu include Hungarian goulash (made with veggies and tofu), Malaysian coconut noodles, and Thai stir-fry. But do save room for their famous des-serts, whether cheesecake, hazelnut torte, or an ice cream sundae. Vegan- and gluten-free options too. Open Thurs through Sat for lunch and early dinner, Sun for breakfast, lunch, and early dinner. $$.

The Del-Bar. 800 Wisconsin Dells Pkwy., Lake Delton; (866) 888-1861, (608) 253-1861; www.del-bar.com. In the late 1930s, two men opened the Del-Bar (between Wisconsin Dells and Baraboo) as a six-table roadside steakhouse, but it was Jimmy and Alice Wimmer who bought it in 1943 and nurtured it into the notable dining destination it is today (their son Jeff now runs it with his wife). With sprawling, Prairie-style architecture by one of Frank Lloyd Wright's protégés, the inviting ambiance adds to the allure. The Wimmers know their audience—hence, the cheese curd appetizer, tender fillets, rib eyes and prime rib, shrimp DeJonghe, and chicken cordon bleu—but they add some international flavors to the mix: steamed dumplings, Mediterranean salad, Wiener schnitzel. Happy hour features $1.99 apps. Open nightly for dinner. $$$.

High Rock Café. 232 Broadway; (608) 254-5677; www.highrockcafe.com. After tast-ing their way across the country for five years, friends and High Rock co-owners Justin

Draper and Wade Bernander opened their "modern American" restaurant in 2004. Amid downtown's souvenir-shop main drag, this local fave carves its own identity. Duck breast, an Airliner chicken breast, pork tenderloin with sautéed bean ragout, and fresh fish, salads, wraps, and pasta detour happily from the norm, as do sandwiches that surprise and impress, like the Soprano (sauteed garlic shrimp with bacon, Swiss cheese, lettuce, tomato, and tomato-basil mayo on toasted honey oat bread) and a much-lauded Monte Cristo. High Rock has since expanded to include a late-night tapas menu and wine bar, but it stays true to its adventurous beginnings. Open daily for lunch, dinner, and late night. $–$$.

Wally's House of Embers. 935 Wisconsin Dells Pkwy., Lake Delton; (608) 253-6411; www.houseofembers.com. You want history? Tradition? Good food too? Then a visit to Wally's is in order. From 1959 to 1998, Wally and Barbara Obois ran their supper-club-style restaurant, famous for Wally's dry-rubbed and hickory-smoked baby back barbecue ribs (with secret sauce) and Barbara's bread-basket cinnamon rolls. After retiring, the couple handed the toque to children Mark, Mike, and Deb, who keep the embers burning. Dining room decor runs from 1980s Miami in the veranda to old-fashioned charm in the Ben Franklin Room. But the Omar Sharif Room gets all the action: an alcove behind leopard-print curtains with reverence for the actor (one of Barbara's favorites), it's known as a popular spot for popping the question. Besides the legendary ribs and rolls, the brothers make a mean coconut shrimp, Austrian veal, rack of lamb, and two types of homemade pizzas. $$–$$$.

where to stay

Baker's Sunset Bay Resort. 921 Canyon Rd.; (800) 435-6515, (608) 254-8406; www .sunsetbayresort.com. It might not have the flash and brash of newer resorts, but this lodging right on Lake Delton does offer the simple, friendly (pet-friendly too) atmosphere of a longtime family-owned and -operated business. It also features a low-key indoor pool with slides, outdoor pool and spray features, whirlpool and sauna, summertime campfire sing-alongs, beautiful lake views, and complimentary tickets to the nearby Kalahari Theme Park. $$–$$$.

Sundara Inn & Spa. 920 Canyon Rd.; (888) 735-8181, (608) 253-9200; www.sundaraspa .com. Get ready to leave water park mania behind and enter nirvana at this adults-only haven set amid a 26-acre pine forest. Sanskrit for "beautiful," Sundara indeed lives up— outdoor infinity-edge pool, stone outcroppings, waterfalls, and warm, woodsy architecture. But it also embodies beauty with its daily yoga classes; holistic skin care services; heavenly spa treatments incorporating Ayurvedic, organic, and botanical healing ingredients and principles; and its luxurious, intimate 26 suites and 12 private villas, most equipped with private fireplaces. $$$.

Waterpark Resorts. No fewer than a dozen water park resorts give the Dells its rollicking reputation. Each one sports its own theme; some are larger, some are smaller; some stay indoors, and others have both inside and outside activity. All of them are masters of the wet and wild. Remember, when you stay at most of these resorts, you're not expected to spend tons of time in your room, so don't expect tons of appeal there. Here's info on a few of them to start:

Chula Vista Resort. 2501 River Rd.; (800) 338-4782, (608) 254-8366; www.chula vistaresort.com. Indoor and outdoor water fun, plus golf course, magic show, steakhouse, and more. $–$$$.

Great Wolf Lodge. 1400 Great Wolf Dr.; (800) 559-9653, (608) 253-2222; www .greatwolf.com. Breakfast and indoor and outdoor water park passes are all included with your stay at this rustic chain. Cute kids' spa for 4- to 12-year-olds too. $$$.

Kalahari Resort. 1305 Kalahari Dr.; (877) 525-2427; www.kalahariresorts.com. See "where to go" for the Kalahari's aquatic offerings. Besides the basics, these rooms feature African-style touches. $$$.

Mount Olympus. 1881 Wisconsin Dells Pkwy.; (800) 800-4997, (608) 254-2490; www.mtolympuspark.com. Enough entertainment for the Roman army with indoor and outdoor water parks and theme parks included in your stay. $$–$$$.

Wilderness Hotel & Golf Resort. 511 E. Adams St.; (800) 867-9453; www.wilder nessresort.com. You need a map just to make your way around this indoor-outdoor multi-activity resort, part of the 600-acre Wilderness Territory and deemed the largest water park resort in the country. Water park passes are included in lodging fees and are only available to resort guests. $$$.

festivals & celebrations

january

Good Midwesterners that we are, we have a good time no matter the weather, right? Like at the weekend-long Waukesha, Wisconsin, **JanBoree** in late January. Ice sculptors work their frosty magic, horse-drawn wagons bring the romance, there's a kids' ice-fishing lesson, and even winter-weather fireworks. (262) 524-3737, www.janboree.org.

Grand Haven, Michigan, thumbs its nose at Old Man Winter too, with its **Winterfest** at the end of the month. A weekend of festivities runs the gamut from a cardboard sled race to the Intergalactic Human Sled Race Championships, a snow-angel contest to an indoor luau. www.winterfestonline.org.

february

New in 2011, Michigan's Harbor Country Chamber of Commerce came up with a month-long event that satisfies sweet-tooths and sweethearts: the **Harbor Country Chocolate Classic,** featuring dessert specials all over the eight-city area, samplings, wine and chocolate pairings, cook-offs, and demonstrations. www.harborcountry.org.

The two-day **Cedarburg Winter Festival** near Milwaukee starts off with a pancake breakfast and, to heat things up later, a chili contest, plus kids' activities and bed races on the ice. (800) 237-2874, (262) 377-9620, www.cedarburgfestivals.org.

march

March means Michigan maple trees are ripe for the tapping. See how it's done at the annual **Kalamazoo Maple Sugar Festival** held at the Kalamazoo Nature Center. Devour pancakes with fresh syrup, dribble some on a bowl of ice cream, take a maple sugar tour, and a horse-drawn wagon ride. (269) 381-1574, www.naturecenter.org.

If you can't be in Chicago for St. Pat's Day, get your green on at **Milwaukee's Annual St. Patrick's Day Parade and Party.** It troops through downtown with marching bands, pipe and drum corps, clowns, drill teams, Irish dancers, and lots of Irish pride. http://shamrock clubwis.com.

april

Get your tickets early to attend Roger Ebert's annual film festival, now called **Ebertfest,** which screens about a dozen overlooked movies (in any genre, any year), as deemed by the famous film critic himself. An Urbana native and University of Illinois grad, Ebert hosts the festival every April at Champaign's Virginia Theater, an elegant 1921 movie palace. (217) 356-9053, www.ebertfest.com.

Taste two of Wisconsin's best exports, beer and cheese, at early April's **Dairy State Beer & Cheese Festival.** Plus, your imbibing benefits the Boys and Girls Club. It's held at The Brat Stop, 12304 75th St., Kenosha; (262) 654-6200, www.kenoshabeerfest.com.

may

Ahhh, finally. . .signs of spring. It's the **Tulip Time Festival** in Holland, Michigan. Beyond the blooms, this weeklong event beginning the first Saturday in May is more than 80 years old and all about Dutch heritage and culture, with parades, dancing, trolley tours, concerts, special dining deals, a marketplace, a quilt show, and more. (800) 506-1299, www.tulip time.com.

Casual Sunday afternoons throughout the summer start this month in Lake Geneva, Wisconsin. It's the **Burnin' Down the Docks** festival at the Abbey Resort, with live entertainment and an outdoor barbecue. (262) 275-9000, (800) 709-1323, www.abbeyresort.com.

Forget the key chains and T-shirts—bring home an arty souvenir from the **Old Capitol Art Fair** in Springfield, Illinois. Typically held around the third weekend in May, its one of the most popular juried art fairs in the country and a tradition since 1962. It features a little of everything and all original items (i.e., no commercially produced stuff here), plus a children's tent, entertainment, and food. www.socaf.org.

june

Jazz enthusiasts converge on Elkhart, Illinois, for the three-day **Elkhart Jazz Festival** at the end of the month, featuring more than 90 performances of every jazz style on six stages throughout downtown. www.elkhartjazzfestival.com.

Got an old Tony the Tiger costume lying around? Pull it out to march in the parade during the Battle Creek **Cereal Festival** in mid-June. This weekend celebration of Battle Creek, Michigan, and its significance to the cereal industry also features the World's Longest Breakfast Table, concerts, food booths, and more. www.bcfestivals.com.

There's something fishy going on during the Fond du Lac **Walleye Weekend.** But it's all good at this second-largest festival in Wisconsin, attracting more than 100,000 visitors to Lakeside Park and the Lake Winnebago fishery. Over the course of four days around the second weekend in June, there are concerts, dodgeball tournaments, bounce houses, bingo games, fishing tournaments, and walleye on the menu. (920) 923-6555, www.fdlfest .com.

Maybe it's not Cannes or Sundance, but the **Waterfront Film Festival** in Saugatuck, Michigan, has been gaining clout since its debut in 1999. Now the early June festival boasts screenings of world and Midwest premieres and plenty of star power with actors, directors, producers, and writers making appearances. (269) 857-8351, www.waterfrontfilm.org.

You can enter the races (foot and bicycle) at the Peoria, Illinois, **Steamboat Sports Festival** mid-June, or just go for the sideline family-friendly entertainment, along with music and food. (800) 747-0302, www.peoriaevents.com.

Started in 1968 and now plugged as the world's largest music festival, the annual **Milwaukee Summerfest** spans 11 days (end of June through beginning of July) and 11 stages and boasts a whopping 800-plus bands. If you can't get tickets to a main-stage performer, take a chance with a lesser-known act on a smaller stage. The ski-lift-like Skyglider takes visitors from the north end to the south end of the grounds. (414) 273-2680, www.summer fest.com.

july

Fifteen thousand fireworks burst into the sky the Saturday before July 4 at the Madison, Wisconsin, **Rhythm and Booms,** claimed to be the largest fireworks show in the Midwest (considering it lasts more than a half-hour, it very well may be). Bring your radio and tune in to WOLX-94.9FM to listen to the synchronized music. (608) 833-6717, www.rhythmand booms.com.

Where can you see a demolition derby, tractor pull, lawnmower races and pig races, award-winning garden vegetables, not to mention farm animals galore? Around for more than 160 years, the late-July **Fond du Lac County Fair** in Wisconsin has all that and more. (920) 929-3168, www.fonddulaccountyfair.com.

Beginning weekends from Independence Day through Labor Day, Kenosha, Wisconsin, goes 16th-century on you with its annual **Bristol Renaissance Faire.** Knights, swordsmen, wenches, jugglers, jesters, a queen, even Robin Hood and his Merry Men. They're all here to entertain amid 30 wooded acres of make-believe. Don't miss the giant turkey legs. (847) 395-7773, www.renfair.com.

At the end of July, Saugatuck, Michigan, hosts its annual three-day **Venetian Festival,** complete with concerts, kids' activities, fireworks, an arts and fine crafts fair, a classic car and boat show, and a lively parade of decorated boats. (616) 886-1162, www.saugatuck venetianfestival.com.

Consider that 28 football fields' worth (in length) of brats are sold at the Milwaukee **GermanFest,** held the last weekend in July. Add that to the 10,000 pounds of potato salad, 500 chickens, and 20,000 tortes and pastries, and that's a lot of happy people. The fest has been one of Brew City's best nods to its German heritage since it began in 1981. And if eating wieners isn't enough, cheer on the racing wiener dogs (dachshunds, of course). (414) 464-9444, www.germanfest.com.

august

An 11-day agricultural extravaganza beginning the first Thursday prior to the first Friday in August, the **Wisconsin State Fair** in West Allis dates back to 1851. Its nearly 200-acre setting features beef and dairy cattle, horses, sheep, goats, llamas, poultry, and more, plus dairy and produce, crafts and textiles, an amazing 30 stages of free entertainment, and extensive marketplaces. You'll get hungry here, but more than 200 food vendors will provide. (800) 884-FAIR (3247), www.wistatefair.com.

Uncensored, unjuried, and totally approachable, the **Indianapolis Fringe Festival** attracts theatergoers for 10 days of nearly 300 diverse, creative, and often thought-provoking shows on six stages with free outdoor entertainment and street-theater performances. It's one of about 25 festivals like it in North America, following the Edinburgh, Scotland, example set back in 1947. (317) 721-9458, www.indyfringe.org.

You might need all day for the annual **Amish Acres Arts & Crafts Festival** in Nappanee, Indiana, in early August. It's a jam-packed schedule of bands, dancing, puppet shows, wagon rides, and, yes, booth after booth of juried artists from around the corner and around the country. (800) 800-4942, www.amishacres.com.

Gurnee Days in the middle of August is like a whole bunch of festivals rolled into one: rib fest, live bands, amusement rides, art shows, bingo, fireworks. It's all meant to bring the Gurnee, Illinois, community together, but visitors are surely welcome to join in on the fun. (847) 249-9613, www.gurnee.il.us/gurnee_days.

It's all blueberries all the time at Michigan's annual **South Haven Blueberry Festival** in early or mid-August. Wake up early on Saturday for the 5K run, head downtown for the blueberry pancake breakfast, then return later for the fish boil (get there early, as lines get long). Don't even think about asking for a strawberry. (800) SO-HAVEN, www.blueberry festival.com, www.southhaven.org.

No one should have to bend your ear or butter you up to attend the late-August **Sweet Corn Blues Festival** in uptown Normal, Illinois (no more corny puns, promise). Fresh sweet Illinois corn takes the spotlight, though there are also live blues, sidewalk sales, and a flea market. (309) 454-2444.

september

From late September through early October, a stroll along Grand Haven, Michigan's Grand River Waterfront or through its downtown business district comes with an eyeful of art—paintings, mixed media, outdoor sculpture, and other artworks in the **Grand Haven ArtWalk.** Vote for your favorite too. (616) 844-1188, www.ghartwalk.com.

Meaning "time of fun," taken from a Native American Ho-Chunk phrase, the Wisconsin Dells' **Wo-Zha-Wa Festival** signals the winding down of summer and the welcoming of autumn. It takes place the second weekend after Labor Day and features Wisconsin's oldest long-distance race (a half-marathon; and there's a 4-mile race too), along with a parade, arts and crafts market, antique flea market, food, farmers' market, and more. (800) 223-3557, www.wisdells.com/wisconsin-dells-attraction/wozhawa.cfm.

The early September **Bonneyville Mill Celebration** in Elkhart, Illinois, brings back the simple life with a bevy of folk singers, storytellers, dancers, mill demonstrations, and candle-dipping. See pumpkin-carving art and sink your teeth into the corn-eating contest; check out the pioneer toys and sit down to a pancake and sausage breakfast. (574) 535-6458, www.elkhartcountyparks.org.

october

Take a big sweet bite out of fall at the Long Grove, Illinois, annual **Apple Festival.** On the must-try list: the brown-bag apple pie, apple doughnuts, and hot apple cider. Face-painting and pony rides for the kids amid the quaint historic town and to a soundtrack of live blue-grass, country, rock, and jazz. (847) 634-0888, www.longgroveonline.com.

Harbor Country, Michigan, doesn't really need more than its spectacular fall foliage, but it adds to the colorful array over Columbus Day weekend during **Harvest Days.** Shop owners pull out the stops with open houses, gallery receptions, cooking demos, discounts, and more. It all coincides with the one-day Harvest & Wine Fest in New Buffalo, with hayrides, local wine and microbrews, and live music. www.harborcountryharvestdays.com.

In and around Kohler, Wisconsin's American Club, the **Kohler Food & Wine Experience** features a weekend of fancy fare from local and international chefs alike. Cookbook signings, food and wine tastings, demos, and seminars. Past celebrity chefs have included Graham Elliot, Sara Moulton, and Bryan & Michael Voltaggio. (866) 847-4856, www.american club.com.

november

It's OK to be a cheesehead at Madison's annual **Wisconsin Original Cheese Fest,** held in the beginning of November at Monona Terrace, the city's convention center. Creamery and farm tours give you behind-the-scenes peeks at the cheese-making process, while cheesemaker dinners, tasting seminars, and the Cheesemaker Gala just cut to the chase and serve up the cheese. (608) 358-7837, www.wicheesefest.com.

The regal Rialto Square Theatre in Joliet, Illinois, gets its halls decked for the annual **Festival of Trees** that starts the week of Thanksgiving and runs through Sunday (closed on Thanksgiving Day). The display of holiday trees, wreaths, and other festive decorations kicks off the Christmas season with good cheer and classic holiday film screenings. (815) 726-6600, www.rialtosquare.com.

december

For a smaller-town version of Chicago's holiday lights festival, join the jolly crowds for the East Peoria, Illinois, **Festival of Lights,** from early December through the New Year. As you drive through "electric park" (actually the VFW Post 2078 Park off Springfield Drive), more than two million lights twinkle around and above you in the form of lighted archways, leaping reindeer, colorful animals, and tin soldiers. www.peoria.org.

Admission is free to the **Christmas in the Air** event at the EAA AirVenture Museum in Oshkosh, Wisconsin, in early December. It's a great opportunity to view the amazing aircraft with merry music makers performing throughout the day, and free cookies and milk in the evening. Topping it all off: Santa arrives by helicopter. (920) 426-4800, www.airventure museum.org.

Chicago may be jaded by its giant trees in Daley Plaza, but perhaps a bit more intimate is the **Madison Capitol Tree Lighting** in early December. The typically 40-foot Wisconsin-grown tree is decorated with garlands, glittering lights, and more than 1,400 ornaments handmade and donated by residents from around the state. (608) 266-5044.

index